MAR   2005

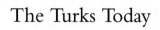

The Turks Today

The Turks Today

ANDREW MANGO

THE OVERLOOK PRESS
WOODSTOCK & NEW YORK

First published in the United States in 2004 by
The Overlook Press, Peter Mayer Publishers, Inc.
Woodstock & New York

WOODSTOCK:
One Overlook Drive
Woodstock, NY 12498
www.overlookpress.com
[for individual orders, bulk and special sales, contact our Woodstock office]

NEW YORK:
141 Wooster Street
New York, NY 10012

∞ The paper used in this book meets the requirements for paper
permanence as described in the ANSI Z39.48-1992 standard.

Cataloging-in-Publication Data is available from the Library of Congress

Manufactured in the United States of America
FIRST EDITION
ISBN 1-58567-615-2
1 3 5 7 9 10 8 6 4 2

To Emily, Anaïs and Emma
the new generation

Contents

CONTENTS

Acknowledgements

I thank the Turkish Embassy in London for supplying me with publications and helping me with contacts, the Turkish Directorate General of Press and Information for arranging for me a trip through provincial Turkey, the Turkish Foreign Economic Relations Board, whose director Mrs Çiğdem Tüzün has encouraged me to write this book, the many universities, think-tanks and study groups in Turkey which have invited me to lecture or take part in panels, and, above all, my friends in Turkey whose voices reverberate in the pages that follow, I hope without undue distortion.

My special thanks are due to Canan and Peter Reeves, my first readers as ever, for their comments and encouragement. I am grateful for the professionalism of my publishers John Murray – my editor Caroline Knox, production editor Caroline Westmore and to Howard Davies for helpful suggestions on the text. My granddaughter Emily Senior took on the heroic task of preparing her first index for this book; I hope that the second will be for her own book. I owe Mary an apology for postponing my retirement yet again. A book like this, which is full of facts, figures and opinions, is bound to contain mistakes. I thank in advance readers who will point them out to me.

A. M.
May 2004

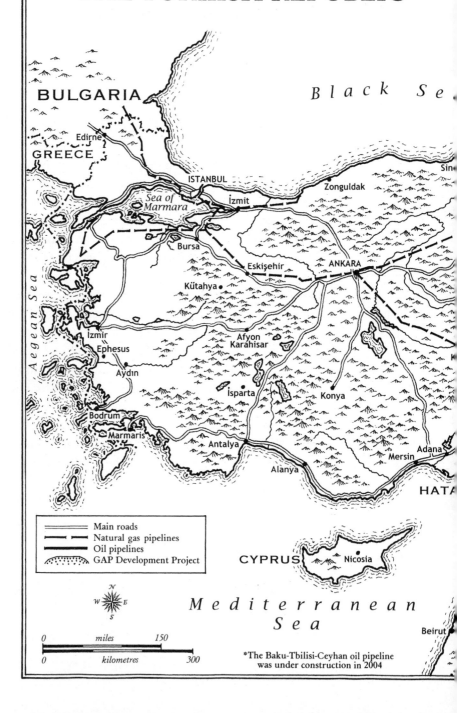

THE TURKISH REPUBLIC

BULGARIA

Black Sea

Edirne

GREECE

Sin

ISTANBUL

Zonguldak

Sea of Marmara

İzmit

İzmir

Bursa

Eskişehir

ANKARA

Kütahya

Aegean Sea

İzmir

Afyon
Karahisar

Ephesus

Aydın

İsparta

Konya

Bodrum

Marmaris

Antalya

Mersin

Adana

Alanya

HATA

	Main roads
	Natural gas pipelines
	Oil pipelines
	GAP Development Project

CYPRUS

Nicosia

Mediterranean Sea

Beirut

0   miles   150

0   kilometres   300

*The Baku-Tbilisi-Ceyhan oil pipeline
was under construction in 2004

Note on Spelling and Pronunciation

Modern Turkish uses the Latin alphabet, modified to ensure that there is a separate letter for each main sound. The spelling thus aims at phonetic consistency. Consonants have more or less the same sound as in English, except that:

> *c* is pronounced as *j* in *j*oy
> *ç* is as *ch* in *ch*air
> *ğ* is silent, but lengthens the preceding vowel
> *j* is pronounced as in French, or as *s* in mea*s*ure
> *ş* is as *sh* in *sh*ip
> *h* and *y* are pronounced as consonants, as in *h*it and *y*ellow

Vowels have the following values:

> *a* as in f*a*ther
> *e* as in p*e*n
> *i* as in p*i*n (the capital also carries a dot, *İ*)
> *ı* is a back, close, unrounded vowel which does not exist in English, the nearest equivalent being the phantom vowel in the second syllable of rhy*thm* (in Turkish transliteration *ritim*)
> *o* as in p*o*t
> *ö* as in German, or in French *eu*
> *u* as in r*oo*m
> *ü* as in German, or in French *u* (in *u*ne)

The circumflex (^) is sometimes used to indicate a long vowel, as in *siyasî* (si-ya-see, meaning political). Used after the consonants *k* and *l*, it indicates that the consonant is soft (palatalized), e.g. *kâr* (k^i-a-r, meaning profit), to distinguish from *kar* (k-a-r, meaning snow).

Prologue

IN JANUARY 2003 a mass-circulation newspaper in Istanbul published a letter from a young doctor who had been put in charge of a health centre in a remote mountain village of south-eastern Turkey. He had been sent there under a programme which prescribes compulsory service in deprived areas for newly registered doctors. But the administration had failed to equip the health centre, which it had set up as a political investment. There was no dispensary in the village, and local people preferred to travel to the nearest market town for medical care. The doctor was underemployed. His living and working conditions were primitive. His only assistant, a nurse, was better off. She was the wife of a serving officer, and the military helped her with transport and supplies. Electricity and telephone connections were intermittent. But the doctor could access the internet through his mobile telephone. Surfing the net one day, he learned of a competition to take part in a seminar organized by the European Union in Brussels. He applied and was successful. A few months later he was in the building of the European Parliament meeting colleagues from other countries.

This simple personal story encapsulates some of the main traits of Turkey at the beginning of the third millennium: an inadequate administration with limited means at its disposal which it uses to provide social welfare and at the same time to garner votes; improved communications which allow villagers to travel in search of better services; working wives; a powerful military deployed in the south-east to defeat a Kurdish nationalist insurgency; a young population eager to reach out to the outside world, enthusiastic for new technology and, above all, determined to achieve success for themselves and their country.

It was Mustafa Kemal Atatürk, the founder of the Turkish republic, who had set the goal of reaching and then going beyond the standards of contemporary civilization. But when he died on 10 November 1938, the country outside the main towns – Istanbul, the new capital of Ankara, the Aegean seaport of İzmir – was poor and primitive, poorer in many cases than it had been under Ottoman rule on the eve of the First World War. Away from the newly extended railway network, villages and even small towns could be reached only by animal-drawn transport travelling along dirt tracks. Most men were illiterate; women almost universally so. Poorly paid public servants and salesmen were almost the only people who travelled within the country. Few foreigners visited Turkey; even fewer Turks went abroad. Any foreigner travelling in the countryside was seen as the repository of knowledge denied to the locals and was besieged by villagers crying out for medicines and advice. The engine for change was gearing up in the metropolitan centres but it had not begun to affect the countryside.

Atatürk's administration had the national territory firmly under its control; it had set out its goals of modernization and prescribed a cultural revolution. But the transformation of a poor and backward country had to wait until the end of the Second World War, when the release of individual initiative, combined with foreign support, propelled Turkey into the modern world.

It is part of this world today. But it is still lagging behind: in 2001 Turkey was ninety-sixth among the 175 countries listed in the human development index compiled by the United Nations Development Programme. While Turkey was in the middle ranks of the second league of countries which had achieved medium human development, the countries of southern Europe, which were members of the European Union – Italy, Spain, Greece and Portugal (in that order) – were all ranked in the first league of forty-eight countries. So too were the countries – from Poland to Greek Cyprus – which the EU had promised to take in as full members in 2004.[1] The overlap between EU membership and advanced development explained why the majority of Turks – some 70 per cent according to surveys conducted in 2003 – wanted to enter the EU. Conversely, Turkey's relative poverty was an important reason why it was the least popular candidate country in Europe. Poverty reinforces the image of the Turk as an alien in the West.

The sense among many Europeans and other Westerners that the Turks belong to a different civilization and culture gives rise to contradictory feelings in Turkish breasts. Some think it is proof of Turkey's shortcomings, particularly in modern education and social organization. Many people in the tradition of Mustafa Kemal Atatürk (known as Kemalists ever since 1919) believe that it is up to their country to rise to the level of contemporary civilization, and that when it does so, when its people become richer and better educated, the West will accept them into its fold. But others have convinced themselves that Western reservations are the product of an ineradicable hostility rooted in the history of wars between the Christian West and the Muslim Ottomans. Thus people who are usually extremely hospitable to any Westerner who comes their way will still believe that the West and its civilization seek to destroy Turkey, that 'the Turk's only friend is another Turk'.

Xenophobia is to be found in most countries. In Turkey it can be Islamic, nationalist or racist. It can manifest itself as anti-imperialism, when espoused by people who forget that the Ottoman state was an empire. It can be fed by the Marxist notion of exploitation, used to explain the higher standard of living in the West as the product of the exploitation of colonial people. The word coined some fifty years ago as the term for a colony – *sömürge*, literally an exploited object – enshrines this notion in modern Turkish.

The feeling that all relations with the West are unequal translates itself into the belief that all transactions with it are a zero-sum game, that if a Westerner makes money or derives some other benefit, it is at the expense of his Turkish opposite number. One can find a historical justification for this attitude. In the past, Westerners and Turks were unequal in their store of modern knowledge, and there were thus grounds for the suspicion that greater access to information enabled the Westerner to outsmart the Turk, who had to defend himself by changing the rules of the game. Although inequality in educational attainment persists to some degree, the dissemination of modern knowledge through Turkish society renders this defensive, and at times xenophobic, attitude anachronistic. In business, diplomacy, often in arts and culture, though not yet in innovation, research and development, and consequently in technology, Turks and Westerners can now draw on similar stores of knowledge. This has already limited the prevalence of aggressively or slyly defensive approaches to the West and Westerners. But it has not eliminated them. Openness to the world and fear of it exist side by side, with openness gradually predominating. As a liberal Turkish newspaper columnist, Şahin Alpay, has pointed out, Turkey has a love–hate relationship with the West.[2]

The human development index measures the average expectation of life, enrolment in education, employment and other quantifiable indicators of the standard of living and, to a lesser extent, its quality. But it does not and cannot measure a society's potential for progress. Factors such as the spread of the spirit of individual initiative, on the one hand, and social cohesion, on the other, are difficult to quantify. Yet they are the foundation of the wealth of nations. Turkey appears well placed in this respect: its citizens are overwhelmingly open to new knowledge and ready to put it to their advantage, and society, unequal as it is and divided in many respects, has held together in times of hardship.

At the beginning of the new millennium, joining Europe is the grand idea in Turkey. But this is unlikely to happen before the year 2010 at the earliest. By then both Europe and Turkey will have changed. According to Turkish Europhiles, their country must choose between Europe and the Third World. Recep Tayyip Erdoğan, leader of the Justice and Development Party which came to power in November 2002, put it better, when he said, 'The alternative to Europe is ourselves.' It is often claimed that Turks are experiencing a crisis of identity, torn between East and West. In fact there are few peoples which have a stronger sense of national identity than the Turks. Their problem is to be accepted for what they are, a distinct people with a Muslim background; a pushy people who, far from being part of the lethargic East, often find the West too relaxed in its comforts. Turkey is not only an aspirant to the European Union, it is also a challenge to it.

The challenge is in the first place demographic. In mid-2002, the population of Turkey was officially estimated at 69,757,000. Although the rate of growth has fallen below 16 per thousand (from a peak of nearly 29 per thousand between 1955 and 1960), the population will grow by approximately one million a year in the medium term because of the large number of women of child-bearing age. By 2010, the earliest date for Turkey's accession to the European Union, the number of its inhabitants is expected to exceed 78 million against 84 million in Germany, the most populous member country. On present trends, Turkey will have a larger population than Germany in 2020: 89 million against 85 million.

Numbers do not tell the whole story. Turkey's eastern neighbour, Iran, is expected to have 70 million people in 2010 and over 80 million in 2020. The population projections for Egypt are even higher: 75 million in 2010 and 85 million ten years later. But these countries are unlikely to match Turkey's growth. True, the achievements of individual Iranians and Egyptians are at least as impressive as those of their Turkish counterparts. There are probably more Iranians than Turks in the ranks of professionals in the USA or in financial services in New York and London. But, taken as a whole, society in Iran and Egypt lags behind Turkey in political development and the dissemination of modern skills. The Iranian economy relies largely on hydrocarbons – oil and natural gas; the livelihood of the Egyptians depends on agriculture and protected manufactures. Turkey, on the other hand, has developed on a wide front. Its economy is more competitive in the global market, its entrepreneurs more numerous and knowledgeable, its contacts with the outside world more extensive. While most Iranians abroad belong to a sophisticated elite in exile, most of the 3.5 million Turks in Europe are workers. Knowledge of the West permeates Turkish society to a degree unmatched in Iran or Egypt. One of the tenets of Atatürk's cultural revolution was that Turkey had to think like the West if it were to catch up with the West. More Turks do so than do their Muslim neighbours to the east and south. There is truth in the statement often heard in Turkey that its people's level of civilization has continued to rise in recent decades and that it is much higher than that in stricter Islamic countries.[3] One crucial difference is that in Turkey women are much more emancipated and better able to realize their potential than in most Islamic countries.

Turkey's superiority vis-à-vis its Muslim neighbours is particularly evident in its level of political development. It is true that the inadequacies of Turkish democracy are proclaimed constantly both inside and outside the country – in the Turkish media and in reports of the European Commission and of many non-governmental organizations. Yet the fact remains that voting has been free in Turkish elections ever since 1950, that elections change governments, that votes count and politicians are therefore responsive to the electorate, that the constitutional and legal framework has by and large been brought into line with EU standards, that the judiciary, although usually slow, and often inconsistent and unpredictable in its judgements, is shielded from direct pressure, that the media enjoy a wide latitude to criticize all and sundry, and that citizens can obtain redress against administrative abuses, albeit sometimes with the help of personal contacts. Turkey is an open country, and faults within its system of government are not difficult to detect and publicize. But the claim that Turkey is a country where human rights are routinely violated, a claim often made by Turkey's ethnic adversaries, and sometimes used as an excuse by opponents of Turkey's accession to the EU, is unjustified. Turkish citizens are at least as free as their neighbours in the Balkans, who attract much less criticism. They enjoy much greater freedom than the citizens of almost any other Muslim country. The spotlight on what is termed 'the democratic deficit' in Turkey should not obscure the country's essentially democratic character.

However, the relationship between democracy and clean government is complex. While democracy exposes corruption, democratic electoral politics can encourage jobbery and the distribution of favours. In 2002, Transparency International, which compiles comparative tables of corruption in public life, placed Turkey sixty-fourth among 102 countries it had studied. Among EU candidates, only Romania was found to be more corrupt.[4] Here again, the campaign against corruption which swept Turkey in the opening years of the millennium may have exposed abuses which are better hidden, and tolerated, elsewhere. However that may be, the origins of corruption are not exclusively political. Bribery and nepotism can oil the wheels of a cumbersome administration. The remedy lies not only in democratization but also in more efficient governance. While the cause of democracy is being pushed forward, the need for better, simpler administration should not be overlooked. The centuries-old Ottoman state tradition, with its concomitant respect for the state, which the Turkish republic has inherited, is part of the country's social capital. But the tradition must be brought up to date. The fact that Turkish private companies often achieve international standards of corporate governance suggests that sufficient knowledge and talent exist to endow the country with a properly functioning public administration.

Life cannot be reduced to politics or to mathematical data. For all the hardships to which the relatively poor people of Turkey are exposed, the visitor is struck by the liveliness of its social life. Turkish society has become progressively more open since the death of Atatürk and, particularly, since the end of the Second World War. It is unequal, but mobile; self-critical, but fundamentally self-confident; friendly, but not submissive to foreigners. One important change since Atatürk is the rediscovery of the recent Ottoman past. In order to carry out his cultural revolution, Atatürk laid stress on the central Asian origins of the Turks who conquered the country, while belittling the Ottoman heritage. Now the two have come together: there is interest in Turkic kinsmen, but also Ottomania – pride in the imperial achievements of local people of diverse ethnic origins who ruled the far-flung Ottoman state from Istanbul.

Development has changed not only the people of Turkey, but also the face of the country since Atatürk's day. Cities have grown at the expense of the countryside. In 1940, two years after Atatürk's death, one quarter of the population of 21 million was urban, three quarters rural. In 2000, two thirds of the country's 68 million inhabitants lived in towns. Just over a quarter of the population is now concentrated in the Marmara region, dominated by the cities of Istanbul (with nearly 9 million inhabitants) and Bursa (over a million). Another quarter lives along the shores of the Aegean (centred on the seaport of İzmir with a population of 2,250,000) and the Mediterranean. Antalya, the centre of the Mediterranean tourist area, is the fastest-growing city in the country (by nearly 5 per cent a year in the ten years to 2000, when its population exceeded 600,000).

These cities and the poles of attraction in the interior of the Anatolian peninsula (among them Ankara, Gaziantep, Konya, Diyarbakır, Kayseri and Eskişehir) are dominated by large concrete apartment and office blocks. They often boast wide tree-lined avenues and busy shopping precincts. Nostalgic observers lament the disappearance of picturesque Turkish neighbourhoods and their replacement by building complexes the likes of which can be found anywhere and everywhere in the world. Tourism has led to ribbon development along the shores of the Aegean and Mediterranean which were virtually empty until after the Second World War. Ownership of a holiday house, usually bought through a co-operative society based on an affinity group, has become the distinguishing mark of middle-class life. In the cities, new estates built to house rural migrants and a large lower middle class surround the monuments of Ottoman architecture. The urban panorama proclaims that Turkey is a young, modern country. Shoddy architecture and inadequate urban planning demonstrate that it is still comparatively poor and poorly administered. Bad building and siting in new cheap developments cause loss of life in earthquakes, floods and fires. Such disasters show up the weakness of an administration which finds it difficult to implement building and planning regulations in the face of social and political pressures.

Villages too have changed dramatically since Atatürk's day. Mud brick has given way to breezeblock, stone and cement. Almost all villages are connected to the national electricity grid. Most have clean water. Almost everywhere all-weather roads provide easy access to rural settlements. All village children are served by local primary schools. These may have only one teacher and a single classroom, but they do teach the three Rs. There are still primitive, poor villages, particularly in the mountains of eastern Turkey, but they do not live in a separate world. National administration, the national economy, national radio and television, reach and affect even the remotest settlement.

Social critics speak of 'the other Turkey' – the Turkey of the poor with poor prospects. But social mobility is high, and a large and growing lower middle class links the Turkey of the indigent with the Turkey of the affluent. The villager is not 'the real master of the country', as Atatürk declared rhetorically. But today he is conscious of his rights as a citizen of the republic.

In the last half-century Turkey has, more or less successfully, muddled through to modernity. Constant patch-and-mend has kept the country going on its inadequate physical and social infrastructure.

The disciplined habits and anonymous relationships of contemporary society have not yet replaced the more lax codes of personal networks which permeate Turkish society. But Turkey is not unique in this respect. It has much in common with other south European countries. Membership of the European Union has helped these countries mend their ways. Whether in or out of the EU, Turkey too must reduce the degree to which it tolerates laxity and irregularity. Muddling through is no longer enough.

The unevenness of modernization and of material progress makes it hard to sum up the state of Turkey today. After arriving in the gleaming, efficient new terminal of Atatürk airport in Istanbul, the traveller may book electronically a seat in a modern Turkish-built intercity coach with a properly trained driver. But he might still face a collision with a tractor driven by a villager on the wrong side of the road or with a private car whose undisciplined driver has bought his way out of previous offences. Personal courage, highly prized in a traditional society, can override the cautious rules of the modern world. Two of the worst disasters in the history of Turkish Airways have been caused by brave pilots determined to show their mettle by landing in conditions which would have forced more cautious Western pilots to turn back.

The number of women in Turkish higher education is fast catching up with the number of men,[5] and the proportion of women is high in most liberal professions. Yet in villages and shantytowns women are still murdered by their kith and kin when they are deemed to have sullied the family honour. One's view of Turks and Turkey depends on which class of people and which part of the country one knows. Is it Turkish workers in Germany and elsewhere in Europe, who are usually migrants from poor areas, or are your friends professionals from Istanbul? Are you familiar with tourist resorts or with inner Anatolia? But the fact that the country and the people are diverse does not mean that they are not changing. With all its contrasts and complexities, Turkey is converging with the West within the one universal modern civilization to which Atatürk committed his countrymen.

That convergence goes on undetected in the realm of religion which is often cited as the main dividing line, or even the front line of a clash between Turkey and the West. A few years ago, Paul Henze, an experienced American observer of Turkey, argued that 'the great majority of Turks are Muslims in the same sense that most Europeans and Americans are Christians.'[6] Apart from the fact that the place of religion in life tends to be different in Europe and the USA, the argument can be refined by saying that the Muslim religion in Turkey today resembles European Christianity in the nineteenth century. Thus the upsurge in mosque-building in Turkey since 1950 is reminiscent of the proliferation of churches in industrial Britain in Victorian times.

The heated argument about religious education in Turkey today echoes the conflict between clericals and anticlericals in France in the nineteenth and twentieth centuries. Atatürk was inspired by the French example when he made the Turkish republic a secular state. After his death, and particularly since the 1950s, this secular state has witnessed what has been termed a 'Sunni [Muslim] renaissance'.[7] This has led the British anthropologist David Shankland to contrast the resurgence of faith in Turkey with its decline in Europe. Where in Europe even an agnostic may wonder whether it is not better to prop up the existing remnants of the Church, in Turkey, he argues, the question is how may the expansion, the vibrant sense of certainty of faith amongst the orthodox Sunni population, be channelled, controlled and led so as to satisfy the twin necessities of freedom of religious belief and prevention of the dominance of their version of religion over other, less numerous and less forceful forms of faith.[8]

A few months after these words were penned, the Justice and Development Party, which had its origins in political Sunni Islam, was elected to power in Turkey. Yet immediately after the election, the winning party declared its allegiance to the secular republic and asked that it should not be considered an Islamic party, but rather a centre-right political party analogous to the Christian Democrats in western Europe. The claim remains to be substantiated. But the appointment of a liberal Muslim theologian, who had studied philosophy in England, to the position of minister of state in charge of the department of religious affairs suggested that the West European model was taken seriously. It is true that religious practice is more prevalent in Turkey than in Europe, and that Muslim fundamentalists, although a

small minority, are more numerous in Turkey than Christian fundamentalists are in Europe (although possibly not in the USA). But the
present divergence in the strength of religious feeling between Turkey
and Europe does not contradict the assumption of a process of convergence. The 'Sunni renaissance' accompanies and is partly a reaction
to the continuing organic secularization of Turkish society, just as
Victorian piety developed in counterpoint to the secularization of
British society. As in Britain after the industrial revolution, the revival
of piety is easing the pain and discomforts of Turkey's modernization.
The phenomenon is, arguably, not a sign of a coming clash of civilizations, but a common feature in the development of our universal
civilization.

Democracy, secularity, impersonal government and management
balanced by an active civil society developed gradually in the West
where they had their origins. In contrast, Turkey is on a forced march
to modernity, a march inspired by Atatürk, and sustained after his
death, not by other reformers of his stature, but rather by the forces
of globalization. In Turkey, as elsewhere, these forces are facing some
resistance. But taken as a whole, Turkey is avid for modernity. It is also
avid for recognition as a modern country, for respect as a member of
the family of advanced nations. The visitor who shows this respect
will soon learn to understand Turkey.

PART I

Turkey Since the Death of Atatürk

Introduction
Origins

THE TURKS MAKE their first appearance in world history in the sixth century AD, when they can be identified among the nomadic tribes on the north-eastern confines of China. Their original homeland lay in and around the Altai mountains between the Gobi desert and the western Siberian plain. For centuries, the vast expanses of northern Eurasia, from Finland to the Pacific, had sustained a shifting population of pastoralists whom historians recorded under different names, Cimmerians, Scythians, Sarmatians, Hephtalites, Huns, Turks, Tartars. They fought each other, formed ephemeral kingdoms, supplanted each other, traded with and raided the settled populations on the edges of the northern steppes and forests. The great plains bred warriors who, at times, seized control of neighbouring countries with sedentary populations, from China in the east to Russia in the west. The ethnic origins and languages of the earliest known nomadic tribes are disputed hotly by historians. Some nomadic peoples are classed as Indo-European, others as Finno-Ugrian, others again as Altaic, a group designed to include Turks, Mongols and, sometimes, Manchurians and Koreans. But the distinctions are blurred, as some peoples absorbed others. The environment, rather than ethnic origin, moulded the way of life and the culture of the pastoralists.

In prehistory some tribes moved from west to east, like the ancestors of the native Americans who crossed the Bering Strait from Asia to Alaska. But in historic times the direction of migration and of conquest was predominantly from east to west and from north to south. The last two great waves of nomadic migrants and conquerors were of Turks and Mongols. The two ethnic strands became confused. As a result, the name of Tartar (more correctly, Tatar), originally applied to the Mongols, now designates Turkic peoples once ruled by

Mongols. The Moghuls who conquered India were also of Turkish origin. Then the direction of conquest changed, and rulers of settled peoples gradually won control over the whole of north Eurasia.

The first inscriptions in Turkish, mentioning the ethnic designation of Turk, date back to the beginning of the eighth century. Carved in runes on stone steles, they were found in the wastes of northern Mongolia. As Turkish tribes spread out, east to China and west to the great northern Eurasian plain, they became subject to diverse influences, and the dialects they spoke hardened into separate languages, which together form the Turkic family. The most important influence came from the Muslim world. The Turks were originally animists, worshipping a sky god (*Tanrı*, in modern Turkish spelling) and deities of soil and water (*Yersu*, a term appropriated by the modern Turkish department of village irrigation). The gods were mediated by shamans, male and female witch doctors, whose descendants survive in Korea and southern Siberia. Some Turkish nationalists claim that in Turkey too the heritage of shamanism can be discerned in folk Islam, particularly as practised by the heterodox Alevi community.

The nine Oghuz (in Turkish spelling Oğuz, in Arabic Ghuzz) tribes, which lived closest to the Islamic world, learnt about Islam from Persian and Arab merchants and preachers. Their conversion in the tenth century opened the great age of Turkish expansion, assertion and, eventually, dominance in the Muslim world. Turkish fighters reached that world at first as mercenaries or slave troops of the Abbasid caliphs in Baghdad. By the beginning of the eleventh century, the slaves had become masters, and the trickle of Turkish recruits had turned into a mass migration of Turks into the old Islamic world. As they travelled through Persia on their way west, the Turks came under the influence of Persian Islamic culture and their language was enriched both by Arabic and by Persian words. The old Turkish vocabulary was preserved and explained to the Arabs in the first Turkish encyclopedic dictionary compiled in the beginning of the eleventh century by Mahmud of Kashgar (now in Xinjiang or Chinese Turkistan) and presented to the Abbasid caliph. The caliph was a puppet in the hands of the Seljuk (Selçuk) dynasty which had arisen among the Oghuz. From Baghdad, the Seljuks pushed their ambitions to the north and west. In 1071 the Seljuk ruler Alp Aslan (Alparslan) led an army into Byzantine territory and defeated the emperor Romanos IV Diogenes at Malazgirt, north of Lake Van in eastern Anatolia. The date marks the beginning of the history of Turkey.

Arabs had raided deep into Byzantine territory ever since the birth of Islam in the seventh century. But they did not stay in any numbers in the territory of modern Turkey. The Turks did and gradually colonized it. They called it at first the land of Rum (of the Romans), a name which they later transferred to the Balkans. But by the end of the twelfth century at the latest, Western Christians had another name for Asia Minor (Anatolia). They called it Turkey – first attested as *Turchia* in Italian spelling.

The Mongol invasions of the thirteenth and fifteenth centuries brought more Turks from central Asia to Asia Minor. As Seljuk power, centred on Konya on the Anatolian plateau, was destroyed by the Mongols, a number of autonomous Turkish principalities arose. One of them, in Bithynia (now the region of Bursa), on the borders of the much diminished Byzantine state, attracted Turkish warriors from far and wide. Under the rule of its warlord Osman, it began expanding into Byzantine territory. Osman gave his name to the Ottoman (in Turkish, Osmanlı) dynasty and to the state, which became an empire when his descendant Mehmet II conquered Constantinople (Istanbul) in 1453. The expansion then continued to the gates of Vienna, to be followed by a decline which lasted from the end of the seventeenth to the beginning of the twentieth centuries.

The Turkish nation took shape in the centuries of Seljuk and Ottoman power. The nomadic Turkish conquerors did not displace the original local inhabitants: Hellenized Anatolians (or simply Greeks), Armenians, people of Caucasian origins, Kurds, and – in the Balkans – Slavs, Albanians and others. They intermarried with them, while many local people converted to Islam and 'turned Turk'. They were joined by Muslims from the lands north of the Black Sea and the Caucasus, by Persian craftsmen and Arab scholars, and by European adventurers and converts, known in the West as renegades. As a result, the Turks today exhibit a wide variety of ethnic types. Some have delicate Far Eastern, others heavy local Anatolian features; some, who are descended from Slavs, Albanians or Circassians, have light complexions, others are dark-skinned; many look Mediterranean, others central Asian or Persian. A numerically small, but commercially and intellectually important, group is descended from converts from Judaism. One can hear Turks describe some of their fellow country-men as 'hatchet-nosed Lazes' (a people on the Black Sea coast), 'dark Arabs' (a term which includes descendants of black slaves), or even 'fellahs'. But they are all Turks.

However, not all the inhabitants of present-day Turkey became Muslim, and not all the Muslims adopted the Turkish language and a common Turkish culture. Paradoxically, it seems that there were at one time more Turkish speakers among Christian Armenians than among Muslim Kurds. Muslims were in the majority in Ottoman Anatolia, while Christians formed the overall majority in Ottoman possessions in the Balkans. The religious communities lived separate lives but came together in an economically and culturally productive society which practised an ethnic division of labour. Dairymen in Ottoman Istanbul were predominantly Bulgarian, gardeners Albanian, grocers and fishermen Greek, glaziers Jewish, potters and jewellers Armenian, porters Kurdish. This mosaic was gradually destroyed by nationalists in the nineteenth century. Almost all the Christians are gone, but there are still traces of ethnic and regional specialization: sailors come predominantly from the Black Sea coast; the central Anatolian town of Kayseri keeps alive Armenian skills in trade; people of Caucasian origin are prominent in senior military ranks; heavy manual labour often falls to the lot of the Kurds. The balance is con-stantly shifting. Turks of Anatolian origin are gaining ground at the expense of descendants of refugees from the Balkans; there is a new class of tough Kurdish businessmen. Today ethnic origin is discussed more openly, but matters less, as the country is brought together by a nationwide economy and a common media culture.

In their heyday, the Ottomans provided law and order over a vast area stretching from central Europe to the borders of Persia, from Morocco to the Persian Gulf, and from Crimea to the Sahara. They perfected a system of government based on the manuals of the Persian viziers of Arab caliphs, adding local practices which had developed in the Eastern Roman Empire, and innovating as the need arose. Their standing army, built round a core of slave troops recruited in the Balkans, was the envy of cash-strapped European monarchs. They imported European military technology in ordnance, fortification, the construction and fitting out of ships; and they welcomed European converts who taught them how to apply it. They dotted their dominions with mosques, almshouses, markets, bridges and other public buildings. In architecture, textiles, carpets, pottery, clothes and interior decoration, they developed a distinctive artistic style, which was a synthesis of all the cultural influences which they inherited and which reached them over the centuries. But the Ottoman empire did not push forward the frontiers of knowledge. The Renaissance and the Enlightenment passed it by. Russia became a great power in the eighteenth century after Peter the Great had opened its windows to the West, and when Catherine the Great recruited West Europeans to apply the philosophy of the Enlightenment. The Ottomans did not follow suit until a century later. But while the Muslim rulers of the Ottoman state lagged behind, their Christian subjects were quicker off the mark. They enjoyed a quasi-monopoly of trade that brought them into contact with the developed world with which they also shared a religious affinity. It is they who imported from Europe the divisive ideology of nationalism, which threatened the Ottoman state from within, while the European great powers, with Russia in the lead, pressed on it from outside. The imminence of disaster finally forced reform on the Ottomans in the nineteenth century.

Reforming sultans and their grand viziers began the process of modernization, starting with the army and navy. But it was the more advanced non-Muslim communities and their outside Christian protectors which were the first to profit from the improvements in administration. As the disintegration of the state continued, albeit at a slower pace, the first generation of Muslims trained in Western ways began advocating and then conspiring to introduce more radical change. France was the fount of new ideas: prominent among them was the concept of a nation state based on a common language and welded together by a common culture. The first conspirators, known as Young Ottomans, were liberal constitutionalists, who came together in the 1880s. When their hope of fostering a multinational Ottoman patriotism was disappointed, as their Christian fellow countrymen decided that they would be better off on their own, the Young Ottomans were succeeded at the turn of the century by the Young

Turks who progressed from multinationalism to Muslim nationalism and finally to Turkish nationalism. The progression started after the Young Turk military coup of 1908 and speeded up after the Balkan Wars of 1912–13 which deprived the Ottoman state of most of its European possessions. The Young Turks were inexperienced. Sir Mark Sykes, remembered as one of the authors of the Anglo-French Sykes–Picot agreement for the division of the Ottoman empire in the First World War, dismissed them as poseurs. But they made up in courage what they lacked in knowledge. When it became evident that the Young Turks, far from saving the empire, had hastened its disintegration, the new rulers sought to make good their losses by a desperate gamble. They took their country into the First World War on the side of Germany and Austria-Hungary, and lost it together with their German allies. Defeat opened the prospect of the final partition of the Ottoman state and the loss of Turkish independence. But who were the Turks?

The Turkish nation, as we know it today, was still taking shape. Already the first Ottoman constitution of 1876 had proclaimed Turkish as the official language, although that official language was so replete with Arabic and Persian loan words that it was unintelligible to the mass of native Turkish speakers. But most people still defined themselves in terms of their religion. They were Muslims and, therefore, Turks in the eyes of their rulers and of their enemies, but not always in their own eyes. Most Young Turks were practising Muslims, although the Islam they practised was the religion of army chaplains, religion seen as a social cement holding the state and the nation together. Islam, even in its national Ottoman form, did not inform their whole way of life as it did for the mass of the people.

Mustafa Kemal, who later took the surname of Atatürk, was a Young Turk officer who was a realist of genius. He was both more prudent than the Young Turk leaders and more radical in his vision. His successful record in the Gallipoli campaign in 1915, when he stopped the advance of British and Anzac troops on two vital sectors of the front, allowed him to rally round him the best commanders of the Ottoman army after its defeat in 1918. His criticism of the Young Turk leaders and of their alliance with Germany won him the confidence of the new sultan, Mehmet VI Vahdettin, who was determined to propitiate the victorious Allies in order to save his throne. Sent to Anatolia as the sultan's emissary, Mustafa Kemal proceeded to organize the forces of resistance to the Allies, against the sultan's wishes, while claiming that his aim was to save his sovereign from captivity. He mobilized the Muslim inhabitants of present-day Turkey who had good grounds to fear the prospect of coming under the rule of their Christian neighbours. Experience had taught them that Muslims who came under Christian rule faced eviction, expropriation and, often, death. Mustafa Kemal won the Turkish War of Independence by appealing to Islamic solidarity, by dividing the Allies and using Bolshevik Russia against them, and by limiting his military objective to the defeat of the Armenians in the east and of Greeks in the west. He then won the peace by limiting his territorial claims to the territory which the Ottoman army still held at the end of the First World War, and renouncing the irredentist and expansionist fancies of his predecessors. He persuaded the Bolsheviks that he would not stir up their Turkic and other Muslim subjects, and the colonial powers – Britain, France and Italy – that he would not interfere in their possessions. The treaties which he signed with all of Turkey's neighbours were usually, and accurately, called treaties of non-aggression and non-interference. He was content that Britain and France should maintain order in the Middle East, and Britain in Cyprus. He maintained friendly, but wary, relations with the Bolshevik rulers of the former Russian empire, while resisting Communist subversion inside Turkey.

Sultan Mehmet Vahdettin fled Istanbul before the Allies departed. During the War of Independence, Mustafa Kemal had established the seat of his government in Ankara, on the Anatolian plateau, safely away from the guns of Allied warships. He made it the capital of the republic, which was proclaimed on 29 October 1923 by the assembly he had summoned. The following year he exiled the Ottoman dynasty, and abolished as meaningless the office of Caliph, which the assembly had bestowed on the Ottoman heir Abdülmecit. With the country firmly under his control, Mustafa Kemal then rolled out his reforms. The abolition of the caliphate ushered in a secular state, which controlled religion, and did not allow it any say in public policy or any role in education. The fez, which had been the headgear of Muslim gentlemen since the early nineteenth century, was banned, and the veiling of women strongly discouraged. Laws were aligned on the practice of West European countries; the Christian common era was adopted, as was Sunday as a day of rest. The Latin alphabet replaced the Arabic script, in which the Turks had written their language since their conversion to Islam, and a largely illiterate country learned to read and write in the new alphabet, with a new phonetic spelling reflecting accurately the sounds of the Turkish language. Women were granted equal rights. The institutions of democracy were set up, while political opposition was suppressed. But as they waited for democracy, the Turkish people benefited from rational government which husbanded the country's resources. Atatürk's policy brought peace to Turkey and laid the foundations of progress. After some initial troubles, his reforms were not resisted. But it is hard to imagine them winning approval in a popular referendum.

Revolutions do not obliterate a landscape, but they configure it anew. Change was greatest in the ethnic composition of the population. The Great War and its sequel, the War of Independence, had resulted in the disappearance of Christian Greeks and Armenians from the territory of Turkey, except for a handful in Istanbul. Many had fled when their armies were defeated, and the foreign armies on which they had relied had departed. Others perished. The rest were transferred in an exchange of populations. Armenia was absorbed in the Soviet Union and its nationalism stifled. With the Greek minority in Turkey reduced to some 100,000, in Istanbul, and a similar number of Muslims (mainly Turks) in Greek Western Thrace, the two countries had little to quarrel about, and by 1930 they had become allies in defence of the status quo. Atatürk described his policy as 'peace at home and peace in the world'. Peace with all his neighbours allowed him to concentrate on fashioning the new Turkish state. But the trauma of creating a homogeneous nation state could not be cured quickly.

The Armenians found it hard to reconcile themselves to the final loss of their historic home, even though they had long been in a minority there. After the Second World War, nationalists in the Armenian diaspora demanded that Turkey should recognize the elimination of their people from Anatolia as an act of genocide. To bring their demand to the attention of the world, violent Armenian nationalists launched a campaign of assassination against Turkish diplomats. It failed in its purpose, and Armenian nationalists concentrated their efforts on securing from various national parliaments resolutions recognizing the genocide of their people. When the small Armenian republic in Transcaucasia gained its independence with the collapse of the Soviet Union in 1990, it seconded the efforts of the diaspora. At the same time it fought and defeated its larger eastern neighbour, Azerbaijan, and occupied a fifth of its territory, causing the flight of up to a million Azeris. Armenia does not pose a threat to Turkey. There are too few Armenians to people the lands taken from Azerbaijan, let alone ancient Armenia in Turkey. But as long as Armenia does not renounce its territorial claims and does not make peace with Azerbaijan, Turkey will not engage in full diplomatic and trade relations with it. As for the genocide campaign, Turkey holds that claims and counter-claims should be examined by historians and not by politicians. In any case, Turks and other Muslims have also been expelled from lands where they used to live and have been killed in their hundreds of thousands. The dispute drags on.

The old devils of ethnic animosity arose also in Greek-Turkish relations, when new assets had to be apportioned after the Second World War. At the time that the two countries made peace in Lausanne in 1923, no one worried about the continental shelf or flight information regions. But in recent years, claims to the waters of the Aegean sea, the air above it and any resources there may be below it, have caused friction which, at times, has threatened to turn into armed conflict. Fortunately, the resources of the sea are limited, and Greece and Turkey should be able to reach an accommodation if they learn to trust one other. It is more difficult to reconcile Greek and Turkish claims in Cyprus. The Greeks do not see why their kinsmen, who form the majority of the island's population, should not be free to determine their – and its – future, provided the Turkish minority is properly treated. Turkey has succeeded in gaining acceptance of its claim that the Turkish community in Cyprus is entitled to its own state within a Cyprus federation. But even if agreement is reached on a federation, it will have to be tested over many years before the dispute can be consigned to history.

In foreign policy, Atatürk's defence of the status quo had to be adjusted when the Versailles settlement was destroyed by the dictators, when the colonial powers left the Middle East, and when, after the Second World War, Stalin revived the Tsars' push to the south. In Atatürk's own lifetime, changes in the international balance of forces allowed him to re-establish military control over the Turkish Straits and to regain the district of Alexandretta (now the province of Hatay) from Syria, to which the French had promised independence. The beginning of the Cold War brought Turkey into the orbit of American power. Now, the expansion of the European Union has created a new pole of attraction. But Turkish policy has retained the cautious, pragmatic character with which Atatürk had endowed it.

At home, Turkish nation-building progressed apace, but had to face the growth of divisive Kurdish nationalism. 'The black cloud of ignorance' which hung over the country was dissipated, as Atatürk intended. A society, vastly expanded in numbers, held together, but while old inequalities were removed, new ones took their place. It seemed that political democracy brought out old problems which Atatürk and his companions had not resolved: the political demands of the Muslims who resisted secularization, and of Kurds who resisted assimilation. The military, from whose midst Atatürk had come, who had been in the vanguard of modernization, and on whom the founding father of the republic had relied to save and defend the state, seemed loath to leave its fate in the hands of elected politicians. Liberals complained that Atatürk's republicanism had perpetuated the authoritarian traditions of the Ottoman state. But if the problems are old, the setting is new. The balance between liberty and order has to be adjusted continuously. Atatürk's priority was order. It is because the order which he established has largely held, that the Turks can now embrace democracy, as the new secular, universal religion.

I

State Before Nation
1938–1945

MUSTAFA KEMAL ATATÜRK did not start from scratch when he founded the Turkish republic in 1923. He had inherited the administrative structures and traditions of the Ottoman empire. But the instrument at his disposal – the officers and civil servants trained under the old regime – was to serve a changed country, which had emerged in ruins from foreign invasion and civil war, and which had seen a massive exodus of skilled non-Muslims and an influx of Muslim peasants from the Balkans. Law and order had broken down and traditional social hierarchies had been upset. Alone Istanbul, the old Ottoman capital, had escaped destruction, and material continuity inspired hopes of political continuity in the minds of Mustafa Kemal's critics in that city. In the atmosphere of Istanbul, a liberal evolution seemed possible. But the view from the new capital, Ankara, was different. Shabby ministries in tumbledown provincial buildings, unhappy and underpaid civil servants lodging in dormitories, bore witness to the country's poverty in material and human resources. The vast task of reconstruction required firm leadership and a coherent policy.

Mustafa Kemal's first task was to extend the control of the republican government and the reach of its laws to the whole of the national territory. He had accomplished this task by the time he died in 1938. The state which he fashioned had a liberal republican constitution, but it was ruled in an authoritarian manner. Authority emanated from the president who exercised civil power through a prime minister and military power through the chief of the general staff. Atatürk sought advice; he knew how to delegate. But it was he who decided policy, and who selected and dismissed prime ministers, and, through the prime minister (and with due regard for constitutional propriety), ministers and senior officials.

Atatürk was also the leader of the single party he had founded – the Republican People's Party (*Cumhuriyet Halk Partisi*/CHP). But he took care not to repeat the mistakes of the Young Turks when party officials compromised orderly public administration by interfering in its day-to-day work. In contrast to contemporary totalitarian regimes, the single party did not dominate the state. It was the state that was in charge of the party, which served it as an instrument of popular mobilization through the dissemination of the ideas and ideals of the modernizers, and also as a weak mechanism of control over the administration – weak because the interior minister and, under him, provincial governors doubled as party leaders.

Immediately after the proclamation of the republic, Mustafa Kemal (as he then was) allowed his personal rivals to form a parliamentary opposition. Then in 1930, when Turkey had to cope with the effects of the world depression, he encouraged a personal friend to form an opposition party as a channel for popular discontent. Both experiments were short-lived, as the president decided that, irrespective of the wishes of opposition leaders, their parties were bound to become a focus of 'reaction', in other words of hostility to his reforms. After the parliamentary opposition had dissolved itself within a few months, the list of candidates put forward by the Republican People's Party, all of whom were elected unopposed, included a number of 'independents'. They were meant to question the government in parliament, but the degree of control they exercised was minimal.

It was within this firm framework of a hierarchical state which was an amalgam of French republicanism and Ottoman authoritarianism that the Muslim inhabitants of Turkey were moulded into a Turkish nation made up of citizens equal before the law, but manifestly unequal in wealth, educational attainment, lifestyle and access to power. Yet the ideal of equal citizenship, superimposed on the traditional concept of the equality of believers under the divine law, did find a place in the national psyche. As in revolutionary France, the rulers addressed the ruled as 'citizens' (*vatandaş*) even as they coerced them, as witness the nationalist slogan 'Citizen, speak Turkish' – and not Kurdish, Arabic, Circassian, Ladino or any other language they had used habitually until then.

The theory and practice of Atatürk's republic were, if anything, reinforced after his death on 10 November 1938, by his successor and loyal lieutenant İsmet İnönü. İsmet had served as Mustafa Kemal's military subordinate in the Great War and in the War of Independence. He became the republic's first prime minister in 1923, withdrew briefly the following year, and returned to serve as Atatürk's chief executive for another twelve years from 1925 to 1937. İsmet was a prudent man. He had taken his time before deciding to join Mustafa Kemal in Ankara at the beginning of the War of Independence. Atatürk relied on him for the meticulous execution of his orders, for sound advice, and, often reluctantly, for his warnings, when the president's enthusiasms threatened embarrassment. Two years before his death, Atatürk tired of these warnings and dismissed İsmet. But he continued to esteem him.

The West got to know İsmet as an extremely tough negotiator at the end of the War of Independence – first in the armistice talks on Turkish soil then at the peace negotiations in Lausanne in 1922–3. Short and sturdy, slightly deaf, a good family man, highly disciplined in his habits, secretive as a politician, a faithful servant of the state, suspicious of businessmen, he valued effectiveness above charm. Foreigners knew him, more often than not, as 'Mr No' (or, at best, 'Yes, but . . .'), an uncompromising defender of what he saw as his country's dignity and national interest. At home his austere policies won him few friends. 'İsmet in, *kismet* [luck] out' – '*Geldi İsmet, gitti kısmet*' – people joked wryly. Of his cunning, they would say, 'İsmet can keep a hundred foxes in his head and stop their tails from becoming entangled.' He was the man who gave away nothing. It was a useful attribute in the years of the Second World War.

Elected president on 11 November, İnönü was given the title of National Leader (*Millî Şef*) at a convention of the Republican People's Party which proclaimed Atatürk the country's Eternal Leader (*Ebedî Şef*). The titles, which sounded distinctly odd in Turkish, reflected the usage of contemporary and subsequent dictatorships. But for İnönü, as for Atatürk before him, absolute personal rule was a temporary necessity rather than a permanent ideal. Like Atatürk, İnönü was a pragmatist. But he was more cautious, more patient and more sober than the founding father of the republic. The presidential palace on Çankaya hill in Ankara became a well-ordered family home. Atatürk's drinking companions were given an honourable discharge; his companions in the War of Independence, who had become political opponents, were conciliated and co-opted into high-ranking appointments – speaker of parliament, minister, ambassador – while being denied effective political power. They were also warned that criticism of Atatürk would not be tolerated.

İnönü's first concern was to safeguard the achievements of the republic: the political and economic independence of the state, the integrity of the national territory, domestic law and order, Atatürk's cultural revolution and the slow but sure development of the national economy. He had to exercise stronger controls in pursuit of these aims, partly because he did not have the unrivalled prestige Atatürk had won, first as saviour of Turkey's Muslim inhabitants from infidel domination and then as founding father of the republic, and, more importantly, because Nazi Germany was about to unleash the Second World War. İnönü needed a disciplined and united home front if he was to parry the dangers which faced the young Turkish republic in an unpredictable international environment. As war threatened, he could not tolerate domestic dissent or economic experimentation. The approach of the World War brought on a siege mentality and a siege economy.

From November 1938 to June 1945, when at the eleventh hour Turkey became a founding member of the United Nations, the conduct of foreign policy was İnönü's main preoccupation and, in retrospect, his least disputed achievement. Atatürk had not been a neutralist. He had formed alliances with neighbouring states and had supported measures for collective security under the League of Nations. More cautious by temperament, İnönü avoided taking sides in foreign conflicts. Germany had become Turkey's main trading partner, and İnönü was loath to antagonize it. But Hitler's occupation of Czechoslovakia (which had already lost part of its territory to Germany) in March 1939, followed by Mussolini's invasion of Albania a month later, proved that the Axis powers were determined to expand in all directions. Fearing that Mussolini would try to dominate the eastern Mediterranean with Hitler's blessing, İnönü sought foreign support for his defences. France and Britain were also looking for allies; the Soviet Union, with which Turkey had a friendship pact, seemed to be trying for an anti-Fascist coalition.

Turkey had been negotiating with France since 1936 in order to make good its claim to the district (*sancak*) of İskenderun (Alexandretta) which had been administered by France, the mandatory power in Syria. In July 1938, France had agreed to the entry of Turkish troops into the territory. In September that year the *sancak* became the independent state of Hatay under a government subservient to Ankara. Turkey then indicated that if France agreed to the union of Hatay with Turkey, it would be willing to conclude an alliance with both France and Britain. On 23 June 1939 an agreement with France on Hatay (which immediately voted to join Turkey) was accompanied by the issue of a common declaration on mutual assistance against aggression in the eastern Mediterranean. As a result of parallel negotiations, a similar declaration was agreed with France's ally, Britain. To procure Soviet support for the alignment, İnönü dispatched his foreign minister Şükrü Saracoğlu to Moscow. But in August 1939 Stalin had abandoned the idea of an anti-Fascist alliance and had come to an understanding with Nazi Germany, Italy's senior partner in the Axis. On 31 August Hitler invaded Poland, launching the Second World War. When Saracoğlu arrived in Moscow on 26 September, there was no longer any common ground between the Soviet Union and Turkey. His negotiations with Stalin's foreign minister Molotov were interrupted by the arrival in Moscow of Hitler's foreign minister, Joachim von Ribbentrop. When Saracoğlu and Molotov met again, not only did the Soviets insist that Turkey's agreement with Britain and France should be void of useful content, but they also made it clear that they wanted joint control over the Turkish Straits. Saracoğlu rejected this on the spot. Faced with clear Soviet hostility, Turkey signed an alliance with Britain and France on 19 October.

By that time Turkey had a new prime minister, Dr Refik Saydam. An army doctor by training, Saydam had travelled with Atatürk to Anatolia as his personal physician at the beginning of the Turkish War of Independence in May 1919, and had subsequently served as minister of health. Atatürk's last prime minister Celal Bayar had resigned in January 1939. Bayar was seen as the patron of the new class of Muslim Turkish entrepreneurs whom he sustained with loans when he became founding director of the Turkish Business Bank (*Türkiye İş*

Bankası). The entrepreneurs were nurtured by the government, which financed them and employed them as contractors. But Muslim businessmen lacked experience, as well as capital. Some of their projects were speculative and the balance of public and private interest was uncertain. İnönü was put off by the danger of speculation and corruption. Bayar took risks, İnönü avoided them whenever possible. Bayar had become minister of the economy in İnönü's cabinet in 1932, at Atatürk's insistence. He then replaced İnönü as prime minister in 1937. But although a rival, he stood aside from plots to prevent İnönü from becoming president after Atatürk's death.

The long-standing clash of personalities between İnönü and Bayar was augmented by policy disagreements. 'The main problem', İnönü wrote soon after becoming president, 'was Celal Bayar's financial and economic policy. It had started by allowing too much room to demagogy and was not based on any [proper] calculations. The state finances were being fundamentally ruined. Trade and the national currency were undermined.'[1] The disagreement between İnönü and Bayar, which was to affect Turkish politics for many years, is often presented as a clash between two rival economic policies – between a preference for a control economy and economic liberalism favouring a free market. But İnönü's contemporary reference to economic 'demagogy' provides a better explanation. Like most developing countries Turkey has always been prey to the temptation to overspend in order to speed up development and please a poverty-stricken population. İnönü resisted the temptation from the start, at the cost of his popularity, opting for sound finances with all the disadvantages of bureaucratic control that his policy implied. But bureaucratic controls could not cope with the economic problems which the World War was about to create.

Soon after the outbreak of the war, the country's administrative capacity and resources were strained by an earthquake which struck the town of Erzincan and the surrounding area on the east Anatolian plateau in the night of 26/27 December 1939: 33,000 people were killed, more than 100,000 injured, and some 120,000 buildings were destroyed. Erzincan, which lies in an upland valley on the invasion route to central Turkey, had often been struck by earthquakes, and it had few monuments of note. This time the devastation was complete, and the town had to be rebuilt on a new site. Aid came from countries fighting each other in the World War as they competed in trying to impress Turkey with their generosity. What, however, created a lasting impression was the response of convicts who left their ruined prisons and took part in rescue operations. They were rewarded with an amnesty.[2]

The spirit of solidarity evoked by the Erzincan earthquake disaster was sadly absent in business conduct. While Turkey was more or less self-sufficient in food, simple textiles and coal, it relied on the import of almost all manufactures. As the war restricted supplies, shortages quickly developed. They were aggravated by hoarding. In March 1940, the government decided to increase the strength of the Turkish army to 1,300,000 men.[3] The call-up reduced the productive capacity of a largely agricultural population. As the government delayed introducing price controls and rationing, a black market sprang up. In February 1940 the government responded by issuing the National Protection Law which allowed it to control the economy by imposing compulsory labour, fixing production quotas and prices, and freezing rents.[4] As popular discontent grew, the government tried to stifle criticism by subjecting the press, which was in any case far from free, to further restrictions in April 1940.[5] The proclamation of martial law in Istanbul and Turkish Thrace in October that year allowed the authorities to exercise full censorship over the national press.

The threat to Turkey drew nearer when Italy declared war on the Allies on 10 June 1940 just as France was about to collapse before the German onslaught. The tripartite pact required Turkey to provide help to the Allies if the war spread to the Mediterranean. But Turkey was absolved of this obligation if it involved a conflict with the Soviet Union. Citing this as a justification, the Turkish government issued a declaration of non-belligerency on 26 June. Whatever the legal position, France's capitulation had reduced the tripartite alliance to a bilateral one between Turkey and Britain, and the latter was in no position to insist that Turkey should enter the war or to help it if it did. İnönü's government stuck to its policy of non-belligerence when Italy attacked Greece on 28 October 1940. In April of the following year the Germans came to the aid of their

Italian allies whom the Greeks had repulsed. The Bulgarians joined the Axis to share the spoils. By May 1941, the Germans, Italians and Bulgarians had occupied Yugoslavia and Greece. German troops stood poised on the Turkish frontier in Thrace. Ribbentrop asked Turkey to allow Germany unlimited transit facilities for troops and equipment and offered some Greek territory in return. İnönü was not tempted, and Nazi Germany had to content itself with a treaty of friendship and non-aggression which it concluded with Turkey on 18 June 1941. A few days later, Hitler invaded the Soviet Union. A secret letter attached to the treaty of neutrality and friendship which Turkey had concluded with the Soviet Union in 1925 promised that friendship should remain unaffected should one of the parties fight a war with any other state.[6] But in 1939, the friendship established by Atatürk had given way to acute Turkish fears of Stalin's expansionism. The initial German victories in the USSR reduced that fear. But the possibility that in an effort to bolster the Soviets the Allies, joined by the United States after Pearl Harbor, might sacrifice Turkish interests preoccupied İnönü's government. Non-belligerence was redefined as 'active neutrality'.

Preserving neutrality was now İnönü's main concern. Turkey had received arms from Britain after signing the 1939 treaty. In the summer of 1942 it received a credit from Berlin to buy German arms. Favours to one side were balanced with favours to the other, depending on the fortunes of war. It was not an easy course to navigate, not least because domestic opinion was divided. There were liberals in Turkey's metropolitan elite who favoured the Allies, but anti-Russian and anti-Communist sentiment was strong also, not least in the armed forces and in the ranks of the government and the single party. The Republican People's Party had been founded by former members of the Committee of Union and Progress (CUP) – Turkish nationalists who had fought on the side of the Kaiser's Germany against Tsarist Russia in the First World War. The leaders of the CUP had espoused the ideals of Pan-Turkists (also known as Pan-Turanians), who dreamt of liberating the Turkic peoples from Russian rule. Atatürk had repudiated both Pan-Turkism and Pan-Islamism, saying that these policies had brought nothing but harm to Turkey. İnönü was of the same opinion, but the prospect of a German victory in Russia could not but encourage Pan-Turkists who had been kept under control since the establishment of the republic. In any case, there were in Turkey many refugees from the Turkic republics of the Soviet Union who were all too ready to aid and abet the Germans. İnönü did not move against them as long as the fortunes of war remained uncertain.

The influence of Nazi racist theories reinforced the policy of discrimination against the religious minorities. In the Ottoman empire, much of the country's trade and manufacture had been in the hands of foreigners and indigenous Christians and Jews. After 1908, and particularly during the First World War, the CUP implemented what it called a 'national economic policy' which favoured Turkish Muslim businessmen. The policy was pushed forward under the republic, which passed a law in 1932 banning foreign nationals from the exercise of most trades and professions. Many of these foreigners were in fact local people who had acquired foreign passports during the years of Ottoman weakness. The period of Nazi ascendance in the Second World War provided an opportunity to destroy the economic power of local Jews and Christians who were Turkish citizens. As shortages and a rising public deficit led to a steep rise in consumer prices (from just over 1 per cent in 1939 to nearly 100 per cent in 1942), and as public anger targeted hoarders and speculators, usually identified as non-Muslim businessmen, the government introduced a capital levy which it justified as a measure to force the wealthy to shoulder a proper share of wartime hardship. A law passed in November 1942 demanded immediate payment of the levy, assessed by *ad hoc* commissions. Defaulters were to be sent to labour camps.

It soon became known that the commissions, made up partly of Turkish Muslim businessmen, had been given the green light by the authorities to eliminate their local Christian and Jewish competitors. These ended up by paying ten times the tax collected from Muslim Turks.[7] Some 1,400 non-Muslim businessmen, mostly Jewish, who were unable to meet their tax assessments, were sent in mid-winter to a camp at Aşkale, on the bleak eastern Anatolian plateau. Surprisingly, almost all survived. The Jewish community feared that public protests would only make matters worse, while hoping that the Allies would intervene tactfully on behalf of the non-Muslims in Turkey. But there were private appeals for help. 'When a gendarme, who turns out to be a brigand, and the state itself threatens an unarmed citizen with a knife demanding his life or his wallet . . . only the public opinion of civilized countries can help him,' wrote the Istanbul correspondent of the American Jewish Committee. Allied public opinion was alerted by a series of articles by C.L. Sulzberger in the *New York Times*.[8] Complaints, however muted, had an effect, but only when the tide of war had turned.

For the first time in Ottoman and Turkish history there was discrimination also against one group of Muslims – the *dönme* (converts) or *Selânikli* (Salonicans). These descendants of Jews who had converted to Islam from the seventeenth century onwards were forced to pay twice as much tax as other Muslims. Vicious cartoons and editorials in papers close to the government attested to the spread of the anti-Semitic virus from Germany.

The capital levy left its imprint on the country's development. The Turkish Muslim mercantile middle class became more numerous and richer. But rather than support the government, it used its new power to demand a greater say in running the country. Enriched by illiberal means it came to demand greater liberalism in politics and the economy. Nearly half of a Jewish community, which numbered some 80,000 people in 1945, left Turkey for Israel, when that state was founded in 1948.[9] Greece, in the throes of civil war after the end of the Second World War, and Soviet Armenia, firmly under Stalin's thumb, did not attract many Greeks and Armenians from Turkey. But some made their way to the United States and other Western destinations. The remaining minority communities, concentrated almost entirely in Istanbul, made good some of their losses when Turkey came under a more liberal regime after the first free elections in 1950.

The author of the capital levy was Şükrü Saracoğlu, who became prime minister when Refik Saydam died in July 1942. But President İnönü must have approved this discriminatory tax. At the end of the Turkish War of Independence he had argued against the exemption of Istanbul Greeks and of Turks in Greek Western Thrace from the exchange of populations agreed at Lausanne in 1923. İnönü had nothing against foreigners provided they made their money in their own countries. He made an exception for foreign experts whose advice Turkey needed, and continued to employ the German Jewish academics recruited by the Turkish authorities in Atatürk's time. But while these academics were held in honour, İnönü allowed local Jews to be dispossessed. At the same time, Turkish diplomats behaved honourably in protecting Jews who were Turkish citizens in Nazi-occupied Europe. Some Jews fleeing from Nazi persecution in the Balkans were allowed to make their way through Turkey, particularly when the British mandatory authorities in Palestine granted them immigration certificates. Others were turned back. Such was the tragic fate of the refugees on board the barely seaworthy Romanian steamer *Struma* which arrived in Istanbul in December 1941. Denied immigration certificates to go to Palestine, they were kept in appalling conditions on board the ship, which was then towed back into the Black Sea where it was torpedoed by a Soviet submarine. Only one of the 769 refugees survived.[10]

The capital levy did not solve Turkey's wartime economic problems. It netted the treasury only half of the sum expected (221 million out of 465 million lira). Tax unpaid under the levy was cancelled in September 1943, and the businessmen deported to Aşkale were allowed to return home. As the government tried to balance its books, it increased to 10 per cent the proportion of farm produce which it demanded in tax. A deputy complained in parliament that this meant the reintroduction of tithes, which had been abolished soon after the establishment of the republic.[11] An attempt had been made in 1938 to protect the peasantry by setting up a public purchasing agency – the Office of Soil Products. However, the prices it paid were too low to ward off rural destitution. Another measure to improve conditions in the countryside was the creation in March 1940 of Village Institutes to train young people who were then expected to spread modern practical skills and a modern world outlook in rural communities all over the country. To this day, many Turkish intellectuals believe that this was one of İnönü's most important achievements, even though it fell foul of nationalists and traditionalists and was cut short when liberal ways were adopted after the end of the war. Another initiative, admired to this day, was the establishment of an office which published translations of the classics of world literature. Apart from helping to realize Atatürk's vision of a Turkey integrated into the mainstream of world civilization, this gave employment to a rising generation of talented writers.

As the war progressed, İnönü began to repress right-wing nationalists who had pinned their hopes on a German victory in Russia. The war had exacerbated conflicts among Turkey's intellectuals and students. When a left-wing writer, Sabahattin Ali, accused the country's leading racist Nihal Atsız of having insulted him in an article and sued him for libel, the supporters of Atsız staged a noisy demonstration outside the courthouse in Ankara, shouting 'Down with the Communists!' The government was alarmed at this open display of hostility towards the Soviet Union, whose armies were winning the war in the east. A committee under the minister of education, Hasan-Âli Yücel, the patron both of the Village Institutes and of the translations of world classics, produced a list of forty-seven people accused of creating a secret society to promote racism and Pan-Turanianism. Twenty-three were put on trial in September 1944. Along with well-known right-wing ideologues, they included an obscure infantry lieutenant, Alpaslan Türkeş, who was to become prominent many years later as a military conspirator and then a nationalist party leader and cabinet minister. The accused were found guilty in March 1945, and most were sentenced to ten years in prison. But two years later, as the Cold War began, they were all acquitted on appeal, as the 'exponents of a nationalist ideology against an ideology which was not national'.[12]

Domestic politics reflected Turkey's stance in a war-torn world. From the end of 1942 onwards Churchill was determined to secure Turkey's entry into the war on the side of the Allies. Faced with the threat that resistance to British demands risked British acceptance of a privileged position, perhaps even a base, for the Russians in the Turkish Straits, İnönü sought to gain time. On 30 January 1943 Churchill arrived in the southern Turkish city of Adana for a conference with İnönü, who argued that he needed military supplies before he could join the conflict on the side of the Allies. On 17 November 1943, İnönü's foreign minister Numan Menemencioğlu declared that Turkey had agreed in principle to enter the war. But when, ten days later, İnönü travelled to Cairo to meet Churchill and Roosevelt he found that disagreements between the Allies allowed him to procrastinate. Stalin, whose armies were in the ascendant, saw that he would find it more difficult to get his way over the Straits if he accepted Turkey as an ally. Roosevelt did not want to be distracted from the

opening of a second front in Europe. The only result of the conference was the dispatch of a British military mission to Turkey in
January 1944.

İnönü continued to ration his concessions to Allied demands. In
April, Turkey declared that it would stop exporting to Germany the
chrome ore used in the manufacture of steel. In June, after British protests at the passage of German military transports through the Turkish
Straits, İnönü arranged for the resignation of his foreign minister
Menemencioğlu, whom the British wrongly identified as an obstacle
to Turkey's entry into the war. In August, Turkey broke off relations
with Germany. Finally on 23 February 1945, when Soviet troops were
within 40 miles of Berlin and Anglo-American forces were nearing
Cologne, Turkey declared war on Germany and Japan, and thus
earned the right to take part in the founding conference of the United
Nations in San Francisco.

İnönü's policy was founded on the assumption, or at least the hope,
that sooner or later the Western Allies and the Soviet Union would
fall out. Events proved him right, but at first he had to negotiate the
dangerous transition from the World War to the Cold War. In March
1945, the Soviet government announced that it would not renew the
Turkish-Soviet friendship pact of 1925. In June, the Soviet foreign
minister Molotov let it be known that the price of Soviet friendship
would be frontier 'rectification' – in other words the cession of territory which Turkey had regained from Russia after the First World War
– and the establishment of Soviet bases in the Straits. Stalin repeated
his demand for bases at the Potsdam conference in July–August that
year. Although this alarmed the Western Allies, it was not clear at first
how far they would go in supporting Turkey, whose image had
suffered from the pursuit of neutrality in the war.

Fortunately for Turkey, it was not the only target of Stalin's expansionism. The Soviets were determined to consolidate their grip on
central and eastern Europe; they supported the Communists in their
attempt to seize power in Greece; they were loath to withdraw from
Iranian Azerbaijan. Harry Truman, who became US President on the
death of Roosevelt in April 1945, came to the conclusion that the
Soviet advance had to be held all along the line. The American decision to support Turkey was symbolized by the arrival in Istanbul of

the battleship *Missouri* in April 1946, ostensibly to repatriate the body of a Turkish ambassador who had died in Washington. Never was a funerary transport received with such an explosion of joy. Popular legend has it that even the prostitutes of Istanbul offered their services free to visiting American sailors. The joy was justified. The *Missouri* was the harbinger of the Truman Doctrine, proclaimed in March 1947, under which the United States pledged to assist Greece and Turkey in their resistance to Communist encroachment. Turkey's image changed from that of a prevaricating neutral to that of a stalwart ally in the containment of Soviet Communism. İnönü had lost nothing through his policy in the World War. First, he had gained Allied arms and then Allied support. He had halted the destruction of war at his country's frontiers. He had safeguarded the country's territory and its independence. He had also shown that Turkey knew where its interests lay and could not be taken for granted.

2

The High Cost of Free Elections
1945–1960

TURKEY WAS A tightly run country when the Second World War ended in 1945. The government budget was balanced; publicly owned utilities showed a profit; foreign trade was in surplus. But economic rectitude was achieved at the cost of depressed living standards. The countryside was poor, not to say destitute. Public employees were badly paid. State enterprises paid their way not because they were well run, but because they could charge high prices for their goods and services. Commercial private initiative was stifled. Discontent was widespread. The government could contain it so long as its Republican People's Party (CHP) had a monopoly of power, the press was censored, strikes were banned and associations and demonstrations subject to stringent controls. But the country was used to authoritarian government: most people resented it, but few challenged it. In politics, centred on the capital, the challenge came largely from malcontents within the ruling party, and was often fed by personal animosity, in the first place against President İsmet İnönü. In Istanbul, which had a tradition of opposition to orders emanating from Ankara, the educated elite, the business community, the press, such thinkers as the country had, were all eager to throw off government controls. But the malcontents were united only in their desire for greater freedom, and often by their personal dislike of the president and his ministers. There were many scores to settle with İnönü, who had been prime minister for many years under Atatürk and then unchallenged second president since November 1938. People knew what irked them. But when it came to proposing remedies, the divided post-war world offered widely differing sources of inspiration.

Although voices were sometimes raised in protest, the opposition was non-violent, even polite. The country was restive but peaceful.

There were few political prisoners – a handful of pro-Soviet Communists, the most famous among them the poet Nazım Hikmet, joined, towards the end of the war, by several pro-Nazi racists. Now and then, the police raided meetings of banned Muslim brotherhoods and detained the organizers. Politics hardly touched the majority – the 14 million people, out of a total population of 19 million, who lived in 34,000 villages. But it is they who became the object of the first political battle which led to the formation of opposition parties.

In May 1945, the government introduced a reform bill for the distribution of land to landless peasants at the expense of landowners and the state domain. It was a typical example of top-down reforming zeal. There had been no agrarian agitation for land. The peasants had suffered from low prices, forced deliveries, compulsory labour, and taxes which they were unable to pay for the construction of schools and roads. Agriculture as a whole had been held back by lack of capital, equipment and skills. But there was no pressure on the land, as left-wing authors were to admit towards the end of the twentieth century after spending years demanding that the government should take on the landlords, and after trying to make political capital out of the few isolated instances of forcible land occupation. In the words of Professor Çağlar Keyder, 'The history of the agrarian structure . . . was conditioned by an abundance of land relative to population.' Some 80 per cent of the peasantry were independent petty producers. Technology had remained unchanged for centuries, and an average family could crop and cultivate an area of only five hectares. 'Anatolian soil was on the whole tired and not very fertile.' But as there was no shortage of land, 'it was always possible to move out of established settlements and start anew with freshly reclaimed land'.[1] Large estates were to be found mainly in the Kurdish areas of eastern Turkey, where the government had earlier tried to break them up. But as the Kurdish peasants rallied round their tribal chieftains on whose protection they relied, the estates survived. In the country, as a whole, holdings larger than 700 hectares represented some 20 per cent of the 20 million hectares of privately owned land. The area of cultivable land belonging to the state was estimated at 3 million hectares. In addition, large tracts were registered as the common property of villages.[2]

The landlords were well represented in the ranks of the Republican

People's Party. They found an eloquent spokesman in Adnan Menderes, a 46-year-old politician whose family farmed an estate in the province of Aydın in the Aegean coastal area. A good-looking man with a smiling face, he was articulate, an orator with a popular appeal, ambitious, nervous, ready to criticize, but himself intolerant of criticism. He had cut his political teeth in the short-lived opposition Republican Free Party in 1930 before joining the ranks of the government party. Menderes argued forcibly that compulsory redistribution was not needed in a country where one could buy a hectare of land for the price of a pair of shoes.[3] He was joined by a handful of other deputies. In spite of this unusual verbal assault on the government, parliament passed the bill unanimously in a slightly amended form on 11 June 1945. There were other amendments later. In the end some state land was distributed, but private landholdings were hardly affected. In any case, registering assets in the name of proxies, usually members of the family, was – and remains to this day – a well-established practice to circumvent the designs of the state.

On 7 June 1945, a few days before the land reform bill was approved, İnönü's best-known rival, Celal Bayar, who had been Atatürk's last prime minister, joined Menderes and two other well-known members of the ruling party in submitting a motion asking that the democratic principles of the constitution should be applied in practice. When the motion was rejected, Bayar resigned from the party, while the other three signatories of the motion were expelled. However, President İnönü, who throughout his long life was accused of being deaf only to what he did not want to hear, decided to respond to the new mood, but in his own good time.

Domestic change in Turkey has always been influenced by the external environment. In 1945 politics developed against the background of the threat which Stalin posed to Turkey's independence and territorial integrity. Democratic reforms, above all free elections, would commend Turkey to the West, whose support was essential to resist Soviet pressure. But there was a danger that greater freedom would be exploited by the handful of Communists and fellow-travellers in Turkey. Although few in number, they were influential in the press and among intellectuals. They were more dangerous than the much more numerous right-wing, religiously motivated opponents of the republic, who had no powerful foreign backers.

There was no law against the formation of opposition parties, which in the past had been checked by administrative means. The first to try his luck in the new environment was a wealthy Istanbul businessman, Nuri Demirağ. He joined forces with Hüseyin Avni Ulaş, a veteran politician who had been a conservative opponent of Atatürk, and with a journalist, Cevat Rıfat Atilhan, known as an admirer of Hitler, and together they registered a new National Development Party (MKP). Before long the founders quarrelled among themselves and the party sank without trace. In the meantime, left-wingers – from Communists to drawing-room socialists – were agitating both for democracy and for a rapprochement with the Soviets. The Russians were universally feared, but democracy was popular and there was a danger that Communist fellow-travellers might find a place in the democratic opposition. All over Europe, Communists had manipulated National Liberation Fronts, which had originally included genuine democrats, in order to seize power. In Turkey this threat was pre-empted. On 4 December 1945, nationalist students of Istanbul University, bearing aloft pictures of Atatürk and İnönü, attacked the presses of newspapers and magazines friendly to the Soviets. The police did not interfere, and the left-wing press was destroyed by rioting students. Turkey's best-known left-wing journalist, Zekeriya Sertel, who had been briefly Atatürk's press chief during the War of Independence, and who later became the editor of the influential left-wing daily *Tan* (The Dawn), and his American-trained, radical wife Sabiha, escaped to the Soviet Union. Shortly afterwards left-wing academics were purged from universities.

With Soviet sympathizers out of the way, Celal Bayar and the three former members of the ruling Republican People's Party (CHP) who had asked for democracy in practice went ahead and formed their own party on 7 January 1946. They called it the Democrat Party (DP). Henceforth, it was hoped, Republicans and Democrats would compete against each other, just as in the United States. It was meant to be a civilized contest: on the day the DP was founded, İnönü invited Bayar to dinner and wished him luck.[4] More importantly, he changed the law which, since Ottoman times, provided for elections in two rounds. In the first round, voters chose an electoral college in each province which then selected the deputies who were to sit in parliament. The change made in June 1946 provided for direct elections. But a flaw remained: voting was public, but the votes were counted in secret. This led to accusations of fraud when elections were held the following month. İnönü had advanced the date in order to shorten the campaign and give the opposition less time to organize. The Democrats had in the meantime been weakened by a split, as some of their right-wing supporters left to form a Nation Party (MP).

In the elections held in July 1946, the Republicans won 400 seats, the Democrats 40. The new parliament re-elected İnönü to the presidency. The Democrats contested the result, saying that electoral officers had stuffed ballot boxes with votes for government candidates. Civilized politics had been short-lived. İnönü tried to ride out the storm, choosing an authoritarian Republican, Recep Peker, as the new prime minister. Peker issued an order banning journalists from contesting the legality of the elections. In parliament, Democrat deputies decided to boycott meetings after Peker had described Menderes as a psychopath. İnönü intervened to cool tempers. On 12 July 1947 he issued a statement declaring that he would deal impartially with the government and the opposition. Peker resigned and was replaced by a moderate Republican, Hasan Saka, and then by another moderate, a former cleric Şemsettin Günaltay who had recited the funeral prayers in the private religious service held when Atatürk died in 1938. İnönü (who used to carry a miniature Koran in his pocket) was a defender of secularism, but he was not blind to political necessity, and allowed his prime minister and his party to court the pious vote. In February 1949, religious instruction, which had been abolished throughout the educational system, was reintroduced in primary schools on a voluntary basis. Four months later, the faculty of theology, which had been closed down in Istanbul for 'lack of demand' in Atatürk's lifetime, was reopened in Ankara under the government's watchful eye.

These concessions to religious sentiment disturbed the secularists, many of whom did not at first doubt the Democrats' loyalty to Atatürk's reforms. The founders of the Democrat Party were not known for their personal piety; their criticism was directed at the government's control

43

of the economy. They argued that cumbersome state controls were the root cause of poverty in the country. These arguments were backed by Turkey's Western supporters. In March 1947 Turkey had secured US military aid under the Truman doctrine. İnönü's government then asked for economic aid. As imports rose after the war to meet pent-up demand, the trade balance swung into deficit and the reserves Turkey had accumulated as a neutral state were melting away. In the summer of that year a private American foundation conducted a survey of Turkey's resources and potentialities. Max Weston Thornburg, author of the survey, concluded that Turkey needed to acquire business and technical experience before it could attract foreign capital.

With no prospect of private American investment, the Turkish government concentrated its efforts on obtaining government aid under the Marshall Plan for European economic recovery. Objections that Turkey did not qualify as its economy had not suffered from the war were overcome, and in July 1948 the Marshall Plan was extended to Turkey, which became a member of the Organization for European Economic Cooperation (OEEC, later renamed Organization for Economic Cooperation and Development/OECD), set up to coordinate disbursements. An American economic cooperation mission arrived in Turkey to supervise the delivery of aid. In May 1949 a ceremony outside Dolmabahçe Palace in Istanbul marked the arrival of the first shipment of American tractors. American engineers drew up a plan for the construction of metalled roads and helped set up an effective Highways Department.

In 1950, a young graduate of the Village Institutes, Mahmut Makal, published a book called *Our Village* (*Bizim Köy*), depicting the backwardness and poverty of rural life. The peasants, he said, went hungry; they were plunged in superstition, and in the absence of medical services, they had recourse to medicine men. It was not the peasants, but the evil spirits (jinns) in which they believed, which were the real masters of the countryside. The book shocked the country, and the author was briefly imprisoned for denigrating his homeland. It was this reality, which could not be denied, that American money and advice helped transform in the following decade. By June 1950, Turkey had received nearly 200 million dollars in American aid.[5] Even as they disbursed government aid, the Americans criticized the bureaucratic constraints on the Turkish economy. The Turkish government, which had moved on to its next objective – admission to the North Atlantic Treaty Organization (NATO) – could not disregard the advice.

Foreign advice and domestic opinion both urged change. For all their misgivings that their ignorant fellow countrymen might be misled by self-interested conservatives and religious bigots, the Republican elite agreed that it was right to set the people free. The government removed the last hurdle to the expression of the popular will by amending the electoral law yet again. Henceforth the vote would be secret and the counting of the ballot would be open to public scrutiny. On 14 May 1950 the first free elections in the history of the republic were held in Turkey.

The Democrats triumphed, winning 408 seats in parliament against the Republicans' 69. It looked like a landslide, but the outcome was exaggerated by the electoral system under which the party leading the poll took all the seats in a given province. The Republicans had polled 40 per cent of the vote against the Democrats' 53 per cent. It was not too bad a result for a party that had been in power since the establishment of the republic. But the fact that the Democrats had done best in the most developed parts of the country – in Istanbul, in the coastal plain round the Aegean port of İzmir, along the Mediterranean coast – suggested that it was they rather than the Republicans who represented the future.

It is said that when the results came in, a leading general came to İnönü and asked him whether the army should intervene to prevent a change of government, and that İnönü refused. He had agreed to free elections and would abide by their outcome. That outcome was hailed at home and abroad as a sign of the soundness of the foundations laid by Atatürk and a proof of Turkey's maturity. The Americans could support Turkey with a clear conscience. Inside Turkey the mood was euphoric. Paul Stirling, the first British anthropologist to conduct academic research in a Turkish village, noted that 'after 1950, officials in villages became more polite, more concerned to please, more willing to discuss village needs and desires, and less peremptory and paternalistic . . . To the roles of maintainer of law and order, legitimate robber and arbitrary universal provider, the government added that of vote catcher.'[6] The Democrat Party had the bulk of educated opinion behind it as it embarked on what it called 'unprecedented development'.

The 1950 elections were a break, but not a revolution. The new president, Celal Bayar, had been prime minister under Atatürk; the new prime minister, Adnan Menderes, and his leading ministers had been members of Atatürk's Republican People's Party. Atatürk's reforms were untouched, while some of the measures taken by his successor İnönü to push them forward were reversed. İnönü had made it a crime to recite the call to prayer in Arabic. After the Democrats' victory, muezzins were allowed to use Turkish or Arabic as they wished. They reverted to Arabic. İnönü had changed the language of the constitution from Ottoman to 'pure' Turkish. The Democrats claimed that the new language was artificial and reinstated the old terminology (which was finally abandoned when they were driven from power in 1960). Ever since Atatürk's language reform in the 1930s, language has been a political as well as a social marker in Turkey. Progressives use 'pure' Turkish; cultural conservatives favour Ottoman. The Democrats, like their successors on the centre right of Turkish politics, were economic liberals but cultural conservatives. However, they took care to show respect for the official ideology of the republic.

When members of a secret dervish brotherhood took to mutilating busts of Atatürk, the Democrats passed a law making it a crime to insult the memory of the republic's founder. In 1953, on the anniversary of Atatürk's death, his coffin was moved to a grandiose mausoleum in Ankara. It seemed that secularism and freedom could march hand in hand. Thousands of mosques were built through the length and breadth of the country. By and large, congregations paid for the buildings, while the state appointed and paid the salaries of clerical staff, who were treated (and controlled) as civil servants. The issue was not state control of religion, as it had been in the Ottoman empire, when state and religion were theoretically one. The question which pitted the Islamists against secularists was whether the state should heed the teachings of Islam in its public policy. Though the Democrats shocked the secularists by invoking Allah in some of their speeches, they disregarded Islamic law just as the Republicans had done.

In foreign policy there was continuity, and also a new dynamism. The effort initiated by İnönü to gain admission to NATO was brought to fruition by the Democrats in February 1952. Menderes' bold and prompt decision to contribute a Turkish brigade to the United Nations forces in the Korean War had helped swing US opinion in favour of Turkey's application. Reports of the Turkish soldiers' courage in battle and steadfastness in adversity gave Turkey an honoured place in the Western alliance. Unfortunately, Menderes believed also that his country had acquired the right to make unlimited claims on the Americans' purse. Turkey, fiercely independent under Atatürk and İnönü, began developing a culture of dependency, which bred resentment when the Americans offered unpalatable advice or rejected demands for additional aid.

Turkey was transformed in the ten years of Democrat rule. The area under cultivation increased from 14 million to 23 million hectares, the number of tractors from under 2,000 to 42,000, the amount of fertilizer used from 42,000 to 107,000 tons. The length of metalled roads rose from under 2,000 to 7,000 kilometres; 14 dams, 15 power stations and 20 harbours were built.[7] Private entrepreneurs were encouraged to invest in factories producing consumer goods. But, far from being reduced, the public sector grew in size. Not only was the state responsible for the building of dams and roads, it continued also to produce goods both for investment and for consumption – iron and steel, cement, textiles and cheap clothes, sugar, cigarettes and alcoholic drinks. Electoral considerations dictated the choice of sites for new state factories. Private companies flourished by working as subcontractors to the state, whose agencies took on more staff. The government thus bought support among entrepreneurs and also among the public at large. It became an employment agency creating jobs and generating profits, in the first place for its own supporters. This policy could be sustained only by deficit financing – that is, by printing money at home, and accumulating debts abroad. But until resources and the patience of foreign creditors – in particular, the United States – were exhausted, it was a popular policy. In the ten years of the Democrats' rule, the gross value of the national product (GNP) rose by an average of 6 per cent a year. Allowing for the increase in population, this was equivalent to a rise of nearly 3.5 per cent per head.

The Democrats' honeymoon lasted for three years. The Korean War had raised commodity prices. Turkey profited by becoming an exporter of wheat. But imports exceeded exports by ever higher margins as ambitious development projects were pushed forward, while consumption increased in line with a rising standard of living. In 1952 imports peaked at 556 million dollars. A record trade deficit of nearly 200 million dollars could no longer be covered by foreign aid and commercial credits. As imports fell back, shortages developed. Rather than devalue the currency, the government introduced a system of multiple exchange rates to subsidize exports. A black market developed in scarce foreign goods and foreign exchange.

As economic conditions deteriorated, the Republican opposition took heart. The Democrats retaliated in December 1953 by passing a law depriving the Republican People's Party of the property it had acquired during its long tenure of power. This property included a countrywide network of People's Houses and People's Rooms set up in the 1930s to foster cultural activities and spread modern knowledge. Many of these institutions were badly managed and provided sinecures for party stalwarts. But in their heyday they had helped shake the torpor of traditional society, particularly in the provinces. The Democrats could have reformed them. Instead they closed them down, allocating the buildings to government departments or allowing them to decay. The government's attempt to impoverish the opposition introduced acrimony into politics which came to be seen as a struggle for power, with no holds barred, between prime minister Adnan Menderes and the leader of the opposition, the former president İsmet İnönü.

In 1954, at the end of the Democrats' first term in office, the fall in commodity prices was compounded by a disastrous harvest. Nevertheless, the electorate was still grateful to the Democrats for the material benefits they had brought and hoped for more to come. Menderes was returned to office with an increased majority of 490 members of parliament, elected on 57 per cent of the total poll, while the Republicans were reduced to 30 seats. Repressive measures against the opposition helped enhance the Democrats' victory: freedom of the press was restricted, the electoral law was amended to prevent opposition parties from forming electoral alliances, and the government gained powers to retire civil servants, including judges and academics. Gradually, educated opinion turned against the Democrats. At this point, domestic disputes were briefly overshadowed by an upsurge of patriotic feeling over the fate of the island of Cyprus.

In 1955, Greek nationalists, who had long sought the union of the island with Greece, launched a terrorist campaign against the British colonial administration. The 80,000-strong Turkish minority, constituting roughly one fifth of the island's population, did not relish the prospect of exchanging British for Greek rule. Turkish Cypriots, who were traditionally well represented in the police force, found themselves in the forefront of anti-terrorist operations. Others enrolled as auxiliaries. Like the mass of Turkish Cypriots, Turkish governments had been content with British rule in Cyprus. Atatürk's ideal, 'Peace at home and peace in the world', translated itself into support for law and order at home and abroad. Britain had ensured law and order in and around Cyprus. Now Greek nationalists threatened it. Cyprus had been ceded to Britain by the Ottoman empire in 1878. A vociferous campaign started in Turkey demanding that if the British left Cyprus, the island should revert to Turkey, which as a member of the NATO alliance was the bulwark of order in the eastern Mediterranean. The campaign was directed by an unofficial association, called 'Cyprus is Turkish', which enjoyed the government's tacit support. The Republican opposition agreed that Cyprus was a national cause.

Turkey's involvement was not unwelcome to the British Conservative government. In September 1955, a few months after the outbreak of the Greek terrorist campaign, it invited the foreign ministers of Greece and Turkey to a conference in London to discuss Cyprus. The 'Cyprus is Turkish' association organized demonstrations to coincide with the conference. On 6 September, as the ministers conferred in London, a report was published in Istanbul that a bomb had been set off in the house in Salonica where Atatürk was supposed to have been born. The house, which had been turned into a museum, had become a shrine in the eyes of Turkish nationalists. Within hours, large crowds gathered in Istanbul and began destroying and looting Greek property, churches and even a cemetery. The police did not stop looters moving from one neighbourhood to another. In

İzmir, the lodgings of Greek officers assigned to NATO headquarters were ransacked.

The Menderes government was later accused of having provoked the pogrom by staging the bomb incident. But nothing could be proved. Immediately after the riot, the government accused the Communists of fomenting the troubles in order to destabilize a NATO ally. The usual suspects were arrested and then freed for lack of evidence. Officials of the 'Cyprus is Turkish' association received the same treatment. It was useless to look for written evidence. As in the case of the destruction of the printing presses of left-wing publications in 1945, it was enough for the police to look the other way, for a demonstration, which was not unwelcome to the government in the first place, to get out of hand. The Istanbul underclass did not need prompting to go on a looting spree.

It was the beginning of the end for the Greek community in Istanbul. There were some 80,000 Greek speakers in the city in 1955. Many had rebuilt the fortunes of which they had been deprived by the capital levy in the Second World War. Their lot had improved when Greece and Turkey both came under American protection. In 1949, the election of Athenagoras, the Greek archbishop of North America, to the patriarchal see of Constantinople (Istanbul) symbolized the new US-sponsored friendship between Greeks and Turks. After the 1955 riots most Istanbul Greeks despaired of ever leading a secure life in Turkey. As the Cyprus dispute dragged on, the Turkish government tried to put pressure on the government in Athens by cancelling the residence permits of Greek nationals, almost all of them Turkish-born. They left together with other Greeks who were Turkish citizens. By the end of the millennium the Greek community in Istanbul had been reduced to less than 5,000.

The 'incident of 6–7 September', as it came to be known, shook the Menderes government, which had obviously failed in its primary duty of maintaining law and order. Compensation was paid; the interior minister resigned, and the cabinet was reshuffled. Liberals within the Democrat Party were not appeased and broke away to form a Freedom Party (HP), which campaigned for 'the right of proof' – the right of journalists to defend themselves by proving the truth of their allegations. But the bulk of Democrat deputies supported Menderes in his determination to stay on. With no prospect of ending the increasingly repressive regime endorsed by a parliamentary majority, the first stirring of conspiracy began among junior officers in the armed forces. The economic situation deteriorated further, but the government could cushion its effects by indulging in inflationary spending in the public sector. With much of the country living in a fool's paradise, Menderes succeeded in winning a third election in 1957, but with a reduced majority. The bubble burst the following year. Under pressure from the IMF, the government devalued the national currency, foreign debts were rescheduled, and domestic overspending was curbed. To tide the country over, the Americans increased their aid.

The economic crisis encouraged both the legal opposition and military plotters. As inflation continued to erode the salaries and undermine the social standing of officers and public employees – among them articulate academics – the defence of secularism, rather than of incomes, became a rallying cry, and the Democrats were accused of making concessions to religious reactionaries. İnönü set out on a tour of provincial protest rallies. There were clashes when the government tried to stop him. Journalists were imprisoned. The government launched a phantom 'Fatherland Front' against the opposition. Long lists of names of recruits to this front filled the schedules of the official radio. It was clear that material inducements helped mobilize these latter-day supporters.

In February 1959, the Greek and Turkish foreign ministers met in Zurich and agreed on a compromise to solve the Cyprus dispute. The island was to become independent and was to be ruled jointly by its Greek Cypriot and Turkish Cypriot inhabitants. The formula was accepted by Britain, which retained sovereign base areas and other facilities. Menderes flew to London to sign the treaties alongside the British and Greek prime ministers. On 17 February his plane crashed as it approached London's Gatwick airport. The accident was caused by pilot error. Fourteen people were killed, but Menderes survived. He returned to Turkey to a hero's welcome. In some places, instead of the customary sheep, camels were sacrificed in thanksgiving. Menderes' judgement, uncertain at the best of times, was further undermined. Buoyed up by demonstrations of popular adulation, he decided to crush an opposition which he deemed contrary to the popular will. President Bayar, affected by his spite for İnönü, failed to steady him. On 18 April, the Democrat majority in parliament set up an extraordinary commission to investigate the opposition, which it accused of subversion. The committee recommended that all political activity should be suspended, that parliamentary reports should be banned and the press censored. 'Even I shall not be able to save you now,' İnönü exclaimed in parliament, addressing Menderes.

First, students demonstrated in Istanbul and Ankara. The government imposed martial law. Then on 21 May 1960 there was an unprecedented protest demonstration by military cadets in Ankara. Menderes had feared a military coup ever since the Iraqi monarchy had been overthrown by a bloody coup in July 1958. The previous December, nine military conspirators had been arrested in Turkey, where local discontent and foreign example combined to encourage plots against a regime which was turning itself into a dictatorship by parliamentary majority. But in spite of his misgivings, Menderes was caught unprepared when the military plotters struck on 27 May 1960. He was arrested on his way from Eskişehir to Kütahya in western Anatolia. President Bayar, ministers and Democrat deputies were detained in Ankara. The coup was almost bloodless. Educated opinion, the opposition press, students rejoiced. Government supporters kept quiet.

The government was taken over by a military National Unity Committee, headed by a respected general, Cemal Gürsel, who had been commander of land forces. Most of the conspirators were junior officers. They had chosen Gürsel late in the day as a counterweight to the chief of the general staff, who had remained loyal to the government and was arrested on 27 May. The motives and the aims of the conspirators varied. They all believed that officers had been undervalued and ill-treated by demagogic politicians. Some military conspirators were liberal constitutionalists, who had come to the conclusion that a coup was the only way to dislodge an increasingly dictatorial government. Others were authoritarian military socialists, like their counterparts in Egypt, Syria and Iraq. Only a military regime, they thought, could redress social injustice, reduce the power of domestic and foreign capital, distribute land and achieve a host of other progressive objectives. They all professed to be Kemalists, but some wanted to push Kemalism further in order to transform the country socially. Most were ambitious; some were naive. Things would be better, the most junior member of the National Unity Committee declared, now that virtue had replaced vice in power.[8]

University professors of law, outraged by the Menderes regime, encouraged the junta to put the ousted Democrats on trial. They were convinced that the Democrats had subverted the constitution and abused their power in order to maintain themselves in government and enrich themselves. The trial was held on the small barren island of Yassıada off Istanbul in the sea of Marmara. A nineteenth-century British ambassador, Sir Henry Bulwer (brother of the novelist Bulwer-Lytton, author of *The Last Days of Pompeii*), had built there a baronial castle, on whose ruins the Turkish military later erected a modern building. Situated beyond the reach of popular clamour, this building served both as a courthouse and a detention centre for the deposed Democrats.

Regular judges and prosecutors drew up an indictment which accused the Democrats of a series of crimes. The most serious was the charge that by setting up an extraordinary parliamentary commission to investigate and, eventually, try the opposition, they had sought to violate the constitution by force. To this charge which carried the death penalty, other charges were added, some clearly intended to destroy the defendants' reputation. The logic of the main charge was tenuous; the others – fraud, provoking the anti-Greek riots of 6–7 September 1955 – could not be proved. President Bayar treated the tribunal with disdain; Menderes sought to ingratiate himself by apologizing for his failure to recognize the wisdom of İsmet İnönü, whom he believed to be the real author of the coup.

The trial lasted for eleven months and ended in a ferocious verdict: fifteen of the accused were sentenced to death, and over 400 (the entire parliamentary group of the Democrat Party) to long terms of imprisonment. In spite of disagreement among the military and pleas for clemency by İnönü, as well as by allied governments, three of the death sentences were carried out. One of Turkey's most experienced and successful diplomats, Menderes' foreign minister Fatin Rüştü Zorlu, and his finance minister, Hasan Polatkan, were hanged on 16

September. Menderes, who tried to commit suicide, was revived and then hanged the following day. Zorlu was killed because he was arrogant, Polatkan because the military wanted to demonstrate their certainty that the government they had ousted had misappropriated public funds. But the main victim, Menderes, was hanged because the military were afraid of his popularity and of the possibility that he would return to power and call them to account.

President Bayar, whose death sentence was commuted, and the other imprisoned Democrats were subsequently released in batches, and eventually regained their political rights. A few re-entered politics, but found themselves superseded by followers who had been their juniors. The Democrats sentenced in the Yassıada trials were never legally rehabilitated, but they could not be denied political rehabilitation. In September 1990, when Turgut Özal was president, the remains of the three hanged politicians were disinterred, and transferred to a mausoleum near the ancient city wall of Istanbul. They are now described as 'martyrs of democracy'. The new international airport of İzmir and many avenues in cities throughout the country have been named after Menderes. The main conference hall of the Turkish foreign ministry bears the name of Fatin Rüştü Zorlu. It is a paradox characteristic of Turkey that respect for the victims of the military has not tarnished the standing of the armed forces as the most trustworthy institution in the country.

The Yassıada trial was a travesty of justice, condoned, if not actively welcomed, by the country's intellectual establishment. They came to hate Menderes and his Democrats as traitors to their caste, people ready to pander to the ignorant masses, demagogues willing to use religion to stay in power. In fact, the Democrats hardly touched the secularist canon. But the charge of irresponsible demagogy was justified. What the coup of 27 May 1960 did was to limit the spread to Turkey of the kind of populist politics which have ruined the countries of Latin America. True, populism which promises to the poor more than the state can afford and sets them against the educated elite, was to find other proponents, but they had to be more circumspect.

Turkey developed unevenly but rapidly in the decade of Democrat rule. The mass of the people realized for the first time that their votes mattered, and that they could barter them in exchange for material

improvements. At the same time, another social group gained importance. The enthusiasm of educated young people had been restrained
by state authoritarianism. Now civilian students and military cadets –
and their mentors – appeared on the political scene as 'the live forces
of the nation'. They had faced the police – and a hesitant and uncertain army – in demonstrations, and they sought their reward in fashioning a brave new world. It was a romantic dream and it caused no
end of trouble.

3

Years of Strife
1960–1980

THE MEMBERS OF the National Unity Committee (NUC), the junta which took over after the military coup of 27 May 1960, quarrelled among themselves long before the Yassıada court delivered its verdicts on the deposed Democrat politicians. On 13 November 1960, the NUC expelled fourteen of its members, most of them junior officers inclined to authoritarian solutions. The best known was Colonel Alpaslan Türkeş, who had made a dramatic public appearance when he broadcast the manifesto of the conspirators on the day of the coup. As a young lieutenant he had been detained, accused of racist politicking, towards the end of the Second World War. Acquitted, he returned to the army and to conspiratorial politics. As a radical member of the NUC, he had threatened an offensive against newspapers which had displeased him. Now he found himself posted as counsellor to the Turkish embassy in New Delhi. The other thirteen were similarly moved abroad out of harm's way.

The rule of the junta was not disputed at home or abroad. Any fears that the United States may have had were set at rest when the new Turkish government pledged its continued support for NATO, while Western donors were pleased at the prospect of order in Turkey's finances. Although the trials of the ousted Democrats had disturbed Western liberals, they were impressed by the assurances of Turkey's new military rulers that their aim was to endow the country with a more democratic regime and then withdraw from politics. Criticism in the Western media of the Menderes government for its attempts to repress the opposition had left its mark, and there was no liberal campaign against the military regime such as the one that started when the Colonels seized power in Greece in 1967, and then when the generals took over in Turkey in 1980.

Soon after the coup, the NUC had compulsorily retired 35,000 officers, including more than 200 generals and admirals. The justice may have been rough, but the move was wise. The armed forces had become top-heavy. Thenceforth they applied the US practice of retiring automatically officers who were not promoted after a specified number of years. Change at the top became brisk. In practice, four-star generals retained their commands only for three to four years before retiring. After the purge of the fourteen, the slimmed down military hierarchy gradually reasserted itself.

The departure of radical officers was followed by the summoning of a constituent assembly. Some of the members were nominated by the junta, others elected by provincial commissions, professional associations, and the parties which had opposed the Democrats (whose party was dissolved). The assembly reflected educated opinion fairly accurately. The constitution which it drew up was meant to eliminate the possibility of an elected majority abusing its power, as the Democrats had done. It introduced checks and balances: a senate (which the surviving members of the NUC joined for life), a constitutional court to test the legality of legislation, a national security council through which the military could channel their advice to the civilian government, autonomous universities and autonomous public broadcasting. It was the most liberal constitution the country had ever had, and it made room also for modern concerns – the republic was defined as a 'social state' with a vague duty to make provision for the citizens' rights to housing, health and education. The electoral law, which implemented the principles of the new constitution, introduced proportional representation. This led inevitably to the proliferation of political parties with shifting constituencies.

When the Democrat Party was in power, the educated class had resented the rising influence of party ward and precinct chairmen. They were seen as venal party bosses who practised pork-barrel politics at the expense of orderly administration, and who inflamed conflict by splitting neighbourhoods into antagonistic political camps. But by banning party organizations below district (sub-province) level, the new law restricted popular participation in politics and perversely strengthened the stranglehold of party leaders. As single-party governments were replaced by coalitions, ministers became responsible not to the prime minister but to their party leader, who could remove them from office at will. Civil power passed into the hands of an oligarchy of self-perpetuating party leaders, restrained by a military hierarchy subject to frequent change. In a country used to decisive, not to say authoritarian, government, rulers would henceforth have to bargain with their rivals, look over their shoulders and heed their step.

The new constitution was approved in a referendum in July 1961. Almost 40 per cent of the electorate voted against it, showing that the ousted Democrats had retained considerable support. This was confirmed by the results of the general election held in October. İnönü's Republican People's Party came first. But its share of the poll dropped below the 1957 level – from 41 to 37 per cent. The Democrat vote was divided between three parties. The strongest was the Justice Party (AP), led by a retired general, Ragıp Gümüşpala, who had been chosen to reassure the military that the legality of their intervention would not be challenged. İnönü teamed up with him and became prime minister of a coalition government. The NUC leader, General Gürsel, was elected president after a contender close to the Democrats was forced to retire. The military were determined to stop the Democrat leaders from re-entering politics. They forced party leaders to promise time and again that they would safeguard the 'achievements of the revolution of 27 May'. The achievements were symbolized by a bayonet wreathed in oak leaves – an ugly piece of statuary which was planted in the central square of Taksim in Istanbul – and 27 May was made a public holiday. Some years later, the statue was removed and the holiday abolished. The military did not object: the symbols of their first intervention were gone, but the threat of intervention continued to hang over civilian politicians.

The policy of the high command to secure an orderly return to parliamentary rule under the new constitution did not commend itself to ambitious officers who wanted to refashion the country according to their own ideas. İnönü's great achievement was to isolate the radicals. As a retired general himself, and a hero of the War of Independence, he had immense prestige in the army. He used it to good effect to thwart two attempts at an army putsch by Colonel Talât Aydemir, commandant of the war college in Ankara. Aydemir was popular with his cadets, but had little support among senior officers and none in the country, outside a small circle of romantic revolutionaries. After the first attempt on 22 February 1962, Aydemir was pardoned along with all who were involved in the plot. After the second on 21 May 1963, he and his chief lieutenant were sentenced to death and hanged. İnönü had no time for 'young hooligans', as he called them. The phased release of imprisoned Democrat leaders could now proceed. In July 1962, İnönü widened his coalition by taking in another group of former Democrat supporters (who had formed the New Turkey Party/YTP). The coalition fell apart in December the following year, but İnönü stayed in power in order to deal with a new Cyprus crisis.

Archbishop Makarios, who had become president of Cyprus, and the Greek nationalists grouped round him, were determined to revise the settlement which a Greek conservative government in Athens had persuaded them to accept in 1960 as the only alternative to the partition of the island. They approached the British government, one of the three guarantors of the settlement, and formed the impression that London would not object if Ankara also agreed to reduce, or even perhaps remove altogether, the entrenched rights of the Turkish Cypriot community. Makarios went to Ankara where İnönü warned him not to tamper with the settlement. But in December 1963, İnönü's government lost its majority; in Athens, power passed from the conservatives to left-wing nationalists, led by the fiery populist Andreas Papandreou. Papandreou shared Makarios's belief that if he struck against the Turks in Cyprus, the Americans would stop Ankara from intervening.

On Christmas Eve 1963, the Turks came under attack throughout the island. Driven from the government, they were forced to shelter in a few enclaves. İnönü appealed to Britain to use its treaty right and intervene in order to restore the constitution. But the British government preferred to call in the United Nations, which stopped the slaughter of the Turks, but did not reverse the Greek gains. When İnönü prepared to intervene unilaterally, as was his right, President Lyndon Johnson warned him that, were the Soviets to take action against a Turkish intervention in Cyprus, NATO would not be bound to come to Turkey's aid. In any case, Turkey had no right to use in Cyprus weapons supplied by NATO for defence against the

Soviets. 'If there is to be a new world, Turkey will surely find a place in it,' İnönü responded. But he was too careful to order a military intervention, for which the Turkish armed forces were, in any case, ill-prepared. However, when a few months later, Greek Cypriots pushed their luck by trying to seize the only two Turkish-inhabited villages on the Cyprus coast, through which supplies could be smuggled to the Turks beleaguered in the interior, İnönü ordered Turkish warplanes to bomb the Greek attackers. An uneasy calm then descended on the island, most of which the Greeks now controlled, except for the few enclaves whose Turkish inhabitants were kept alive by Turkish government aid and the presence of a United Nations Peace force (UNFICYP). UNFICYP assembled in Cyprus in 1964. It was still there at the turn of the millennium.

The new world – a term which meant that the common interests of NATO and the national interests of its members did not always overlap – had in fact arrived before the outbreak of intercommunal violence in Cyprus in December 1963. France learned the lesson in 1956, when the United States doomed to failure the Anglo-French Suez expedition against the Egyptian president Gamal Abdul Nasser. This led eventually to General de Gaulle's decision to remove NATO headquarters from French soil and withdraw from the military command structure of the alliance. Turkey could not do this, as it could not afford to arm and maintain an effective defence from its own resources. Membership of NATO was not a burden on the Turkish economy, as left-wing critics argued. On the contrary, it provided affordable security. But although Turkey's allegiance to NATO was never in doubt, there were signs even before the fall of Menderes that Turkey could occasionally follow its own counsel.

In May 1953, soon after Stalin's death, his successors sent a note to the Turkish government declaring that the Soviet Union made no claims on any part of Turkish territory. Turkey, which had been admitted to NATO the previous year, was not tempted to renegotiate the non-aggression treaty denounced by the Soviets in 1945. In 1959, Turkey disregarded Soviet protests and allowed the United States to station on its territory fifteen nuclear-armed Jupiter ballistic missiles. But in April 1960, the Turkish press announced that Menderes would visit Moscow to discuss bilateral relations.[1] The fact that Menderes was overthrown the following month gave rise to the conspiracy theory that the Americans had engineered, or at least encouraged, the military coup in order to prevent closer relations between Turkey and the Soviets.

In fact the Americans were not privy to the plot, although the fall of the increasingly erratic Menderes administration did not cause them undue chagrin. In 1962, Turkey was not consulted when the Kennedy administration agreed to the removal of nuclear-armed US missiles from Turkish territory as part of the settlement of the Cuban missile crisis with the Soviet Union. The Johnson letter in June 1964 reinforced the growing impression that the Americans were taking Turkey for granted. The following November, İnönü sent his foreign minister to Moscow where he signed a cultural agreement with the Soviets. It was the beginning of a 'many-sided foreign policy', demonstrating that Turkey did not rely totally on its NATO allies for the protection of its national interests. The West had been Turkey's sole source of aid. Now the Soviets took a hand in their neighbour's development. They built a steelworks, a petrol refinery, an aluminium smelter. Apart from a honeymoon in the early 1950s, the US–Turkish alliance has always been troubled. The crisis which it underwent during the Iraq war in 2003 was by no means the first of its kind.

Anti-Americanism was fanned by the emergent, legally tolerated Marxist movement in Turkey. A significant part of the intelligentsia came to believe that foreign capital, whose presence in Turkey was minimal as a result of Atatürk's and İnönü's nationalist economic policy, was responsible for the country's backwardness. To forge ahead, they argued, Turkey had to follow the path of non-capitalist development and pursue an independent foreign policy. In 1961, a number of left-wing trade-union leaders and intellectuals joined forces to set up the Turkish Workers Party (TİP). Left-wing intellectuals could hardly contain their joy when they heard the first electoral broadcast on behalf of TİP. They had grown up in an atmosphere in which anyone who mentioned class conflict could be accused of being a Soviet agent. When they came together they amused themselves with apocryphal stories of official intolerance. 'How dare you become a Communist?' Nevzat Tandoğan, governor of Ankara at the end of the Second World War, is supposed to have shouted at a left-wing student who had been hauled before him. 'It is up to me to decide whether the country needs Communists. If it did, I would appoint them myself.' In the event, Nevzat Tandoğan became an early victim of liberalization. Newspapers, enjoying a degree of freedom not seen before, had accused him of covering up the involvement in a murder case of the son of the chief of the general staff. Summoned to give evidence in court, Tandoğan could not bear the indignity and shot himself. Today a square in the capital is named after him, in recognition of his many improvements to the city's amenities.

Another hoary story which made the rounds of left-wing drawing rooms was about the police chief who banned the French Larousse dictionary because he read the title as 'La Russe', the Russian woman, and assumed that it was by definition Communist. There were many similar stories: 'Did you hear the one about the headmaster? He was sacked when he said "The classes need changing". He meant the classrooms, but the education inspector was convinced that the headmaster wanted to change the class structure of society.' Now class conflict was aired for the first time on the public broadcasting service. However, the dictatorship of the proletariat remained a taboo subject, as the law made it a crime to advocate the domination of one social class over another.

Turkey was not faced with the threat of a dictatorship of the proletariat – a term which did not correspond to any social reality in the country. The danger lay in the prospect of a dictatorship by radical military officers. Marxists in TİP and authoritarian radical nationalists in the armed forces found common ground in their belief that the social objectives of the 1961 constitution were betrayed by the civilian governments to which the military ceded power after the coup. Their propaganda influenced the 'live forces of the nation' – the younger members of the secularist establishment – but made little impact on the bulk of the people. As the elite became radicalized, the electorate turned increasingly to conservative parties. The Soviets saw in the rise of radicalism the prospect of undermining Turkey's membership of NATO; the West hoped that stability would somehow be safeguarded.

Retired General Ragıp Gümüşpala, the first leader of the Justice Party, died in 1964. He was succeeded by a new name in politics,

Süleyman Demirel, a 40-year-old engineer who had directed the programme of dam building under Menderes. Demirel had been born in the province of Isparta into a poor peasant household of refugees from the Balkans, and had studied at state expense; a practising Muslim without being a bigot, he was also a voracious reader of English-language books on politics. Demirel was a fat man, homely of speech, with a big head and a smiling face. Nicknamed 'Sülü [little Süleyman] the Shepherd' by the elite and lampooned by left-wingers as 'Morrison Süleyman', after the name of the American firm which he advised when the 1960 coup deprived him of a job, Demirel soon proved himself a consummate popular politician, and an expert in deficit-financed economic development. Gradually he built up the Justice Party as the main successor of the Democrat Party of Menderes and Bayar. The military banned the use of the name Democrat by any new political formation. But a symbol based on a pun made the point. 'Democrat' had become '*Demirkırat*' – the Iron-Grey Horse – in the language of the unlettered. The Justice Party chose the white horse as its symbol, copying it from the label of a famous brand of whisky. Demirel won back the old Democrat constituency without yielding power to former Democrat leaders. He was a realist. 'I know I am occupying the seat of a hanged man,' he said when he became prime minister.[2] To avoid the same fate, he was determined to play politics by the new rules.

In the 1965 elections Demirel won his party an absolute majority in parliament (with 50 per cent of the total poll) and formed a single-party government after four years of coalitions. But under the watchful eye of the military he enjoyed much less freedom of action than had Menderes. Public broadcasting had become relatively independent; the universities were autonomous, and often critical; the press too had much greater freedom to criticize. More importantly, economic policy had to conform to five-year plans, prepared by the new State Planning Organization. Planning was fashionable in the West, and Turkey followed the fashion. In the 1930s, the model of five-year plans had been imported to Turkey from Soviet Russia. Now, the ideas of Keynes replaced the ideology of Marx. Even so, the new five-year plans were seen initially as mandatory and not indicative. They established guidelines which had to be followed, rather than giving general advice on how to proceed. They set targets for investments, taxes, prices, foreign trade. Foreign donors within OECD, with whom the US now shared the burden of assisting Turkey, formed an Aid to Turkey consortium, with annual pledging meetings to help finance planned development.

Working within these constraints, Demirel achieved respectable results. The gross national product increased by an annual average of 7 per cent between 1960 and 1970. Allowing for the increase in population, the national product per person rose by 3 per cent a year. The improvement was particularly marked after Demirel assumed power. Shortages eased. Inflation, it is true, rose under Demirel (from under 5 to under 7 per cent), but it was still much lower than in the last years of the Menderes government. Moreover, Turkey had found an additional resource.

In 1961 West Germany began to recruit Turkish workers. By 1971 there were nearly half a million of them in Germany. By the end of the millennium the number of Turks in western Europe reached three and a half million. Most lived in Germany. But there were sizeable communities also in France, the Low Countries and Scandinavia. The remittances of these emigrants eased Turkey's balance of payment in times of crisis. Returning workers brought with them skills and new ideas. But the new Turkish diaspora was also a source of trouble for the home country. The liberal laws of western Europe allowed Turks to engage in political activities banned at home. Western Europe became a haven for Turkish revolutionaries. There they could find shelter, organize, publish their tracts, lobby foreign governments. The earnings of Turkish workers could be mobilized (or extorted) to finance revolutionary Marxism, Kurdish separatism, radical political Islam. It was not a phenomenon peculiar to Turkey. Emigrant communities often have a soft spot for extremists from the home country. Where would the IRA have been without the money donated by Irish Americans?

The improvement in the economy after the return to civilian rule in 1961 did not, however, satisfy either civilian or military radicals. Income inequalities, which had not been reduced, offended them more than they did the mass of ordinary people. They were convinced that planning which made room for private capital was not enough, that 'non-capitalist development', in other words a command economy, could produce even faster growth. Behind these arguments there was a thirst for power which free elections denied the radicals. Revolutionary fervour, which the coup of 1960 had stirred up, found a source of foreign inspiration when students revolted in France in May 1968. Istanbul university students were the first to follow the French example and stage boycotts, sit-ins, strikes and demonstrations. Student unrest quickly spread throughout the country. By June, 80,000 students were unable to take their examinations. On 16 July 1968, one student was killed when riot police broke into the hostel of the Istanbul Technical University, from which students had mounted raids on sailors of the US Sixth Fleet. American sailors, who had been welcomed as saviours when the battleship *Missouri* visited Istanbul in 1946, were now in danger of a ducking in the Bosphorus. A right-wing backlash was not slow to manifest itself, and right-wing nationalist students came to blows with left-wing revolutionaries. More ominously, bombs began to explode. Prime Minister Demirel took the troubles in his stride. 'The demonstrators will not wear out the streets,' he said when pressed to take action. But his sympathies were with the nationalists.

Demirel won a second victory in the elections of 1969. The vote for his Justice Party dropped slightly, but a change in the electoral law, reducing the scope of proportional representation, allowed the party to increase its strength in parliament. The victory brought trouble. Within the Justice Party, rivals, denied cabinet posts by Demirel, broke away and, claiming to be the true heirs of Menderes, founded a short-lived Democratic Party (since the name of the old Democrat Party had been outlawed). At the same time, radicals began to despair of the parliamentary process. The vote for the Workers Party dipped below 3 per cent, and with the change in the electoral law, the number of its parliamentary deputies was reduced from 14 to 2. It was clear that the country would never vote for socialism. In the eyes of the radicals, the system was to blame: it was a simulacrum of democracy, imprisoning the people in 'false consciousness'. Orthodox Marxists were challenged by advocates of a National Democratic Revolution, a movement that, far from being democratic, tried to provoke a military coup in order to establish a People's Republic on the basis of a national version of Marxism. Left-wing students who had formed a federation of Think Clubs and had supported the Workers Party, now set up a Federation of Revolutionary Youth (*Dev-Genç*) advocating direct action.

The situation had become dangerous. The National Democratic Revolution appealed to some officers. Student radicals began escaping abroad to organize and train. The Soviet Union helped them through proxies – Bulgaria and Syria – where revolutionaries had training camps and from which increasing quantities of weapons were smuggled into Turkey. Kurdish separatists, who had been few in number, were now armed with Marxist fervour and weapons procured in Syria. The high command of the armed forces decided to take pre-emptive action. On 12 March 1971 it sent to parliament a memorandum demanding the formation of a national government to carry out reforms – changes which Demirel's government had been unwilling to introduce. Demirel resigned, but allowed his party to support the new national government in parliament. He took his hat off the peg in the prime minister's office and went, believing that in so doing he was stopping the military from dissolving parliament. When Demirel was later ejected from office once again, the hat became his symbol. As leader of the opposition, İnönü too chose to cooperate with the military. This decision heralded the end of his long political career.

After the first military coup in 1960, İnönü had tried to rejuvenate his Republican People's Party and move it cautiously to the left. He had heard of a promising young Turkish intellectual, Bülent Ecevit, who came from a staunchly Republican family, and had gone to London to study, while earning his living as a junior official in the press department of the Turkish embassy there. A man of slight build, Ecevit was a European intellectual, steeped in the canon of Western literature. Only his bushy moustache proclaimed him a true Turk. His intense wife Rahşan came from an artistic family. Like Demirel, Ecevit had no children, which gave the two leaders all the more time to pursue their political ambitions. They strove for power by all the means at their disposal, using questionable tactics at times. But they were not insincere in their belief that they served the people. Demirel measured his achievement by the delivery of services under his rule –

increased access to water and electricity, better roads. 'The people want a government that will meet their needs,' he said. Ecevit's ideal was more elevated – a fairer society, 'neither oppressor, nor oppressed; neither exploiter, nor exploited'. 'But we all exploit each other,' Metin Toker, a popular Turkish journalist, objected.[3]

In London, Ecevit wrote romantic poetry, moved among Hampstead intellectuals, discussed his hopes for his country with a group of like-minded middle-class Turkish students, and attempted to study Sanskrit, in order then to learn Bengali so as to be able to read in the original the work of Rabindranath Tagore, with whose univer-salist message he was greatly taken. Ecevit never completed his degree course in Sanskrit and returned to Turkey, where he started writing for the newspaper of the Republican People's Party. A spell of study in the United States followed. On his return, Ecevit was elected to parliament. After the 1960 coup he became a member of the constitu-ent assembly. Impressed by his work, İnönü appointed him minister of labour in the first civilian government after the interlude of mili-tary rule.

In 1963 Ecevit piloted through parliament a law which legalized strikes for the first time in Turkish history, and replaced the restrict-ive legislation compiled in the late 1940s, again at İnönü's behest, by Nihat Erim, a German-trained professor. Asked whether he was not concerned that strikes might curtail production at a time when the country needed economic growth, Ecevit replied: 'No, the right to strike increases production, because the workers produce more when they are happy, and they are happy when they win their rights.'[4]

Ecevit became the darling of the Turkish liberal left, and the leader of the left-of-centre movement within the Republican People's Party. Liberal conservatives, who had battled against Menderes in the late 1950s, were gradually dislodged from the party hierarchy, which Ecevit dominated when he became secretary general in 1966. When İnönü decided to support the army-backed national government in March 1971, Ecevit dissented. Resigning his party office, he chal-lenged İnönü for the leadership. In 1972, the protégé ousted the pro-tector, and İnönü became a backbencher in the party he had led. This rare occurrence was applauded by 'the live forces of the nation'. The young who cried 'One solution, revolution' and 'Islam – the Only Way' as they fought each other, could now shout in unison 'Ecevit, the Only Hope!' (*Tek Ümit, Ecevit!*).

With his background in poetry and journalism, Ecevit became a highly effective orator, using 'pure' Turkish as it had never been used before. For thirty years, from 1970 onwards, Ecevit, the romantic urban poet, who stood for the left, and Demirel, the wily village fixer, representing the right, fought each other and succeeded each other in power. Demirel won on points: his tenure of power was longer, and he ended a notch higher, as president when Ecevit was prime minister. Demirel retired from active politics with his reputation intact; Ecevit left a broken man after a crushing electoral defeat.

The language of the memorandum, by which the military removed Demirel from power in 1971, seemed to reflect some at least of the demands of the radicals, who were at first hopeful that the army had moved against their conservative enemies. Their hopes were disappointed. The liberal journalist Hasan Cemal, who was then a young plotter in the cause of the National Democratic Revolution, was to write in his memoirs: 'We were waiting at the wrong stop. We thought that history would pick us up there. But it was in vain. We did not see where history was going, and it passed us by.'[5]

The high command immediately purged its ranks of officers who were preparing to stage their own coup to usher in the National Democratic Revolution. To head the national government, the army chose the conservative lawyer, Professor Nihat Erim. Erim declared that the 1961 constitution had been too liberal. 'It should be wrapped up in a shawl,' he said one day, meaning that the constitution should be hidden away for possible future use. The remark earned him the nickname of 'the shawl merchant' (*şalcı*). Erim made changes which, he argued, would counter threats directed at the country's national unity and territorial integrity, sacred concepts for the military. True, he introduced into the government a number of foreign-trained left-of-centre reformers – a senior official of the World Bank, a Turkish academic resident in New York, and others. But 'the brains trust', as they were called, soon found that parliament, which continued to sit, would have nothing to do with their schemes, and left the government.

As arrests continued of revolutionaries and their intellectual mentors, the radicals took to terrorism. The Israeli consul general in Istanbul was kidnapped and murdered when the authorities refused to free arrested revolutionaries. Three radar technicians, two British and one Canadian, were kidnapped from a NATO monitoring station on Turkey's Black Sea coast, and died in a firefight when their captors were cornered in a remote village. Martial law was declared and the army set about restoring law and order with a heavy hand. Weapons caches were found, suspects were arrested, radical parties (including the Workers Party) and associations were banned. Three militant students involved in the kidnapping of the NATO radar technicians were hanged. Suspects, left-wing journalists among them, were maltreated in military interrogation centres. Şahin Alpay, at the time a radical student at the Ankara faculty of political science and now a prominent liberal academic and columnist, was to write later:

> The coup of 12 March [1971] lowered the curtain on the rebellious generation of 1968. The 12th of March marked the beginning of the mass imprisonment of the rebellious young. The authorities, devoid of the slightest feeling of tolerance for the young, mercilessly killed or sent to the gallows those who had evaded arrest and had attempted to engage in urban or rural guerrilla warfare. The young rebels proved incapable of explaining themselves to the people. The vast majority sided not with them, but with the state. A very small proportion of the revolutionaries escaped arrest and joined the Palestinian resistance movement or found shelter in the democracies of western Europe. The cream of the generation of 1968 spent time in prison until the amnesty of 1974.[6]

The country was pacified. But politics proved more difficult to control. The Justice Party withdrew its support and Nihat Erim resigned, to be followed by short-lived national coalition governments more amenable to parliamentary pressure. Parliament refused to elect to the presidency of the republic a politically ambitious general who had resigned his commission in preparation for the election, and chose instead a retired admiral who could be trusted not to exceed the president's limited constitutional powers.

In 1973, the army withdrew from the political scene. General elections were held under the amended constitution. The moderate conservative vote was split between the Justice Party and the Democratic Party (which rejoined it soon afterwards). But, significantly, many conservatives voted for political Islam, which had attracted few supporters until then. The Turkish constitution bans the use of religion for political purposes, and pious Muslims usually voted for centre-right secular parties like the Democrats or the Justice Party, which, they felt, were sympathetic to their way of life. But when the centre right splintered and appeared incapable of meeting the wishes of the conservatives, a minority of practising Muslims, mostly associated with religious brotherhoods (*tarikat*), sought for their own party which would move the country in the direction of Islamic law, the *sharia* (*şeriat* in Turkish).

The strictly orthodox Nakşibendi brotherhood encouraged a new politician, Necmettin Erbakan, to form such a party. A pot-bellied, German-trained professor of engineering of provincial background, Erbakan had become a strict Muslim while studying at the Istanbul Technical University. Demirel, another provincial who was a fellow student, was also pious, but the two men did not take to each other. The breach came out into the open in 1969, when after returning from Germany Erbakan was elected chairman of the union of chambers of commerce (TOBB) against Demirel's wishes. A Turkish party leader who tolerates open defiance loses his authority. Demirel retaliated: his Justice Party government found an irregularity in the election and annulled the result. Erbakan then decided to challenge Demirel on the political stage, and in 1971 he formed the National Order Party (MNP). When this was dissolved a few months later, after the military had intervened in government, Erbakan tried again. The following year he re-established his party under the name of National Salvation Party (MSP), and won 48 seats in the 1973 elections. In a divided parliament, the two main rivals, Demirel on the centre right and Ecevit on the centre left, needed the MSP to secure a majority. The MSP logo was appropriately a key – the key to successful coalition-building.

At first Demirel would have nothing to do with Erbakan. It was Ecevit who broke with the secularist tradition of his Republican Party and formed a coalition government with him in February 1974. He justified the move by saying that he wanted to end the feud between secularists and Islamists, which, he argued, had been the result of a 'historic mistake'. But he had another, less elevated, reason to court Erbakan. The use of the oil weapon by the Organization of Petroleum-Exporting Countries (OPEC) in the Arab-Israeli war in October 1973 had brought immense wealth to Turkey's oil-producing Arab neighbours, and done immense harm to Turkey's weak economy. With little oil of its own, Turkey found it difficult to pay for Arab oil at the new higher price. Ecevit believed that he could cover the foreign trade deficit by persuading oil-rich Arabs to invest in Turkey. Erbakan, who had good contacts with Saudi Arabia and other Muslim countries, could be a useful intermediary.

In the event, even if some Arabs liked Erbakan, he counted for little in their investment decisions. A few rich Arabs bought property in Turkey; some chose it for their holidays; but Arab investment in the Turkish economy never amounted to much. Oil-rich Arabs preferred to invest and deposit their money in safer Western economies. It is the rich, not the poor who attract money, and Turkey was poor. Eventually Turkey was to balance its books, and even achieve a surplus with oil-producing Arab states by increasing its exports to them and winning construction contracts. It was a slow, but useful process, which taught Turkish business to compete on price instead of relying on favours.

Ecevit's first major decision after coming to power at the beginning of 1974 was to declare an amnesty for the revolutionaries imprisoned by the military and those who had fled abroad. Some of the beneficiaries of the amnesty put their revolutionary past behind them. A few middle-class revolutionary intellectuals were gradually converted to the merits of parliamentary politics and became prominent in the media as advocates of liberal reforms. But many more, people who came from modest or poor backgrounds, used their newly-won freedom to renew the revolutionary struggle in a more violent form. Young revolutionaries who found the radical Dev-Genç too moderate set up Dev-Sol (Revolutionary Left), which later became DHKP/C (Revolutionary People's Liberation Party/Front), an organization dedicated to acts of terror. Marxist Kurdish separatists, who had found their voice in the Turkish Workers Party (TİP), regrouped in the Eastern Revolutionary Cultural Hearths (DDKO). On the right, Colonel (by now retired) Alpaslan Türkeş returned to Turkey and took control of a small party which he renamed Nationalist Action Party (MHP) in 1969. The youth organization of the party, officially called Idealist Hearths, but generally known as the Grey Wolves, prepared to do battle with left-wing revolutionaries. While prime minister Bülent Ecevit dreamt of a reconciliation between secularists and Islamists, of Turkey becoming a bridge between the Middle East and the West, of the resettlement of disadvantaged villagers in modern agro-towns, parties to an incipient civil war were arming and organizing.

It was at this point when Ecevit needed all the help he could get at home and abroad that he antagonized the United States by lifting the total ban on the cultivation of the opium poppy which had been imposed by the military-backed government of Nihat Erim. The opium poppy is a traditional crop on the western edges of the Anatolian plateau, where an important town, Afyon Karahisar (Opium Black Castle), is named after it. The ban was naturally unpopular with local voters. While Turkey served and serves as a corridor for opium-based narcotics (morphine base and heroin) produced in Afghanistan and Pakistan, and while imported morphine base is sometimes refined into heroin on Turkish soil, control over Turkish growers of the opium poppy had been adequate. Ecevit's assurance that, after the ban had been lifted, locally produced opium would be used exclusively for medical purposes was honestly meant, and appears to have been implemented. But it was the wrong time to anger the Americans, for it was at this juncture that the Cyprus problem erupted once again, overshadowing all other considerations.

Having failed in his first attempt to subdue the Turkish Cypriots in 1963–4, Archbishop Makarios had settled to a slow process of wearing them down. It was too slow for the Greek junta in Athens, now dominated by the impetuous Brigadier Dimitrios Ioannidis. On 15 July 1974 Athens backed a coup against Makarios by veteran Greek Cypriot terrorists in Nicosia. The Archbishop escaped capture and was airlifted to a British sovereign base area from which he went abroad to appeal for help. The 1960 Cyprus constitution had already been breached by Makarios himself in 1964. It was now in tatters. Bülent Ecevit flew to London to persuade the British government to intervene jointly with Turkey, using their rights as guarantor powers.

The foreign secretary, James Callaghan, refused. Fearing that Britain and America would end by accepting the regime set up in Nicosia by the terrorist gunman Nicos Sampson, Ecevit ordered his troops to land in Cyprus. He had the full backing of his deputy Necmettin Erbakan, the leader of the Islamist MSP, and of all shades of opinion in Turkey. When they landed on 25 July 1974, Turkish troops met some resistance before they succeeded in establishing a bridgehead and linking up with the Turkish Cypriots besieged in the old city of Nicosia.

The junta in Athens collapsed, and was succeeded by the conservative democratic politician, Constantine Karamanlis. His foreign minister travelled to Geneva to work out a new Cyprus settlement with the other two guarantor powers, Britain and Turkey. Turkey could not wait for the conclusion of long-drawn-out negotiations. Its bridgehead in Cyprus was vulnerable to a Greek counterattack. The old pattern of mixed settlement on the island had collapsed ten years earlier in 1964. Now ethnic hatred peaked as Greeks fled from areas under Turkish control, while Turks outside them were rounded up by Greeks and, in places, slaughtered. Turkey insisted on the immediate establishment of a viable Turkish sector. When Greece refused, the Turkish army effected it by force, extending the area under its control to one third of the island. Greeks fled before the Turkish advance. A little later, Turks detained by the Greeks were allowed to move to the Turkish-held northern part of the island. As there were not enough of them to cultivate all the land, villagers were brought in from Turkey. Their number is hotly disputed. Thirty years after the event, it is almost impossible to give exact figures, as the settlers, some of whom have married locals, now have Cyprus-born children.

Ecevit gave to the Turkish military intervention the name of 'Operation Peace'. The Greeks derided it, citing the number of casualties and of refugees. But, although both communities remain dissatisfied, not only has Cyprus been at peace since 1974, but it has prospered: the Greek south prodigiously, having absorbed all the refugees, while in the north the Turks live more comfortably than they had ever lived before, but not as well as their Greek neighbours to whose riches they aspire. In 2003, the European Union decided to admit Cyprus as a full member in the hope that this would promote a settlement. Conditions on the island eased, as the border was opened between north and south, but there is much unsettled business left.

The military intervention in Cyprus cost Turkey dear. Yielding to pressure from the powerful Greek American lobby, an unwilling US administration banned military aid and sales to Turkey in February 1975. The ban, which was often circumvented, was not lifted officially until August 1978. Turkey retaliated by limiting US access to bases in Turkey, but it had to spend more on weapons. One effect of the US arms embargo was the establishment of a Turkish aerospace industry, paradoxically with US aid, and the expansion of a local defence industry which had previously been limited to the production of small arms.

Turkey's military presence in Cyprus complicated relations also with the rest of the world. United Nations member states, many of which have restive minorities, are unwilling to recognize partition and secession anywhere. Europe hoped that if Cyprus were reunited, relations between Greece and Turkey would become amicable and peace would reign on its eastern approaches. While the stationing of Turkish troops in northern Cyprus did not involve much extra expenditure, it was expensive to sustain the economy of northern Cyprus. Turkish northern Cyprus came to live largely off the salaries paid by the Turkish treasury to a bloated civil service which employed almost all the Turkish Cypriots with any kind of education. Turkey paid also for improvements in the physical infrastructure: roads, water supply, power stations. The relentless Greek campaign against what it called the illegal Turkish occupation of northern Cyprus cut off Turkish Cyprus from the rest of the world. Tourism, the island's main resource, stagnated in the north; farmers could not sell their produce direct to Europe.

Inside Turkey, however, the military intervention in Cyprus was hailed as a victory for an assertive, independent policy. Ecevit decided that his newly-won popularity would ensure him an absolute majority in parliament if new elections were held. In September 1974 he dissolved his coalition with Erbakan's Islamists and tendered his resignation. But parliament did not vote for early elections. Discarded by Ecevit, Erbakan teamed up with Demirel, who formed a right-wing coalition which became known as the Nationalist Front. The fall of the first Ecevit government let loose a wave of violence throughout the country. The new government was implicated, since it included the Nationalist Action Party of Alpaslan Türkeş, whose Grey Wolves fought left-wingers in the streets. 'You will never make me say that nationalists commit crimes,' prime minister Demirel declared defiantly. But they certainly did. On May Day 1977, thirty-four people were killed in Taksim square in Istanbul when left-wing demonstrators were fired on by their right-wing opponents. In the same way revolutionary Marxists killed 'class enemies' and 'class traitors' with little discrimination.

Elections in 1977 were again inconclusive. Ecevit's Republicans achieved their best results ever, but were nevertheless outnumbered by right-wing parties. Demirel formed a second Nationalist Front government, which collapsed after a few months when a handful of Justice Party deputies abandoned their party and joined Ecevit as independents. Having thus secured a narrow majority, Ecevit rewarded the renegades with ministries in his new cabinet. Three of these ministers were later sentenced to prison for corruption. Ecevit's behaviour in January 1978 dealt a heavy blow to his reputation. Incorruptible himself, he had made friends with corrupt politicians in order to return to power. It was a power he could not exercise effectively.

Violence, which had started among university students, spread to the countryside, where the left–right antagonism translated itself into intercommunal violence. In the eyes of Sunni militants, membership of the heterodox Alevi minority became synonymous with leftism, not to say Bolshevism. In December 1978, 105 people, most of them Alevis, were killed by Sunni militants in the city of Kahramanmaraş. Much against his inclination, Ecevit declared martial law. But the killings continued. There were some 3,000 political murders in the year to September 1980. The most famous victim, whose death came to symbolize Turkey's years of the bullet, was Abdi İpekçi, the liberal editor of the daily *Milliyet*. A provincial terrorist, Mehmet Ali Ağca, was charged with the murder. Sprung from the military prison where he was detained, Ağca escaped to western Europe. He achieved world-wide notoriety when he shot and gravely injured Pope John Paul II in Rome in May 1981. Sentenced to life imprisonment, he was eventually extradited to Turkey, where he was later to benefit from the abolition of the death penalty.

Violence spread from universities, which were practically paralysed, to high schools. People were killed in the street for reading the
wrong newspaper. Strikers closed down factories. The formation of
the Marxist Workers Party in 1960 had been accompanied by the
establishment of a breakaway Confederation of Revolutionary
Workers Unions (DİSK, whose leaders later preferred to translate
their name as Confederation of Reformist Unions). This led to
intense rivalry with the older, mainstream union federation,
TÜRKİŞ. Private employers, particularly in successful companies,
were faced with exorbitant demands by union leaders trying to
outbid each other in radicalism. Unionized workers, who represented
the minority of the labour force, became a privileged class (dubbed
'the worker aristocracy') at a time of acute economic distress for the
mass of the population.

Ecevit's economic and foreign policies were wildly impractical.
While union leaders beggared the private sector, Ecevit and Demirel
competed against each other in debauching public finances. Inflation,
which had risen gradually since the return to civilian rule in 1961,
accelerated after the end of the second military intervention in 1973.
Prices rose by nearly 50 per cent in 1978, then by 70 per cent in 1979.
With the trade deficit widening as a result of successive rises in the
price of imported oil, Demirel tried to attract foreign money through
convertible lira accounts which earned a high rate of interest. By the
time Ecevit came to power, the principal was at risk.

Turkey had become an associate member of the European
Economic Community in September 1963. The agreement looked
forward to Turkey's full membership after a phased process of convergence. But implementation was repeatedly delayed by both sides. In
the meantime, Greece was advancing steadily towards membership.
The Greek application was lodged in June 1975 by the conservative
government of Constantine Karamanlis. The failure of the Americans
to stop the Turkish intervention in Cyprus had led to a rift between
Greece and the United States. Greece, like France before it, withdrew
from the military command structure of NATO – a decision which,
unlike France, it later reversed. Karamanlis chose Europe to redress the
balance. He was helped by his friend, the French president Giscard
d'Estaing. Until 1975, Turkey and Greece had kept in step in their

moves towards the European Community. Some European officials would have welcomed a Turkish membership application, which would have made it easier for them to reject both Greece and Turkey. But Turkey did not follow suit.

In 1979, Greece signed its accession treaty with the European Community. The previous year Ecevit had declared in his programme that the terms agreed earlier with the European Community had proved an obstacle to Turkey's development, and that his government would make sure that the country's economy would not be crushed by the Common Market. He proposed that the European Community should absolve Turkey of its obligations for five years and grant it 8 billion dollars in aid and credits.[7] Europe did not oblige. Neither did anyone else. With mounting debts, and its foreign credit exhausted, Turkey was unable to pay for essential supplies of oil. As the winter of 1979/80 set in, Turks froze in unheated flats, lifts stopped working, hospitals were deprived of essential power. Long queues formed not only for petrol, but for domestically produced goods – light bulbs, cooking oil, cigarettes, even salt. The mismanagement of the economy had produced shortages which had not been seen during the Second World War. Only the West could help now. Zeki Kuneralp, an experienced Turkish diplomat who retired from the diplomatic service in 1979, wrote in his valedictory report: 'We were in need of support: practical, real and urgent support. We cast around on all sides. We went and embraced one, then hugged another, but in the end we went and knocked on the same door. And that door was neither in Cuba, nor Mecca, nor yet Moscow. It was in the West.'[8]

Ecevit's enthusiasm for the third world had brought the Turkish economy to its knees. He paid the price in September 1979, when he lost all five mid-term by-elections and suffered a setback in Senate elections. He resigned and was succeeded by Demirel who formed a minority administration, which other right-wing parties promised to support. But when his foreign minister, worried by the accession of Greece, asked the European Community to note Turkey's intention to become a member as soon as possible, Erbakan joined Ecevit in a motion of no-confidence which forced the minister to resign. The survival of the Demirel administration hung by a thread. Nevertheless, he was able to take a decision that changed the face of Turkey. When he returned to power, Demirel appointed Turgut Özal, a 54-year-old fellow graduate of the Istanbul Technical University, to head the State Planning Organization. Özal, a plump provincial in rumpled clothes, had, like Demirel before him, risen rapidly in the technical civil service; he had also worked in the World Bank and in the private sector in Turkey. He had made an unsuccessful move to enter politics, when he failed to be elected to parliament on the list of Erbakan's Islamist party. A self-made man, he was a practising Muslim, a liberal and an admirer of the wealthy West. It was a winning combination which represented the aspirations of the mass of his fellow countrymen.

On 24 January 1980, Demirel put into effect a new economic programme worked out by Özal. The Turkish lira was devalued; the state increased steeply the prices it charged for its goods and services; farm subsidies were reduced. The promise of putting an end to chronic government overspending allowed Özal to negotiate with Turkey's Western creditors a rescheduling of debt repayment. Other measures were to follow, culminating in the scrapping of all foreign exchange controls. The Turkish lira became a convertible currency. For as long as anyone could remember, a Turkish resident could be arrested if he carried foreign currency. Now, people could open dollar accounts at home or abroad. It was a risky policy which later gave rise to recurrent crises. But at first it proved spectacularly successful. The earlier policy of protecting domestic industry in a closed market had failed, because it increased, instead of reducing, the demand for imports, as new factories relied on foreign suppliers for their equipment and other inputs. Instead of trying to cut down on imports, Turkey began to increase its exports and learned to compete on the open market.

The programme of 24 January could not, however, have succeeded if trade union militancy had continued, or if farmers had been able to put pressure on their elected representatives to milk the treasury for subsidies. Only a suspension of parliamentary democracy could prevent resistance to measures whose initial effect was to lower the living standards of a large part of the population. The economy had not been the only victim of party politics. Demirel's minority government could not put an end to acts of violence. Parliament was unable to agree on the choice of a new president of the republic. 'How much longer are we to suffer for the sake of democracy?' a senior Turkish diplomat asked.[9] Not much longer, as it happened.

In December 1979, the commanders of the Turkish armed forces called publicly on the political leaders to collaborate in order to restore order. But the leaders would not act together. On 6 September Ecevit, now leader of the opposition, addressed a rally and appealed to the workers 'to come down from the stands and on to the pitch'. The generals took this apparent call to the workers to take to the streets as the final legitimation of a coup.[10] On 12 September 1980, the high command of the armed forces suspended the constitution, dissolved parliament and all political parties, and substituted itself for the government. In the words of Professor William Hale, 'In retrospect, what is surprising about the coup of 12 September 1980 is not that it happened, but that it took so long in coming, and that the politicians did so little to prevent it.'[11]

The coup enjoyed the overwhelming support of the middle classes, while the rest of the population found some comfort in the restoration of old-fashioned authoritarian government. The low-intensity civil war which had raged in the 1970s is estimated to have caused some 5,000 deaths. But its impact went well beyond the number of victims. 'When our young people left home in the morning, we were never certain that we would see them again,' parents complained. They thanked the military for banishing that fear.

4

Conflict Contained
1980–2003

THE GENERALS WHO came to power on 12 September 1980 took their time to lay the foundations of the new order. For three years the country was ruled by the high command of the armed forces. General Kenan Evren, the chief of the general staff, became head of state. His prime minister was a retired admiral, Bülent Ulusu. Law and order were restored by draconian means. Nearly 180,000 people were detained, 42,000 sentenced to various terms of imprisonment, 25 found guilty of political murder and hanged. A large arsenal of illegal arms was confiscated, including 7,000 machine-guns, 48,000 rifles, 640,000 handguns and 26 rocket launchers[1] – enough to equip an army, the generals said. After restoring order, they turned their attention to a new constitution. The country had been riven by ideological conflict. The military decided that the remedy lay in confining politics to the inner councils of a few, preferably only two, polite political parties, just as religion had been confined to the interior of mosques under state control. Society was to be depoliti-cized. Trade unions, voluntary organizations of all kinds, universities were forbidden to have anything to do with politics.

An advisory council produced Turkey's longest and most detailed constitution. It outlawed any activity which could be construed as a threat to the indivisible unity of the state and nation. The generals blamed the leaders of the old parties for the near-civil war of the 1970s. Demirel was detained, set free, then detained again when he tried to re-enter politics. Ecevit was sentenced to four months' imprisonment for a statement to the foreign press. Türkeş was detained, put on trial and eventually acquitted. All the leaders of the old parties were banned from politics for ten years. The ruling generals allowed the establish-ment of new political parties, provided they approved the credentials of their founding members. When İsmet İnönü's son, the nuclear physicist Professor Erdal İnönü, sought to form a social-democratic party, he was vetoed until after the first free elections. Eventually only three parties were allowed. Two were sponsored by the military: the Nationalist Democracy Party (MDP), led by a retired general, to represent the centre right, and the Populist Party (HP), led by a retired senior civil servant, to represent left-of-centre voters who fancied stronger state control of the economy. But a third party, which stood for exactly the opposite – for free enterprise at home and the country's integration in the world free market – slipped through the net. It was called the Motherland Party (ANAP) and it was led by Turgut Özal, whom Demirel described dismissively as 'my civil servant'. Turkey's parties are held together by loyalty to the person of the leader. Özal's decision to found a party in his own right, and without his former boss's permission, started a feud which bedevilled Turkish politics for nearly two decades.

Özal was the man whom Turkey's foreign creditors trusted. The generals had little option but to keep his services when they took over. They put him in charge of the economy as deputy prime minister. The immediate result of Özal's stabilization programme, agreed with the IMF, was to reduce the growth rate of the Turkish economy from an average of 7 per cent over the preceding fifteen years to 2 per cent. The gross national product per person fell from 1,300 to 1,000 dollars; 1.5 million people lost their jobs.[2] Consumer prices doubled, while wages were held down. The pain caused by the economic stabilization programme dented the popularity of the generals, while its subsequent success enhanced the reputation of Özal. In any case, he distanced himself in time from the military regime by resigning in 1982, when his tight money policy led to the bankruptcy of a speculative banking venture, into which thousands had poured their savings in the hope of earning absurdly high returns. Özal then joined an association of private employers and, with their help, established his own party. On the eve of the elections, the military issued a veiled, but nonetheless unmistakable, warning to people not to vote for him. It had the contrary effect, as Özal became the beneficiary of the resentment which the generals had earned by three years of austerity.

The new constitution was submitted to a referendum on 7

November 1982 and approved by 91 per cent of the voters. The unusually high 'yes' vote had a simple explanation: rejection would have meant the continuation of military rule. The generals had done their job in re-establishing order; people now wanted their concerns to be taken up by democratically elected politicians. Under a provisional article, approval of the constitution entailed the election to the presidency of General Kenan Evren for a six-year term. Although the rule of the generals was harsh, Evren, who was 65 years old at the time, was a popular, paternal figure. His father had been a regimental *imam*, and the outlook of military chaplains, which shaped his approach to the country's problems, chimed in with the conservative feelings of most of his countrymen. He appealed to their sense of patriotism, solidarity and common sense. Even where his conclusions were stern, many shared them. He said:

> The death penalty exists not only in our laws, but also in our religion. It is even to be found in the Gospels [he meant the Bible]. It is in the book sent by God [the Koran]. Now we are being urged to abolish something that is in God's book. I tell you why: if there's no death penalty, it becomes easier to stage anarchic and ideological incidents. That's what opponents of the death penalty have in mind.

On another occasion, Evren declared: 'Turkey can't allow a Communist party, just because some countries do. A Communist party has no business in Turkey.'

Intellectuals made fun of Evren's homely advice. 'When you prostrate yourself in prayer, make sure you don't stick your feet in the nose of the worshipper behind you,' he told a congregation. Shown a Picasso painting in America, Evren commented:

> It seems he traced a black line with his brush here, and drew a circle next to it. A black spot here, and white in between. There, a black spot with circles in between. I had a good look and said to myself: when I go back to Turkey I'll take up painting. I can do as well. These here are so expensive, only because they are signed by Picasso.[3]

Evren did take up painting when he retired in 1989 to a villa in the seaside resort of Marmaris. On occasion, he travelled to Istanbul to show the landscapes he painted (not in Picasso's style) or to act as a witness at the weddings of the children of prominent families.

Demands by angry radicals that he should be called to account for complicity in the violation of human rights fell on deaf ears. The human rights lobby could not dent his popularity.

In the elections in November 1983, Özal's Motherland Party won an absolute majority of 211 seats, against 71 for the Nationalist Democracy Party which had been created by the generals. The Populist Party, which was equally artificial, did better with 117 seats. In local elections the following year, Özal increased his share of the vote at the expense of the Nationalist Democrats, who then disappeared from the scene. Özal thus succeeded in reuniting the centre right, which had ruled the country for most of the preceding thirty years.

But there were early signs of a challenge. Demirel re-established his party under a proxy. He called it the True (more correctly, the Right) Path Party (DYP), a name which had a religious resonance, as the opening words of the Koran are: Guide Us along the Right Path. However, it could not count on the hard-core religious vote, for the Islamist leader Necmettin Erbakan had also found a proxy and had revived his National Salvation Party under the name of the Welfare Party (RP). On the centre left, Erdal İnönü was finally allowed to contest local elections at the head of a Social Democracy Party (SODEP), which absorbed the Populist Party. But he too was not unchallenged, as Mrs Ecevit, acting as the proxy of her banned husband, became soon afterwards the leader of a new Democratic Left Party (DSP).

So, instead of reducing the number of political contestants, the generals ended up by multiplying them. Two parties disputed the votes of the centre right, and another two of the centre left. The policies of all these parties resembled each other in their vague formulation. The divisions between them were not ideological, but personal. The parties were mutual protection societies among which the voters made a choice on the basis of affinity and in the hope of personal benefit. On the extreme right, the Islamists soon found an adversary in a party set up on behalf of the nationalist leader, Alpaslan Türkeş. The extreme left continued to be insignificant in electoral terms.

The new divisions took some time to establish themselves. In 1983 Özal had his chance to impose his vision on the country, and he took it. After a brief recession, the stabilization programme which he had introduced in 1980 with the blessing of the IMF produced impressive results. During Özal's first four-year term of office, the economy grew by an average of 7 per cent a year. The export drive proved a resounding success: the value of Turkish exports rose from under 3 billion dollars in 1980 to more than 10 billion in 1987, and the trade deficit was reduced, as imports rose more slowly from 8 to 14 billion dollars. This opening up to the outside world encouraged a spirit of enterprise which spread throughout the country. As factories working for export were set up in provincial cities, people began to talk of 'Anatolian tigers' rivalling the feats of the Asian tigers of the Far East. Tourist revenue climbed sharply.

Realizing that Turkey's infrastructure was out of date, Özal concentrated his efforts on energy and communications. New power stations were built and telephone lines laid until every village gained access to electricity and telephone services. Exchanges had been so antiquated that long-distance calls had to be reserved beforehand, and were then graded 'lightning', urgent or ordinary. Even a 'lightning' connection could take hours. Özal's investment programme provided business with the essential facility of automatic long-distance and international dialling. Finding that the civil service was too set in its ways and the laws too restrictive to accommodate rapid change, Özal recruited outside specialists, tempting over from the United States Turks with degrees from American universities and practical experience in management. Where he could not or did not have time to liberalize the law, he disregarded it. 'What does it matter if I violate the constitution just for once?' he is reported to have said.

Even his enemies did not deny that Özal was a man of vision. But Özal did not invent this new approach. It was the ideology to which the West had turned in the 1980s as it reacted to the failures of social and economic engineering – the vision of Margaret Thatcher and of Ronald Reagan, the ideology of the open society, of free enterprise and free markets, and eventually of globalization. There was, of course, a price to pay and it was higher in Turkey than in the West. As strikes were first forbidden by the generals and then restricted under new laws, the lot of wage earners worsened. Turkey became acquainted with schoolteachers who supplemented their income by working as cab drivers after hours. But moonlighting was not the only way to make ends meet. 'My civil servants know how to look after themselves,' Özal remarked memorably. People took it as an invitation to public employees to look after themselves by taking bribes.

It was not only the needy who learned how to look after themselves. While Turks are not more averse to riches than anyone else, moneymaking is despised in Turkish tradition. To serve the state as a soldier or an administrator was the proper career for a gentleman. Özal gave social status to moneymaking. This had been tried before. Atatürk had hoped that successful, honest merchants would appear among the Turks. They were slow in coming. In the 1950s Adnan Menderes dreamt of a Turkey in which every neighbourhood would boast a millionaire. Menderes wanted his country to become 'a little America', a country which he had never seen. His dream was derided when the romantic socialism of the 1968 generation became the dominant ideology.

Özal – and his two brothers – had lived in America. They admired its business spirit, but also its respect for diverse religions. It is said that Turgut Özal's brother, Korkut, became a strict practising Muslim after living among Mormons in Utah where he had been sent for training.[4] Couldn't business and piety combine in Turkey too to the benefit of society as well as of individuals? Turkey's two main business dynasties – the Koç and the Sabancı – had done so when they established their fortunes step by step from the 1950s onwards. They had moved on from small-scale trading to manufacturing, marketing, banking, tourism and other activities. But patience was in short supply when Özal came to power. He admired achievers – people who completed a job quickly. For many, the job was 'to turn the corner', in a phrase which has become associated with the Özal era – in other words, to get rich quickly. 'I blame Özal for taking ethics out of Turkish society by idealizing money,' said one Turkish academic. 'The state of Turkey should not surprise you: capitalism without the Protestant ethic equals the mafia,' said a senior civil servant.[5]

Özal introduced export incentives. They were widely abused, as dishonest businessmen produced fraudulent invoices (colloquially known as 'nylon invoices') for phantom exports and then collected the government subsidy. State revenues were hypothecated for specific programmes which were financed through separate funds. Thus when imports were freed, they were subjected to a levy payable to a Mass Housing Fund which provided cheap houses for the poor. The trouble was that the special funds were open to political manipulation and suffered from lax accounting. As expenditure by the funds eventually equalled one third of the official government budget, fiscal discipline went by the board. Local councils were given a greater share of tax revenue which they spent very much at the discretion of local politicians. 'It was an era of expansion, but also of plunder. Bribery secured public contracts and the contractor then overcharged the state,' a Turkish journalist remembered. As inflation picked up, low-interest credits by state banks offered a road to instant riches for friends of the government who could lay their hands on cheap money for their investments and then charge high prices for their goods and services.

Özal's own family typified the new spirit. His high-living wife Semra set up a Foundation for Women's Empowerment, whose emblem was the daisy. Businessmen's wives hastened to become daisies, while their husbands bought political influence by supporting the foundation. When the Istanbul Stock Exchange was opened in 1985, Özal's son made a fortune on it. 'He is an ordinary citizen, so why should he be excluded because he happens to be the son of the prime minister?' his mother said in reply to criticism. The state broadcasting monopoly was circumvented by beaming television programmes from Germany and then relaying them inside the country. Özal's son was a partner in one of these enterprises of dubious legality. In the words of the American historian of Turkey, Professor Heath Lowry:

> Özal introduced economic liberalization without putting any kind of legal infrastructure or controls in place to regulate and limit its excesses . . . His failure to provide ethical references for his new Turkey weakened the public fabric of the nation. Corruption, though always a factor in Turkey, was generally shunned as evil prior to the Özal era. In the last two decades it became more or less an accepted way of life.[6]

At the end of his first term, Özal realized that he had to address the complaints of wage earners if he was to stay in office. Demirel, Ecevit and the other old political leaders re-entered politics, when the ban on them was lifted by a razor-thin majority in a referendum in September 1987. Özal, who had tried to keep them out, had to outbid them in promises to the electorate. Characteristically, he increased the pay of public employees without cutting government expenditure elsewhere. He also changed the election law to give an extra premium of seats to the leading party. As a result, in the 1987 parliamentary elections his Motherland Party won 292 seats, after receiving 9 million votes, while the opposition Social Democrats, who were supported by 6 million voters, were allocated only 99 seats. The economy continued to expand and prices to rise. Growth accelerated just before elections: 7 per cent in 1986, 10 per cent in 1987, but only 1.5 per cent in 1988. The rise in prices was more relentless. In the year following the election, consumer price inflation rose to 74 per cent; it then settled at 60+ per cent a year.

In 1989 General Kenan Evren's term as president of the republic ended. When Özal declared himself a candidate, the opposition accused him of trying to make good his escape before the bubble burst. He was elected by the votes of his party, the second civilian to become head of state in the history of the republic (the first being Celal Bayar, deposed by the military in 1960). When political opponents declared that they would never accept him as president, Özal replied, 'They'll get used to it.' They did. But Özal's elevation to the presidency did not end his interference in day-to-day government. He chose as his successor a little-known provincial lawyer, Yıldırım Akbulut, who became a figure of fun for the intelligentsia. When Akbulut went to Moscow, a typical story went, he was invited to *Swan Lake*. 'But isn't it too cold for a swim?' he is supposed to have asked his hosts. With its founder no longer in direct control, the Motherland Party replaced Akbulut by a more serious figure, the former foreign minister Mesut Yılmaz. Özal fell out with him, when the new prime minister disregarded the president's advice. Working on his own, Yılmaz was unable to hold together the disparate elements which had come together in the Motherland Party: religious conservatives, nationalists and economic liberals. Identifying himself with the liberals, he decided to advance the date of the elections in order to win the mandate to retrench and lay sounder foundations for economic progress. The voters had other ideas.

Menderes had advanced the country's development by freeing domestic private enterprise, while continuing to subsidize it from state funds. Özal spurred on economic progress and raised living standards by opening up the country to foreign competition, while also continuing to subsidize local entrepreneurs and maintaining a bloated public sector. Whenever he went abroad – which he did much more frequently than any of his predecessors – he was accompanied by a planeful of businessmen. He took personal charge of foreign policy, making it an instrument of economic expansion.

In April 1987, Özal took the step contemplated by Demirel in 1979, and applied formally for membership of the European Economic Community, disregarding the advice of the German Chancellor Helmut Kohl that neither Turkey nor Europe was ready for it. Özal put his case in *Turkey in Europe and Europe in Turkey*, a book published under his name, which was in fact ghost-written by an up-and-coming Turkish diplomat.[7] He argued that Turkey had always been part of Europe, because European civilization was born on its territory. The claim was made with a rhetorical flourish: 'Homer – our countryman,' Özal wrote, 'signalled the beginning of what would later be called "the Greek miracle" in Anatolia.'[8] The Greeks were incensed: Homer belonged to them and no one else. But Europe was interested in the present, not the past. In his argument, Özal moved on from glorious past to radiant future. 'Energies', he wrote, 'which for centuries have been repressed are now released, enabling Turkish businessmen and engineers to establish themselves in the outside world. Economic stability is assured by the operation of market forces . . . Attaining the same economic level as Europe is only a matter of time, perhaps only a short time.'

The European Commission was not convinced. After taking two years to examine the Turkish application, it concluded that 'at the present time, Turkey and the Community cannot be easily integrated.' But it promised to re-examine the Turkish request for membership at intervals, yet to be determined.[9] Özal was disappointed, but not surprised. As it put off Turkey's accession to an indefinite future, Europe had at least recognized that Turkey was eligible for membership. 'The reason we applied for membership', his finance minister Adnan Kahveci explained privately, 'was to attract foreign investors who would be more likely to come to Turkey if they believed that we abided by European business rules and practices.'[10] That hope too was disappointed, as foreign investors came to the conclusion that, contrary to Özal's prediction, the operation of market forces did not produce economic stability in Turkey. Market forces could not operate freely so long as the government's free-spending policies fed crony capitalism at the expense of sound business.

Özal's election to the presidency coincided with the fall of the Berlin Wall and the beginning of the collapse of the Soviet Union. The end of the Cold War reduced Turkey's importance as the south-eastern bulwark of NATO. But this loss, Özal believed, could be made good if Turkey played its cards right. A vast area of instability had opened up to the east of the European Community. Özal bent his energies on persuading the West that Turkey was the only bastion of stability 'between the Adriatic and the Wall of China'. He secured the establishment of a Black Sea economic cooperation area with its headquarters in Istanbul. It provided a useful venue for the discussion of regional problems, but had little impact on the economies of its disparate members.

A more important opportunity to prove Turkey's importance arose when the Iraqi dictator Saddam Hussein occupied Kuwait in August 1990. Overcoming considerable domestic opposition, Özal closed down the pipeline from the Kirkuk oilfield in northern Iraq to the Turkish Mediterranean terminal at Ceyhan (Yumurtalık) in the gulf of İskenderun. He allowed the use for offensive operations against Iraq of the NATO base at İncirlik, near the southern Turkish city of Adana. Professor Erdal İnönü, the leader of the Social Democratic opposition, led peace marches to the base. Two foreign ministers resigned in succession in protest at the takeover of foreign policy by the president. But Özal was not deterred. However, he was unable to commit Turkish armed forces to military operations against Saddam Hussein. The resignation of the chief of the general staff, General Necip Torumtay, whom Özal had selected personally, disregarding the preferences of the high command, did not reduce the generals' opposition to an active participation in the war. When, after his ejection from Kuwait, Saddam Hussein suppressed the rebellion of Kurds in northern Iraq, an estimated half a million Kurdish refugees pressed against the Turkish frontier. Rather than admit them, Özal won acceptance of a proposal to create a safe haven to which the refugees could return. Up to the time of the Second Gulf War in 2003, this safe haven was patrolled by US and British aircraft operating from the base at İncirlik. Kurdish self-rule developed under their protection.

Özal's support of the Allies in the First Gulf War has been widely criticized in Turkey. His prediction that Turkey's winnings would be three times greater than its stake in the war has been derided. True, under US pressure, Saudi Arabia and other Gulf states supplied Turkey with concessionary oil to make good the losses caused by the closure of the Kirkuk pipeline. In all, Turkey received some 4 billion dollars in grants and credits at the end of the war. Critics argue that its losses were much greater, as the economic sanctions against the regime of Saddam Hussein, which survived for another twelve years, virtually ended Turkey's lucrative trade with Iraq. The Iran–Iraq war which had preceded the First Gulf War had made both countries dependent on supplies from Turkey, and Iraq had become Turkey's second largest export market. The loss of that market was blamed on Özal. At the same time, the Kurdish area in northern Iraq, created at Turkey's instance and maintained with its cooperation, proved to be a safe haven not only for local inhabitants but also for armed bands of separatists who used it as a launching pad for forays into Turkey. Turkey's armed forces crossed the frontier repeatedly, but could not put an end to the terrorists' presence.

The fact is, however, that, whatever policy it pursued, Turkey was bound to suffer from the First Gulf War. The Allied effort to eject Saddam Hussein from Kuwait and the economic sanctions against him had the backing of the United Nations and of NATO. Turkey had no excuse to stand aside. Özal may not have won all the advantages for which he had hoped, but, unlike his domestic critics, he saw clearly that backing the winner was the more promising course. The flourish with which he followed this course endeared Turkey to the US administration, which did not cavil at the absence of Turkish armed forces from the combat.

The Allied victory in Kuwait did not help the Motherland Party in the elections held in October 1991. Özal's rival, Süleyman Demirel, led an effective campaign accusing the government of mismanagement and corruption. His words, 'They have one hand in the honey pot, the other in grease', were applauded by large crowds to whom he had become 'Papa' (*Baba*, a term used also for mafia godfathers). Demirel outbid the government by promising to lower the pensionable age. Asked how a government, which was already deeply in the red, could afford to pay pensions to 50 year olds (and in some cases even to people in their forties), Demirel said privately, 'You've got to promise something if you want to win an election.' He made use of public anger at the rise of terrorism in the south-east of the country. 'The state has ceased to exist there,' he said.[11] It was an exaggeration, but security in the south-east had deteriorated even before the First Gulf War. The rise in terrorism is usually blamed on the repression practised by the military regime during its years in power between 1980 and 1983. But the repression had forced the Kurdish rebel leader Abdullah Öcalan to flee to Syria, and it was under Özal's more tolerant rule that Öcalan launched his insurgency inside Turkey. To fight it, the military used much more reprehensible methods than they had employed when they were in full control of the country. Kurds suspected of assisting the insurgents were targeted by death squads; villages in which insurgents found shelter were evacuated and destroyed; the torture of suspects became more widespread.

Demirel's True Path Party emerged from the 1991 election as the strongest single party, with 178 seats against Motherland's 115. The Social Democrats came third with 88. True Path and Motherland appealed to roughly the same conservative constituency, but Demirel had sensed that the country wanted change. He provided it by teaming up with Erdal İnönü's Social Democrats. This ended, supporters claimed, the feud between centre right and centre left. But at the same time it perpetuated the new divisions within both camps between parties of the same ideological hue but with rival leaders. The younger İnönü was an ideal partner, unfailingly polite and a stickler for coalition protocol. Working with President Özal was more difficult. Both Demirel and Özal believed in a Turkey great and free. After the military had closed down his Justice Party in 1980, Demirel wanted to name its successor 'The Great Turkey Party'. He had promised thereafter to 'add a second Turkey' to the one that existed – in other words, to make the country twice as rich. But Demirel was cautious, while Özal was bold in pursuit of the same ideal. After the election, Özal continued to run his own foreign policy, as Demirel grappled with economic problems which his electoral promises had aggravated.

In 1992, consumer prices rose by 73 per cent, while the foreign debt which stood at 19 billion dollars in 1982 increased to 56 billion dollars. This did not cramp Özal's style as he toured the newly independent Turkic republics of the Soviet Union, from Azerbaijan to Kyrgyzstan. When the Armenians wrested from Azerbaijan the autonomous district of Nagorno-Karabakh, within which they were in the majority, and also much adjoining territory, Özal suggested in a private conversation with journalists that they might be restrained if Turkey bombed them on the quiet. The Turkish establishment, civil and military, was horrified: the Russians stood behind the Armenians.

In June 1992, Özal easily outshone Demirel as he presented his vision to the Third Economic Congress in İzmir. The first congress had been summoned by Mustafa Kemal (Atatürk) in 1923 to determine the economic policy of the new Turkish nation state. Özal harked back to it in 1981 when he addressed the second congress, also in İzmir, to explain his philosophy of an outward-looking competitive Turkey. Now he looked back to his achievement and forward to the future:

> I tell you that the main objective of Turkey in the next decade is to become one of the world's ten or fifteen most advanced countries. I tell you that Turkey must enter and can enter the league of first-class countries . . . Together with the new states from the Balkans to Central Asia – states that are Muslim, and mostly Turkish – we can make our power more effective . . . If we do not make serious mistakes, the twenty-first century will be the century of the Turks and of Turkey.[12]

It was Turgut Özal's swansong. He died of a heart attack in April 1993 on his return from yet another trip to the former Soviet Turkic republics, and was buried in a specially constructed mausoleum just outside the walls of Istanbul. Under his rule, Turkey had punched above its weight: his bravado concealed the country's weaknesses. Disillusion was bound to follow.

Özal was succeeded in the presidency by the more cautious Demirel, who made good his departure from the prime minister's office as a crisis was about to hit the economy. Before winning the 1991 elections, Demirel had recruited into his True Path Party Tansu Çiller, an attractive, US-trained woman economist on the staff of Boğaziçi University in Istanbul. She had a round, smiling face, which concealed a strong ambition and a harshness towards her subordinates. She was married to a banker who had emerged blameless – and rich – from the failure of a small bank he had managed. Çiller was not popular among her academic colleagues, who relate how she was determined to make her way in politics, but was uncertain which party to back. Demirel thought that she would look good on election posters and would help modernize his party's image. Tansu Çiller joined Demirel's True Path Party and charmed the electorate with an ingenious economic model which purported to show that Turkey could advance to prosperity while continuing to overspend. Demirel called her 'my girl' and appointed her minister in charge of economic policy. Impressed by the filial respect which she showed him, he took the decision of recommending her to his party as his successor, when he gave up the leadership on becoming president of the republic. Perhaps he had thought that she would act as his obedient executive; perhaps, as cynics claimed, he had become soft in his old age and had fallen for the flattery of an attractive young woman. Whatever the true explanation, Demirel came to regret his decision.

Tansu Çiller thus became Turkey's first woman prime minister. She saw herself as a Turkish Mrs Thatcher: her opponents preferred to compare her with Imelda Marcos of the Philippines. As overspending continued, Turkey's foreign debt rose to 67 billion dollars by the end of 1993. With Russia about to default, Western creditors were disinclined to lend more money to its neighbour, Turkey. In 1994 Tansu Çiller tried to engineer a fall in interest rates in order to reduce the burden of debt service. Financial markets panicked and there was a massive flight of capital. Tansu Çiller sought the aid of the IMF, which imposed its usual recipe of devaluation and retrenchment. She agreed, and the value of the gross national product fell by 8 per cent, while prices rose by 106 per cent. It was seen as the gravest economic crisis in the history of the republic, but the economy had become resilient and growth bounced back to 6 per cent the following year. Tansu Çiller then forgot her promises to the IMF and steered the country towards a new crisis. She badly needed a success and sought it in two areas.

The first was the fight against the Kurdish insurgency in the southeast of the country. Tansu Çiller's rule witnessed further serious violation of human rights – more targeted assassinations, more villages destroyed – as she gave free rein to military repression. She established strong links with the security services and recruited into her party a former chief of the general staff and the former head of the intelligence service. 'The parliamentary group of the True Path Party is beginning to look like the passing-out parade of the police academy,' an observer noted with a degree of exaggeration. The insurgency was contained, but continued to smoulder.

At the same time Tansu Çiller strained every muscle to secure a customs union with the European Union. She enlisted the help of President Bill Clinton, who was responsive to her sweet smiling face, and impressed the European Community with her promises of liberalization. The European Parliament agreed to the customs union which came into effect on 1 January 1996. Tansu Çiller presented this as a crucial step towards full membership, almost a guarantee of it. But critics argued that henceforth Europe would be less inclined to agree to membership, which would burden the EU budget, since the customs union gave it all it needed – free access to the Turkish market at no extra cost. True, there was some provision to compensate Turkey for the loss of customs revenue, but Greece vetoed disbursements. The customs union had important consequences. Trade with EU member countries increased and came to account for roughly half of Turkey's commercial exchanges. On the positive side, Turkish industry learnt how to compete with European products. On the other hand, Turkey bound herself to abide by rules which had been made and could be changed in her absence. But then any agreement with Europe was bound to be an unequal treaty: Turkey could not punch above its weight in a match with hard-headed rich Europeans immune to Tansu Çiller's charm.

Tansu Çiller hoped that the signature of the customs union would endear her to the voters. Early elections had been forced on her by her Social Democrat coalition partners, who had reverted to the old name of Republican People's Party and acquired a less accommodating leader in the person of the veteran politician, Deniz Baykal. In appealing to Europe, Tansu Çiller had claimed that she provided the strongest barrier to political Islam. In 1994 Necmettin Erbakan's Islamist Welfare Party had alarmed the secularists by gaining control in local elections of Ankara, Istanbul, and many other cities. Çiller attacked the Islamists in her election speeches. But she made little impression on the electorate. Many people had suffered from the 1994 recession which signalled the failure of Çiller's development policy. Voters, fickle in their preferences, were willing to try another leader who promised to put more money in their pockets.

The Welfare Party emerged as the single strongest party in the parliamentary elections held in December 1995. In the political horse-trading which followed, the main concern of party leaders was to block a parliamentary investigation into corruption charges levelled against them by their political rivals. After an interval of six months, Erbakan and Çiller proved to be the only two leaders willing to protect each other against their accusers. Çiller, the self-professed champion of secularism, agreed to serve as deputy to Erbakan, who became the first Islamist prime minister in the history of the republic.

The performance of the Erbakan–Çiller coalition did not redeem its flawed birth. When he had served as Ecevit's deputy in 1974, Erbakan had been notorious for littering the country with foundation stones for factories which were never built. Now he was ridiculed by the business community for discovering phantom sources of revenue to finance grandiose projects. Nor did his tours of Muslim countries produce the money to build an 'Islamic car', an 'Islamic submarine', even less an 'Islamic aircraft-carrier'. The Libyan dictator Muammar Gaddafi received him in his tent and harangued him on the shortcomings of Turkey's Kurdish policy; the Turkish establishment was outraged. In Cairo, he advised the Egyptian leadership to deal more kindly with the political organization of Muslim Brothers; 'Take them back with you to Turkey,' the Egyptian president is reported to have replied. In Teheran he signed an agreement for the supply to Turkey of Iranian natural gas. The ground had already been prepared, but, through no fault of Erbakan's, the terms had to be renegotiated later when demand fell in Turkey and the price proved to be too high. 'Our job now is damage limitation,' a Turkish diplomat complained privately.[13] But a remedy was at hand.

The Islamist mayor of an outlying suburb of Ankara had invited the Iranian ambassador to mark Jerusalem Day – a day of protest against the Israeli occupation of the old city of Jerusalem with its Muslim shrines. The ambassador obliged and made a speech extolling the virtues of Islamic government. The following day, the army sent its tanks to the suburb, ostensibly on exercise, but, as the generals put it later, in order to 'readjust the balance delicately'. In a campaign orchestrated by the general staff, universities, employers' organizations and trade unions demanded the resignation of the government. At a meeting of the National Security Council on 28 February 1997 Erbakan was presented with a list of demands which included the curtailment of religious education. He agreed, but failed to carry out his promise. Thereupon some members of Erbakan's coalition partner, Çiller's True Path Party, broke away to form their own political group. Çiller withdrew from the coalition in the hope that she would be invited to form the new government. But President Demirel had lost patience with his former protégée, and asked the Motherland Party leader Mesut Yılmaz to try his hand at coalition-making. After serving for sixteen months, Yılmaz resigned when parliament censured him for his part in a suspect privatization deal. In January 1999 he was succeeded by Bülent Ecevit, leader of the Democratic Left Party, the smallest in parliament, as head of an interim government to prepare for new elections.

Thus began what became known in Turkey as 'the process of 28 February' – a campaign, concerted by the military, to eradicate political Islam from education, business and other activities. 'Green capital' – that is, businesses suspected of financing political Islam – was penalized. They included the country's largest biscuit manufacturer (Ülker), who lost the contract to supply the military. Professors accused of 'reactionary views' were barred from university posts of dean or rector. Clever commentators called it 'Turkey's first postmodern coup'. But, whatever its description, it was supported enthusiastically by the majority of the intelligentsia. The constitutional court, a stronghold of the secularist establishment, banned the Welfare Party as 'the focus' of reactionary activity. Recep Erdoğan, who had been elected mayor of Istanbul on the ticket of the Welfare Party, was deprived of his post and sentenced to ten months' imprisonment for reciting a poem by a nationalist poet who wrote at a time when Turkey was fighting foreign invaders: 'The mosques are our barracks, their minarets our bayonets, their domes our shields.' The court held that by declaiming these verses at a provincial rally, Erdoğan was guilty of fomenting divisive religious passions. Many Islamists were demoralized, convinced that the military would never allow them to exercise real power. But others decided that they had brought misfortune on themselves and began devising new policies. The process took time. As a first step, the Welfare Party was replaced by a largely similar, but more soft-spoken Virtue Party (FP), under Recai Kutan, an elderly lieutenant of Erbakan.

Ecevit was lucky. In September 1998, the Turkish military took the bit between their teeth and threatened Syria with force if it did not expel the Kurdish rebel leader, Abdullah Öcalan. The Syrian dictator Hafez al-Asad, who could no longer rely on Russian support, gave way. In February 1999, a team of Turkish commandos, alerted by friendly intelligence services, snatched Öcalan from Kenya, where he had been hiding on Greek diplomatic premises under cover of a passport procured by the Greek Cypriot authorities, and brought him back to face trial in Turkey. Ecevit, a staunch nationalist as well as a social democrat, was the beneficiary of the surge of nationalist pride which Öcalan's capture evoked. In elections held in April 1999, Ecevit won 136 seats – more than any other party leader. He was followed by the far-right Nationalist Action Party (MHP) with 129. Neither party had been in government since the late 1970s (if one disregards Ecevit's brief return to power before the elections) and neither was, therefore, involved in recent corruption scandals. MHP, which had languished after the death of its Supreme Leader (*Başbuğ*), the military plotter Alpaslan Türkeş, had found a new untried leader, Devlet Bahçeli. An economist by training, he was a fussy bachelor, who told his backwoodsman supporters not to wear white socks with blue suits. A much reduced Motherland Party under Mesut Yılmaz completed the coalition.

At first all went well. But success in defeating the insurgency of Kurdish separatists was matched by a growing realization that a decade of short-lived coalition governments, not to say half a century of vote-seeking policies, interrupted only by brief intervals of military rule, had left the administration in tatters. The lesson was driven home in

August 1999 by an earthquake which devastated Turkey's industrial heartland in and around İzmit, on the eastern approaches to Istanbul. The death toll of 17,000 demonstrated that laxity, political pressure and bribery had allowed a massive violation of planning and building regulations. The tardy and confused response by the authorities was contrasted with the efficiency of foreign rescue teams which arrived promptly, overcoming bureaucratic obstacles, not to mention the objection to 'foreign blood' by a nationalist minister of health. Even the army, applauded for its success in crushing Öcalan's Kurdish rebellion, was slow to swing into action. Clearly, reforms were urgently needed. The electorate hoped that nationalists, of the left and right, would do the job.

Ecevit relied on the political sense of his erstwhile opponent President Süleyman Demirel, who crowned his career as the grand old man of Turkish politics. Reforms were put in hand with a will. In 1997, the European Union had excluded Turkey from the list of candidates with which it proposed to start accession negotiations. The list included, in the first wave of candidates, Cyprus, represented by the Greek Cypriot government which ruled the southern two thirds of the island, and in the second, Turkey's neighbours, Bulgaria and Romania, still bearing the marks of more than half a century of Communist rule. Turkey, a long-time associate member and recent partner in the customs union, was outraged. But the earthquake disaster had softened animosity on both sides. European countries had actively expressed their sympathy. Greece, which could earlier be relied on to put every obstacle in the path of Turkey's accession, changed its policy under the moderate leadership of prime minister Costas Simitis, who realized that a Turkey negotiating its membership with the European Union would be unlikely to pose a threat to Greece, and might even make concessions – over Cyprus, in the first place – as a price of admission. Greek sympathy was expressed by a campaign of donations for Turkish earthquake victims and by the dispatch of a Greek rescue team. Turkey reciprocated by sending its rescuers when Athens was hit by a smaller earthquake. The term 'earthquake diplomacy' was born to designate the attempt to use the new atmosphere of goodwill in order to solve long-standing problems between the two countries. Progress was slow, but it was better than the stalemate that had threatened to erupt in military clashes as the two countries squabbled over drilling rights, flying rights and the ownership of uninhabited outcrops of rock in the Aegean, in addition to the much more substantial clash of interests in Cyprus.

In December 1999, the European Union offered to start accession negotiations with Turkey, provided the latter met European criteria of democratic governance, administrative competence and economic management. It was a tall order, which, Turks complained later, had not been met by other candidates when they had begun negotiating their membership. Ecevit agreed to enter the process, after receiving assurances that although Cyprus and problems with Greece had to be resolved, they were not part of the criteria of acceptability which applied to all candidates. It was a fine and, in the last resort, meaningless distinction. But Ecevit and his partners were satisfied, and he flew to Helsinki to appear in the family photograph of prospective candidates.

Helsinki speeded up the reform process. At the same time, the Ecevit government negotiated a new aid agreement with the IMF. Under its supervision, Turkey began implementing a programme designed to stop politicians from playing fast and loose with the economy. The initial results were promising and interest rates fell steeply, easing the burden of servicing a mountainous public debt. But the programme underestimated the difficulty of regulating an economy fed by an unsound banking system. Government subsidies to farmers and tradesmen were covered by unfunded advances from state banks and did not appear on the government budget. Some private banks made unsecured loans to companies which they controlled. In 2000, which was supposed to be the first year of retrenchment, the economy grew by a surprising 6 per cent, pulling in more imports and making it difficult to limit the devaluation of the Turkish lira to targeted (rather than actual) inflation. In November the markets panicked and capital fled abroad. Private banks began to fail. In the 1994 crisis, Tansu Çiller had tried to prevent panic by guaranteeing all bank deposits. As the policy continued to be applied, the treasury had to take over failing banks saddled with debts of billions of dollars.

Ecevit's task was made more difficult by the departure of Demirel from Çankaya palace at the end of his seven-year presidential term in

May 2000. Ecevit had tried to secure a constitutional amendment to allow Demirel a second term or, at least, to extend his first term. Parliament refused, reflecting public pressure for change. Change came with a vengeance. As a last resort, Ecevit persuaded parliament to vote for a candidate outside politics and the army, which had until then supplied presidents for the republic. The new president was Ahmet Necdet Sezer, the president of the constitutional court. Sezer saw himself as a defender of legality against dishonest politicians. A stickler for rules and regulations, he won popularity by making sure his driver obeyed traffic lights. Being thrifty, he reduced to a minimum the large staff of advisers Demirel had assembled in the presidential palace, and paid the price by floundering when political decisions had to be made. His principle was *fiat justitia, ruat coelum*. The heavens collapsed on 19 February 2001.

At a meeting of the National Security Council, held that day, President Sezer accused the government of covering up corruption scandals. Ecevit, the most austere of Turkish politicians, who nonetheless tolerated less scrupulous colleagues as a matter of political necessity, took it as a personal affront. The assistant prime minister, springing to his master's defence, hurled a copy of the constitution at the president, who, he claimed, had exceeded his powers. Ecevit walked out of the meeting and announced to journalists waiting outside that the state, not the government, was facing a crisis. The chief of the general staff, who had been present at the meeting, succeeded in calming tempers, but it was too late. The markets, already shaken by a crisis of confidence the previous November, collapsed. As capital fled abroad, the government floated the Turkish lira, which immediately halved in value.

To salvage the situation, Ecevit secured the services of a Turkish national, Kemal Derviş, who was assistant president of the World Bank, and put him in charge of the economy. While President Sezer and Prime Minister Ecevit stayed away from each other, Derviş negotiated with the IMF additional credits to back up a radical economic reform programme. Its immediate aim was to cut back public expenditure and produce a large and continuing surplus which would serve to reduce the public debt. More banks failed. As the treasury took over their debts, the public debt rose steeply until it exceeded the gross national product, which plunged by nearly 10 per cent by the end of the year. More than 2.5 million jobs were lost in the two crises of November 2000 and February 2001.

The programme worked, and by the following year the economy had begun to recover. But confidence was not easily restored and new jobs were slow in coming. The IMF had insisted that the leaders of all the coalition parties should sign an assurance that they would abide by the terms of the economic programme. They did so with a heavy heart, but squabbled over measures to implement it. They disagreed also on the political reforms demanded by the European Union as a condition for beginning accession talks. Confidence was further shaken when Ecevit fell seriously ill in May 2002. His refusal to appoint an acting prime minister, let alone to stand down, led to a wave of resignations from his party. First his deputy prime minister, then his foreign minister and, finally, his economic coordinator, Kemal Derviş, left the government and joined the opposition. Even so, Ecevit, who discharged himself from hospital against the advice of his doctors, tried to soldier on, realizing that the pain caused by the IMF programme would destroy the electoral prospects of the coalition parties.

His partners were more rash. The Nationalist Action Party leader, Devlet Bahçeli, had already broken ranks by opposing the abolition of the death penalty, cultural rights for the Kurds and concessions in Cyprus as the price of EU membership. He now declared that he would leave the coalition unless elections, due in April 2004, were advanced to November 2002. Ecevit was obliged to give way before the economic reform programme had a chance of producing the first signs of success. He had inherited the sins of his predecessors – the maladministration, corruption and growing debt which demagogic politicians had allowed in a vain effort, at first to raise, and then simply to maintain living standards. Although Ecevit was damned by the electorate, his last government had achieved an impressive record of reforms. But it would take much longer than the three years which he had spent in office at the head of a fractious coalition to clean the Augean stables of Turkey's political economy.

In the elections held in November 2002, none of the three coalition parties – Ecevit's Democratic Left, Bahçeli's Nationalists and Yılmaz's

Motherland Party – could win the minimum of 10 per cent of the total poll, which under Turkish electoral law a party needs in order to qualify for representation in parliament. Ecevit's Democratic Left Party's share of the poll was a derisory 1.3 per cent. Only two parties entered the new parliament. In first place was the youngest, known as Justice and Development (whose initials AK mean 'white, clean or pure' in Turkish). It won an absolute majority of 362 seats in the 550-member parliament. The opposition was now represented by the country's oldest party, the Republican People's Party, which Kemal Derviş had joined. The results had been distorted by the 10 per cent barrier, as votes cast for parties which fell below it were wasted to the benefit of those which crossed the barrier. Justice and Development, which had won only 34 per cent of the vote, and the Republican People's Party, with 19 per cent, had a disproportionate number of members of parliament. No matter, Turkey now had the prospect of a stable government.

The leader of Justice and Development was Recep Tayyip Erdoğan, the former mayor of Istanbul, who gathered round him the reforming wing of Islamists after their Virtue Party had been banned by the constitutional court, as had all other previous expressions of political Islam. A constitutional amendment allowed Erdoğan to stand for parliament in a by-election in February 2003. He won it handsomely and became prime minister. Forty-nine years old, tall, good-looking and well-dressed, Erdoğan was a man of the people – a German journalist called him a 'flower sprung from a marsh'. He had a chance to realize their aspirations.

PART II

Turkey and the Turks Today

5

Catching Up

'WE WERE NOT brought up in crystal mansions,' the leaders of the Justice and Development Party are fond of saying. But neither were the leaders of the political parties which they replaced in power in November 2002. Of the four pre-eminent popular politicians who have ruled Turkey since the end of the Second World War, only the first, Adnan Menderes, was born into a comparatively wealthy family of landowners. His successors, Süleyman Demirel and Turgut Özal, came from humble provincial backgrounds. Both owed their careers to the free secular system of education introduced by Atatürk. In a country which was still short of technical staff, both rose quickly to senior positions in the service of the state before entering politics. Although their early career was in the civil service, their social background made them aware of the dead hand of bureaucracy. Nurtured by a paternalistic state, they wanted, nevertheless, to remove the restraints which it placed on the energy of the people they genuinely wished to serve. But as they relied on the resources of the state to promote their political careers, they were unable to prune its tentacles.

Recep Tayyip Erdoğan, the founder and leader of the Justice and Development Party, who became prime minister in March 2003, rose by a different route. He was born in 1954 into metropolitan, rather than provincial, poverty in a run-down neighbourhood of Istanbul. The district of Kasımpaşa, on the northern shore of the Golden Horn, had grown round the Ottoman admiralty and a shipyard which remained in use until recently. Senior officials who worked there gradually moved away, and Kasımpaşa became dilapidated. Before the Second World War it was the last neighbourhood with open sewers in Istanbul. Kasımpaşa was notorious for its bullies, who prided themselves on an exclusive code of honour. Recep Tayyip's father typified their behaviour in his family setting. One day he hung up his young son from the ceiling as a punishment for swearing.[1] Recep Tayyip learnt to humour his father and go his own way.

The family had migrated to Istanbul from the eastern part of the Black Sea coast, near the old frontier with Russia (now with Georgia). Here the mountains come close to the sea leaving little room for farming. Until the cultivation of tea was introduced at state expense some fifty years ago, and the mountain slopes were terraced for the new crop, local people had little choice but to migrate in search of work or go to sea. Known as Laz, they were of Caucasian origin, and spoke a language akin to (the Mingrelian dialect of) Georgian. They had been converted to Islam comparatively late, after the conquest of their region by the Ottomans in the fifteenth century, and they retained the religious fervour of late converts and of frontiersmen. In the nineteenth century many worked in the Russian empire where they were renowned as bakers. But they found their main employment as sailors and fishermen. As the only Muslim community with a maritime tradition in Turkey, they provided the bulk of sailors to the Ottoman fleet, after the Greeks had gone their own way, and then to the merchant and naval fleets of the Turkish republic. Recep Tayyip's father found employment in the state shipping lines and was eventually promoted to captain of ferries plying the Bosphorus and the sea of Marmara. Even so, his salary was barely sufficient to house, feed and clothe his family. A man of the geographical periphery, he had come to the centre. His son would continue the move from the social periphery to the political centre of affairs.

In the early 1950s, the Democrat government of Adnan Menderes had chipped away at the universal system of secular education by opening seven-year high schools for prayer-leaders and preachers. These schools multiplied until they constituted an alternative religious stream of education. By the time he had finished his five-year primary school at the age of 12, Recep Tayyip had a choice of a religious or a secular high school (*lycée*). He was a pious boy and his headmaster recommended that he should go on to the *lycée* for prayer-leaders and preachers, situated on the opposite shore of the Golden Horn in the heart of Ottoman Istanbul. Young Recep earned money to buy books by selling bagels (*simit*) in the street: he bought stale bagels in the evenings and his mother heated them for sale as fresh the following morning.

The religious *lycée* was not a somnolent seminary. 'You are not here to learn how to wash the dead,' new boys were told. They joined sports teams and took part in poetry recitals and other social activities. Recep Tayyip had played football with neighbourhood boys, unbeknown to his father who was ambitious for him and, like many Turkish parents, wanted to see his son's nose permanently stuck in schoolbooks. During his years in the religious school, young Recep Tayyip became a talented footballer and was tempted to turn professional. His father would not, of course, hear of it. There was another obstacle. After graduating from the *lycée*, Recep Tayyip had grown a beard as a sign of Muslim piety, and he refused to shave it off when offered a place in one of Turkey's top football teams which insisted on clean-shaven players. Religious observance was, after all, the main purpose of his schooling, and religion was turning political.

Necmettin Erbakan had founded his first Islamic party, the National Order Party, in 1970, when Recep Tayyip was sixteen, and its successor, the National Salvation Party, two years later. Erdoğan, who was combative and ambitious, joined its youth branch. Islamic fundamentalism had few adherents in Turkey: what inspired young practising Muslims like Erdoğan was the desire to gain recognition for the repressed culture of Muslim believers in Turkey, and to advance their social status. He had by then suffered a disappointment: he did not get high enough pass marks for entry to the faculty of political science in Ankara and had to content himself with a place in a college of lesser standing – the academy of commercial and political sciences in Istanbul (which later became part of Marmara University). As an Islamic militant, Erdoğan took an active part in the ideological struggles of the 1970s. But, unlike some of his companions, he avoided involvement in armed clashes, and thus survived the clampdown on violent Islamists after the military coup of 1980. When the military regime ended and political activity resumed in 1983, he became a full-time politician in the ranks of Erbakan's third party, the Welfare Party (RP), and was elected chairman of its Istanbul provincial branch. He concentrated his efforts on changing the party's previous image as a dour defender of Islamic values, telling his members:

Greet everyone. Don't forget to greet all your neighbours in the block where you live or passers-by in the street. If you say *es-selâmü aleyküm* [Peace Be Upon You – the traditional Muslim greeting] and get no response, you must understand that the man you address doesn't like this form of greeting. Then say *merhaba* [Hello – a word of Arabic origin]. If again there's no sign of understanding, substitute *İyi günler* [Good day – the modern pure Turkish form]. If there's no response either, then perhaps you are speaking to George [an English-speaking foreigner]. So, greet him [in English] with 'Hello, good morning!'[2]

In the 1994 local government elections, Erdoğan beat Zülfü Livaneli, a radical musician popular with secularized young people, who had been chosen by the secularist (and elitist) Republican People's Party in an attempt to retain control of the council. The secular centre-right parties also put up strong candidates. Thanks to the split in the secularist vote, Erdoğan won the election and became mayor of Turkey's largest city at the age of 40. He had by then shaved off his beard and taken to wearing bespoke suits. His wife had helped mobilize support among women, while continuing to wear the Muslim headscarf.

Erdoğan managed Istanbul better than had his predecessor, the Republican mayor Nurettin Sözen, whose reign was marred by a major corruption scandal involving bribes to the director of the municipal waterworks. True, jobs and contracts now went to Islamic sympathizers, but no illegality could be proved. As mayor, Erdoğan learned to work effectively within the system. His subsequent setback in 1997, when he fell victim to 'the process of 28 February' launched by the military against the Islamists, rubbed off such rough edges as he had retained. The few months which he spent in prison (for violating the ban on the use of religion for political purposes by reciting a poem appealing to Muslim feeling) and the loss of his post as mayor and of his political rights, taught him a lesson in prudence. He developed further the inclusive approach which he had advocated in the run-up to the Istanbul local elections. Prison did not embitter Erdoğan; on the contrary, he emerged as a more moderate politician. He broke with his former master Necmettin Erbakan, in a rare act of political parricide reminiscent of the deposition of İnönü by Ecevit thirty years earlier, and together with a group of innovators he founded in 2001 the Justice and Development Party, whose ideology he described as 'democratic conservative'. He declared his allegiance to the secular state which, he said, should deal impartially with citizens of all faiths and none, while helping meet people's basic religious needs (by paying the salaries of mosque staff). After he became prime minister, Erdoğan challenged Europe to prove its secularist credentials by omitting any mention of Christianity from its new constitution. The boot was now on the other foot, and Erdoğan took to making impeccably liberal statements which made some impression on a basically sceptical Turkish secularist establishment. But his more important message was that he was a modernizer. This appealed to almost everyone.

It is often said that Turkish voters brought Erdoğan to power out of disgust at the widespread corruption that the leaders of the other parties appear to have tolerated when they were in power. Certainly, before the elections in November 2002, the Turkish press was full of allegations of high-profile corruption scandals. Some involved official inaction in the face of fraudulent or irregular operations by private banks. Others detailed large losses incurred by the state as a result of unfortunate investment decisions which were attributed to corrupt politicians. But in a pre-election survey only 10 per cent of respondents listed corruption as the country's most pressing problem.[3] It is unlikely that many Turkish voters were naive enough to believe that Erdoğan and his party differed substantially from their predecessors in their attitude to corruption or were less inclined to favouritism. During the electoral campaign in 2001, Erdoğan was asked to explain a large increase in his personal wealth. He replied that the money had been lent to him by his young son who had received gifts of gold when he was circumcised. It was a more credible story than the explanation offered by Tansu Çiller, leader of the True Path Party, that she had found some of her money wrapped in a bundle in her mother's bedroom. Later, when Erdoğan sent his son and two daughters to study in the United States, he let it be known that the expense was met by a businessman.

It seems that most people found it acceptable that politicians should receive personal gifts. After he had become prime minister, Erdoğan threw a huge reception in an Istanbul hotel to celebrate his student son's wedding and invited the Italian prime minister Silvio Berlusconi to witness the ceremony. Again, in the eyes of most Turks this is what any successful man would have done and would have been expected to do. That the successful man was a prime minister who made much of his closeness to the people made little difference. In any case, Erdoğan had distinguished himself by including in his list of guests humble trades- men who had served his family. After Erdoğan's victory, parliament in Ankara set up a committee to investigate corruption allegations. The committee examined – and publicized – accusations levelled against the government's predecessors in power. But Erdoğan's supporters resisted pressure to limit parliamentary immunity, which makes it difficult to institute proceedings against sitting members of parliament. None of this means that the campaign against corruption will produce no results and will serve only political purposes. Attitudes are changing, but the change will be gradual and this is what most people expect.

The survey conducted on the eve of the elections in November 2002 showed that people's main preoccupation was unemployment (31 per cent of respondents), followed by inflation and the high cost of living (22 per cent). Prices are in fact much lower in Turkey than in the West, but so are salaries. In September 2003, the average pay of civil servants was 440 dollars a month,[4] while prices were roughly half as high as in the West.[5]

'Build us a factory!' was the demand most commonly heard when Erdoğan addressed public rallies in the eastern province of Siirt, which sent him to parliament in a by-election in February 2003. Most inhab- itants of the province are of Kurdish origin, yet state-sponsored employment comes before Kurdish cultural rights in their priorities. In the third quarter of 2003, unemployment in Turkey stood at 9.4 per cent – lower than in France (9.5 per cent) and Spain (11.2 per cent), and less than half the unemployment level in Poland (20 per cent) on the eve of its accession to the European Union. But the official figures flatter Turkey's performance. Many of those considered employed do casual work in marginal or even unpaid occupations. Unpaid family members (women and young people) make up about a fifth of the work force. Six per cent of those in employment are counted as 'underemployed' and are looking for additional work. Of the total number of people in employment in the third quarter of 2003, 54 per cent were not registered with any social security institution and hence had no job security, health or pension benefits. A better measure of the employment situation is the proportion of the working age population which is actually employed. In Turkey in 2003 it was under 45 per cent. If unpaid employment were excluded, the employment ratio would work out at only 35 per cent. In the European Union the average employment ratio is 63 per cent (55 per cent for Spain). Only in some Middle Eastern and North African countries is a lower proportion of the population of working age employed than it is in Turkey.[6]

In these circumstances, it is not surprising that three quarters of all Turks believe that the opportunity to work anywhere in Europe would be the greatest benefit of EU membership.[7] Unemployment in the EU does not discourage Turks who dream of moving to Europe. They are prepared to work harder and be paid less than European citizens. If they gain access to European-type unemployment benefits, they would be better off than on the Turkish minimum wage. Dissatisfaction with conditions at home and willingness to seek a fortune abroad is particularly high among the educated: according to one survey, nearly 60 per cent of them want to work or study in a foreign (meaning a Western) country.[8]

In the 1970s and then again after 1987, when Turgut Özal won a second election by jettisoning the policy of economic austerity inherited from the 1980 military regime, trade unions were able to secure comparatively large wage increases for their members, while preventing overmanned state economic enterprises from shedding their labour. Trade union membership, which was always low, fell at the turn of the millennium, and union power was eroded by the rise in unemployment. In the year 2000, when there were 8 million regular wage earners and 2 million casual labourers in the country, only 100,000 were covered by new collective wage agreements. As these agreements run normally for two years, one should add in the 500,000 workers on whose behalf wages had been negotiated the previous year. Even so, the total of 600,000 represents only a small fraction of wage earners. In 2000, 19,000 workers were involved in strikes, causing the loss of some 370,000 working days.

That year there were 106 trade unions, grouped in three confederations which reflected old ideological divisions: TÜRKİŞ (Turkish

Labour Confederation), DİSK (Confederation of Revolutionary Trade Unions) and the Islamic Hakk-İş (Workers' Rights). TÜRKİŞ, which is politically close to the Republican People's Party, draws much of its strength from employees in state economic enterprises. At the beginning of the new millennium, civil servants were allowed to negotiate collectively through staff associations, but not to strike. They publicized their demands by staging marches, go-slow or hunger strikes. These tactics made little impression when the government stuck to its guns. However, as Turkey begins implementing all the conventions of the International Labour Organization, trade union power will increase. In the meantime union leaders are affected by the prevailing enterprise culture: they seek political careers for themselves and profitable investments for union funds. Thus the metalworkers' union Metal-İş, which acquired a large building in northern Cyprus for a staff-training centre, later turned it into a commercial hotel.

Employers have their own organization (TİSK/Turkish Confederation of Employers' Unions) to conduct wage negotiations. But the two main business organizations are the Union of Chambers of Commerce and Commodity Exchanges (TOBB), to which all businesses must belong, and TÜSİAD (Turkish Association of Industrialists and Businessmen), which represents big business. TÜSİAD, which finances research and has an impressive range of publications, has become an important pressure group, and its pronouncements on home and even foreign affairs carry weight. It is an active campaigner for liberal causes and for membership of the European Union. In this it overlaps with the Economic Development Foundation (İKV), also financed by big business, which has become the unofficial leader of the European cause. The private sector supports also the Council for Foreign Economic Relations (DEİK) which organizes meetings between Turkish and foreign businessmen, country by country.

Research foundations and think-tanks have proliferated in recent years. Their sponsors include business, political parties and the military. Some receive grants from European and other foreign research funds. They thus have the means to conduct public opinion polls and social surveys, which are also staged by commercial polling organizations working mainly for advertisers. The major political parties conduct their own polls and have research departments. The Justice and Development Party has sought to demonstrate its modern outlook by setting up an electronic communications centre, which deals with questions and requests sent in by voters, and is therefore able to determine their priorities. Never have Turkey and its people been surveyed, measured, questioned and quantified as thoroughly and as frequently as they are now. It is a sign of modernity, but no replacement for leadership.

As in many Western countries pocketbook politics prevail. Ideological commitment takes second place to calculations of personal advancement. The generals who ruled Turkey between 1980 and 1983 have succeeded largely in their aim of depoliticizing their countrymen following the general trend in Europe where ideological politics have lost their allure. Foreign affairs preoccupy the media. But they interest most people in Turkey only to the extent that events abroad affect their livelihood. Foreign and domestic strategists speculate on the role Turkey could or should play in the Middle East, the Balkans or the countries of the former Soviet Union. But for most ordinary people it is a subject of platonic interest, something to discuss idly in front of the family TV set, unless jobs and livelihoods are threatened or, alternatively, some personal benefit is in prospect. Hundreds of thousands of people in Turkey are descended from refugees from Bosnia, which gave its name to the Istanbul suburb of Yenibosna (New Bosnia). Yet few people turned up at a rally in Istanbul in defence of Bosnian Muslims who were fighting for their lives in former Yugoslavia in 1994.

At the turn of the millennium the mood is sober. It is a far cry from President Turgut Özal's confident prediction ten years ago that the twenty-first century would be a century of the Turks. Expectations that living standards would rise without interruption were disappointed when the country ran out of credit in the late 1990s. Times are hard for most Turks, who take for granted the progress the country has achieved and think more of the distance which still separates them from rich Western societies. The number of motor cars on Turkish roads has increased from only 300,000 to 4,600,000 in the last twenty years, but even so the number of people per vehicle in Turkey is 15, while in Greece it is 3 and in Spain 2. Consumption of electricity in Turkey has nearly doubled in the last ten years from 60,000 to 110,000 million kw/hr, but consumption per person is still under 2,000 kw/hr against 4,500 kw/hr in Greece and 5,000 kw/hr in Spain. The media are full of depressing reports that Turkey spends less on education and health than many Third World countries. When economic progress stalls, as it did in 2001, people lose hope that they will reach the level of 'contemporary civilization' in their lifetimes. 'I've never known people so depressed,' an Istanbul publisher confided in 2003. One reason is that while earlier economic crises had little impact on the middle class, the crisis of 2001 destroyed the jobs and blighted the prospects of some of the best educated and articulate members of society.

The mood is caught perfectly in the novel *Kar* (*Snow*) by Turkey's best-known writer, Orhan Pamuk. The novel, which was published in 2002 with an initial print order of 100,000 copies, is set in the city of Kars, which the Ottoman empire lost to Russia in 1878, and Turkey won back (from Armenia) in 1920. The protagonist, a radical left-wing poet who has spent many years in exile in Germany, visits the city on behalf of an Istanbul newspaper in order to investigate stories of suicides by young women. The Turkish press did in fact carry reports of such suicides, not in Kars, but in Batman in the Kurdish south-east, and attributed them to intolerable pressures by a repressive patriarchal society. In the novel, the suicides seem to be motivated by the insistence of the authorities on Muslim girls discarding their headscarves. While the real cause is left uncertain, Kars itself emerges as the embodiment of melancholy. The city, set on the harsh, high Anatolian plateau, is being emptied by emigration. Buildings put up under Russian rule, many by rich Armenian merchants, are crumbling. Unemployed Kurds fill the tea-houses. Violence is ever present – whether between Islamic and secularist militants, the authorities and Kurdish nationalists, or in personal feuds. Snowstorms obscure and isolate the city, just as conspiracy theories produce a mental fog and make it impossible to understand people's real motives. The unresolved tensions of a society ill at ease with itself are carried into the modern age, when fatal shots are fired during a live transmission from a local television studio. The protagonist, who had been an outsider in Germany, is an outsider in his own country. Like the author, he had grown up in a comfortable middle-class neighbourhood of Istanbul: 'poverty began where our home ended.' He now tries to break out of the limits set by his background. The novel is an exploration of poverty and alienation. It is also a meditation on the possibility that love (between the protagonist and an educated local woman) and an effort to understand 'the other Turkey' – the Turkey that progress has left behind – might redeem a time and a country that are out of joint.

Orhan Pamuk deals imaginatively with a crisis which press and academic pundits explain in terms of deep-seated faults in tradition, social organization, education and governance. Yet people's will to better themselves is as vibrant as ever, and their ability to do so is growing. Like Atatürk, when the republic was founded, and Turgut Özal, who sought to integrate it into the world economy, Recep Tayyip Erdoğan, after he became prime minister, made constant appeals to people to have confidence in themselves and, of course, in the state and his government. Interestingly for a politician with roots in political Islam, he referred repeatedly to Atatürk's vision of a modern Turkey. He also laid special stress on education in general, and the education of women in particular, and put his full weight behind the campaign launched in conjunction with UNESCO under the slogan, 'Come on girls, go to school!'[9]

In fact, according to official statistics, the percentage of girls in primary schools is only slightly lower than that of boys: 87 per cent against 92 per cent. The gap widens in secondary schools, where 47 per cent of boys, but only 39 per cent of girls of the appropriate age group are shown as attending in the year 2002. As a result, while boys spend an average of seven years being educated, the figure for girls is five years. Where there is a noticeable difference is in work outside the home. In 2002 only 21 per cent of women were classed as wage earners (outside agriculture where women work mainly on family farms).[10] Overall, women's participation in the labour force stood at 24 per cent in the year 2000.[11] In Istanbul, according to a report of the metropolitan municipality, more than half the women do not work outside the home and rely on their husbands' wages. Of these 44 per cent had less than 5 million lira a day to spend (3 to 4 dollars at the official rate of exchange, twice as much in purchasing power).[12]

Averages conceal wide variations. In 2000, of 1.6 million people classed as scientific, technical and professional workers, 555,000 were women, but 1 million employers included only 42,000 women. There is genuine gender equality in middle-class metropolitan society, while elsewhere equality is often only theoretical. Men and women mix easily in metropolitan restaurants, clubs and in private receptions. But many provincial restaurants have a 'family room' for women, and neighbourhood coffee- and tea-houses remain a male preserve. A survey revealed that in the poor working-class district of Ümraniye in Istanbul, whose half a million residents are mostly migrants from the villages, 44 per cent of women stated that they needed the permission of a male member of the family to leave the house alone in daytime. In the evenings the proportion rose to 96 per cent. In the 1990s only 9 per cent of all registered property was owned by women.[13]

Allowing for the inevitable time lag between legislation and implementation, the condition of women in Turkey should improve as a result of the new civil code which came into force on 1 January 2002, when the Ecevit coalition government was in power.[14] The new law meets Turkey's obligations under the United Nations Convention on the Elimination of All Forms of Discrimination against Women (CEDAW). The terms 'head of the family', 'husband' and 'wife' disappear from the statute book to be replaced by the single term 'spouse'. Spouses have equal rights over property acquired during marriage (after the entry into force of the law) and equal rights to represent the family unit, to petition for divorce and to claim alimony. Wives can keep their maiden names. All children, whether born in or out of wedlock, have equal rights (the term 'illegitimate' is abolished). Single persons may adopt children. Provisions which reduced sentences on men found guilty of causing harm to 'sex workers' or of so-called 'crimes of honour' have been abolished.

Islamists were not happy with the law when it was discussed in parliament. But their objections that it violated traditional morality and constituted a gold-digger's charter were overruled. The Justice and Development Party made no attempt to put the clock back when it gained power in November 2002. Its only suggestion was that the clergy (*imams*) should be allowed to register marriages. Under current secularist legislation, only a civil marriage is valid in law, and a religious wedding ceremony may be held only on production of a civil marriage certificate; otherwise, the parties and the officiating *imam* are guilty of an offence. In practice, religious marriages without a preliminary civil marriage are common in the countryside, and are periodically legalized after the event under special amnesties.

Campaigners for women's rights continue to press for further reforms in law and practice. They are well organized. In 2001, 126 women's groups throughout the country joined forces to campaign for the new civil code. Now one of their main objectives is to increase women's role in the country's political life. Turkey has had one (controversial) woman prime minister, and there is usually at least one woman minister in the cabinet. But the proportion of women members of parliament is still extremely low: 4.4 per cent in 2002 (up from 1.9 per cent in 1990). To redress the imbalance, women's rights campaigners are pressing for quotas for women, a proposal that only the Republican People's Party is inclined to accept. More could also be done to end gender discrimination in employment. In 2003, some public agencies attracted criticism by excluding women from applying for such jobs as hydraulic engineer, technician and accountant in the state agricultural purchasing agency, or electrical engineer in provincial distribution networks.[15] Subsequently, the government announced that public agencies would not be allowed to advertise men–only jobs. Islamist campaigners are, in the meantime, demanding as a human right that women should be allowed to wear the Islamic headscarf in schools, colleges and government offices. Secularists object that wearing Islamic dress is a political statement likely to cause division in society. Authorities in France tend to the same view.

Polygamy has been banned in Turkey since the adoption of the Swiss civil code by Atatürk. In the three main metropolitan areas (Istanbul, Ankara and İzmir) it has been eliminated in practice, but it still survives in pockets in the countryside. There are no recent reliable statistics, but a survey conducted in 1963 found that 2.7 per cent of marriages in villages were polygamous. The incidence was lowest in the western part of the country (0.2 per cent), and highest in eastern Anatolia (5 per cent).[16] Islamist politicians are often asked whether they wish to bring back polygamy. The stock answer is that Muslims are not obliged, but are allowed to have up to four wives under certain strict conditions, among which Muslim apologists tend to include the agreement of the first wife. Taunted with this question on a visit to Germany in the summer of 2003, prime minister Erdoğan incurred ridicule when he blurted out, 'Well, one condition might be if the first wife was old and sick.' A Muslim apologist might claim that in this sad eventuality a Westerner might seek consolation with a mistress, while in Turkey adultery was a punishable offence until decriminalized under the family law reforms of 2002.

In fact, the way of life, including the sexual behaviour of the Turkish middle classes, follows with a certain time lag the pattern of the European bourgeoisie. Although divorce is easier in the Islamic tradition, it was fairly rare in Turkey until recently when Turkey caught up with European trends. Again, until recently society did not tolerate unmarried couples living together. Now it is gradually becoming part of a 'modern' lifestyle. Islamic tradition did not allow Muslim women to marry non-Muslims, while it often encouraged Muslim men to have non-Muslim wives, in the hope of converting them, and, in any case, because the children would be Muslim. This tradition survived secular legislation again until recently. As in some European countries in the nineteenth century, military officers and civil servants were not allowed to marry foreigners. This ban was circumvented when the foreign woman converted (often only formally) to Islam, acquired a Turkish name and was, illogically, treated as a Turk. Refusal to use this subterfuge could end a career, as was the case with İrfan Orga, a Turkish airforce officer, who settled in England and became a writer after marrying an Irish girl. Turkey's best-known actress, Yıldız Kenter, made a hit with her autobiographical play *It Was Only for Love* in which she described the plight of her father, who had to resign from the diplomatic service when he married an Englishwoman, and then destroyed himself with drink. The ban on civil servants marrying foreigners has now been lifted, and Muslim Turkish women who marry local or foreign non-Muslims are accepted in society without question.

Brothels are licensed and inspected. In Ottoman times prostitutes were usually non-Muslims. This is no longer so, but at the beginning of the millennium the wealthiest *madame* in Istanbul was an Armenian, who was ranked high in the league table of the city's taxpayers. The social dislocation which followed the collapse of Communism brought a flood of prostitutes from East European countries. Russian girls are described generically as 'Natashas' and incur the anger of Turkish wives who accuse them of ruining their families. There had been similar campaigns against Russian women after the First World War when thousands of White Russians fled to Turkey from the Bolsheviks.

The Turkish media speak openly of (and social anthropologists study) transsexuals and transvestites who congregate in a central neighbourhood of Istanbul.[17] Characteristically, transsexuals take their cue from their counterparts in Europe. Homosexuality has, of course, always existed. Troupes of dancing boys (*köçek*) were banished from Ottoman palaces in the nineteenth century, but survived in the countryside. They are now extinct outside folk festivals. Effeminate men continue to make their mark in the entertainment industry. One such was the country's best loved singer, Zeki Müren, one of the most skilful interpreters of Turkish music in the Ottoman classical mode. The object of love in Ottoman court poetry was of indeterminate gender or none (if one believes that the loved one is a mystical representation of the divine). Now people are more explicit. Nevertheless, as in other south European countries, macho values continue to permeate Turkish society.

In the countryside, social disapproval at times manifests itself in the form of 'honour killings'. Both men and women are at risk if their respective families consider that their honour has been sullied. The aggrieved family sometimes uses a minor to kill the offender, and thus reduce the risk and, in any case, the length of imprisonment for murder. A survey conducted by a Canadian sociologist estimated the number of 'honour killings' at twenty-five a year.[18] The new family law allows spouses to apply to a court for a protection order in cases of family violence. There is no reason to disbelieve press reports that violence against women is still widespread. The survey by the Canadian sociologist claims that between 50 and 67 per cent of Turkish women are assaulted by males in their household. Shelters for women victims of violence have recently been opened in Istanbul. But, as usual, the problem is worst in the backward Kurdish regions of south-eastern Anatolia, where violence of all kinds is endemic.

The system and administration of justice have proved ineffective in checking the prevalence of violence, which is rooted in, and sometimes sanctioned by, tradition. The Turkish justice system is inspired by the French model based on the Code Napoléon. It has been brought up to date piecemeal by the addition of family courts and special courts for children. State security courts, established in the 1970s when terrorism became a major problem, were abolished in 2004. There are parallel systems of military courts and administrative tribunals. The main complaint is that cases take too long to decide, as they wind their way from investigation to prosecution, and then from court of first instance to various levels of appeal. Justice is starved of money: magistrates and judges are badly paid, court buildings poorly maintained, clerical support inadequate. At the beginning of each judicial year in September, the president of the court of appeal makes a ritual plea for more speed, more money and better drafted legislation. But with money hard to find, there is often a stark contrast between professionally presented petitions by lawyers of rich clients and badly drafted verdicts, typed on cheap paper by inexperienced clerks. Verdicts are often quashed on appeal, and cases are then returned down the line, with lower courts sometimes insisting on their original verdicts which the court of appeal then re-examines. The whole process can be dragged out until the case is dropped under the statute of limitation or an amnesty. In the circumstances, detention during trial often becomes the main or even the only sanction. In 2001 of the 55,600 inmates of Turkish prisons, slightly less than half (27,500) were convicts, while the rest were awaiting sentence. Turkish laws often prescribe lengthy sentences, but extenuating circumstances can usually be produced, and, in any case, overcrowded prisons are at intervals emptied by amnesties, before filling up again. Thus the prison population dropped from 52,000 in 1986 to 26,500 in 1991, and then climbed to 72,500 in the year 2000.[19] In 2002/3, 43,500 prisoners were released under an amnesty introduced by the Ecevit government.[20] By July 2003 the prison population had climbed back to 63,500.[21]

The media rejoice when a high-profile businessman is arrested for fraud and sent to prison pending a trial which is more likely than not to end in his acquittal. Orhan Pamuk parodies the public perception of criminal justice, as he relates the legal consequences of a murder in a television studio:

The detailed report compiled by the hard-working major sent as an inspector by the general staff was considered with extreme respect by the military prosecutor and judges in Kars. As a result, Kadife was convicted not for politically motivated murder but for causing death through carelessness, and sentenced to three years in prison. She was freed after twenty months. As for Colonel Osman Nuri Çolak, he received a heavy sentence for forming a band for the purpose of committing murder and for [responsibility for] murder by persons unknown . . . and was freed under an amnesty six months later.[22]

The accidental death of the baby son of a Scottish father and a Turkish mother, who was killed in 2003 in a café in a Turkish holiday resort when an argument at a neighbouring table turned into a gunfight, drew attention to a widespread gun culture. Although in theory all firearms should be licensed, unlicensed handguns abound, whether for self-defence or as a sign of manliness. Parliament finds it necessary to stipulate that members should not enter the chamber armed. There are periodic campaigns for tighter gun control, but Turkey's Wild East tradition will not disappear overnight.

A survey conducted in 2001 into public perceptions of corruption showed that the traffic police and then the police in general are considered particularly suspect (along with customs and revenue officials).[23] Official figures confirm the findings: nearly 40,000 policemen were disciplined and nearly 1,000 expelled from the force in the two and a half years to July 2003.[24] These figures show also that action is being taken to improve the service and re-establish public trust.

Turkey has signed and ratified the UN convention against torture and has agreed to allow individual complaints to the UN Committee Against Torture.[25] Although successive governments have declared their determination to stamp out torture in Turkey, international organizations, such as Amnesty, and domestic pressure groups, like the active Turkish Human Rights Association (İHD), have continued to list cases of violence against people detained in Turkish police stations and prisons. The wide publicity which surrounds allegations of torture and other violations of human rights in Turkey, and the frequent use of these allegations for political rather than humanitarian purposes, make it difficult to determine whether Turkey is indeed more blameworthy in this respect than, for example, other countries awaiting admission to the European Union.

There is little doubt that the authorities did respond in kind to the violence of the terrorist organizations – leftist, rightist, Islamist and Kurdish separatist – which the Turkish republic has had to fight since the 1970s. Everywhere, civil wars are notorious for their cruelty. Nor is it easy to eliminate the effects of anti-terrorist operations on the behaviour of security forces. In Turkey several forces are involved: in towns, the national police, controlled by the interior ministry; in the countryside the gendarmerie; and, particularly when martial law is declared, the regular army. As in some European countries, the gendarmerie is a part of the armed forces which the general staff puts at the disposal of the interior ministry. As a separate service, it has its own intelligence organization and specialist anti-terrorist teams. These have often been accused of the worst violations of human rights. In addition to regular security forces, the Turkish state has armed and paid village guards to ward off attacks by armed gangs of Kurdish separatists. As a result, the war against the separatist insurgents has at times assumed the character of inter-tribal fighting, and resulted in abiding blood feuds.

At the turn of the millennium, the authorities are responding to demands for better policing and better coordination of intelligence in order to contain terrorism. At the same time they are pressing liberal democracies in the West to play their part by denying shelter to terrorists who target Turkey. While the threat of terrorism persists, new areas of concern arise, such as urban crime and drug-trafficking. In the past, the police was effective, largely because it enjoyed public cooperation, and partly because it was feared. Now the fear is diminishing, and the number of complaints against the police is rising. They are investigated by magistrates, but convictions are rare. At times there are gaps in evidence; more generally the state protects its own, even though the government professes a policy of 'zero tolerance' on torture. Between January 2000 and April 2001, some 1,500 policemen were prosecuted for mistreating prisoners; only 113 were convicted. Another 160 faced the more serious charge of torture; 29 of them were convicted.[26] Although the conviction rate is low, it is bound to have had an effect on police behaviour. Instruction in human rights has now become part of training throughout the security forces. The effect of all these reforms will be gradual. As a Turkish civil servant dealing with human rights said privately: 'We have to educate law-enforcers from poor backgrounds who were themselves subject to violence in their homes and who have seen their fathers beat not only their children, but also their mothers.' For all that, violations of human rights are an exceptional rather than a constant feature of life in Turkey.

It is because people do not always trust the authorities to address their concerns impartially and effectively that they rely first on the extended family and then on networks based on mutual obligation. The extended family is the original environment of socialization. 'Our family is not like your family,' a young Turkish worker explained in London. 'I'm going back because I miss my younger brother.' A Turkish psychologist, trained in Istanbul and London before going to Harvard, noticed that British students had a more critical approach to their lecturers than had their Turkish counterparts and thought more independently, but were ill at ease when they first went to university. 'It was as if they had social acne.' Turkish students, on the other hand, who had been brought up in the wider environment of the extended family and the neighbourhood, treated the university like their family home and were perfectly comfortable in it. In this respect, Turkey does not differ substantially from other countries of southern Europe. Like them, it is changing, and change will improve efficiency at the expense of social cohesion and social control.

Traditional moral training instils two basic values: respect (*saygı*) for elders and kindness (*sevgi*, literally love) for the young. Children are expected to kiss the hands not only of their parents, but also of an elder brother (*ağabey*, literally 'lord and master', contracted to *âbi*) or elder sister (*abla*). On the two main religious holidays (*bayram*), one marking the end of the Ramazan fast and the second the beginning of the pilgrimage to Mecca, families visit the elders of the extended family (grandparents, uncles, aunts) and kiss their hands. Children receive presents in return. The terminology of kinship is elaborate. It distinguishes between paternal and maternal uncles and aunts; it has four separate terms for sister-in-law (depending on whether the relationship is on the husband's or the wife's side of the family), but only two for brother-in-law. On the other hand, the same term (*enişte*) is used for sister's husband and uncle-in-law, and similarly one term (*yenge*) for brother's wife and aunt-in-law. These two words, which distinguish newcomers to the family circle, can be applied metaphorically to an outsider who becomes a close family friend. Thus a foreign woman taken to heart by a Turkish family might find herself described as *yenge* (sister-in-law). In the same way, a taxi driver would call an older passenger *âbi*, while an elderly one might be described colloquially as *amca* (uncle). As the Turkish sociologist, Mübeccel Kıray, has pointed out, these attempts to establish personal links in terms of kinship resist the advent of an impersonal society.

Respect and kindness are duties which evoke obligations. An uncivil person (*terbiyesiz*, a term of opprobrium which translates the French *mal élevé*) is one who is deficient in showing proper respect or fulfilling his obligations. Family members, neighbours, members of affinity groups (based on place of birth, schooling or profession) have rights (*hak*), which can also be earned by helping or protecting a person. A weaker form of rights is 'consideration' (*hatır*), as in the expression 'a cup of coffee offered earns forty years' consideration'. The duty incumbent on a person in authority to protect his charges is described by the expression 'to assume mastership' (*sahip çıkmak*). The term 'without a master' (*sahipsiz*) denotes not a person who is free, but someone abandoned to his fate in a friendless world.

As in all traditional societies, social control relies on the concepts of honour (*namus*, *şeref*) and shame (*ayıp*). They overlap with religious values. A Turk need not be religious to exclaim as he narrowly escapes a mishap, 'I must have given alms to someone' (and thus earned a reprieve). The idea of reciprocity, of the wages of good deeds as well as of sins, of a proper balance between personal rights and obligations, underlies traditional morality, which continues to sustain Turkish society even though it is in retreat before the forces of the modern world. The apocryphal story which evokes the full horror of the loss of civility has for its villain a young man who calls his father 'dodderer' (*moruk*). This extremely unlikely scene symbolizes the final death of respect in society.

In spite of shortcomings in the administration of justice, Turkey is a relatively safe country. According to police statistics, the incidence of murder is 3.5 per hundred thousand inhabitants, of sexual offences 24.8, of theft 253.4 and of fraud 9.4 per hundred thousand. Turkish police believe that these figures show their country to be safer than Germany and Russia. But there are danger signs. Mugging, at one time almost unknown, is becoming a major preoccupation in Istanbul, to judge by press reports. Poverty alone does not explain the growth in inhalant abuse by children, which did not occur when the country was much poorer. Children sniffing solvents (paint thinner, *tiner* in Turkish, hence the name *tinerci* given to addicts) are a pointer to the erosion of family discipline. These are modern afflictions which Turkey is unlikely to escape, just as Spain did not escape them when a conservative dictatorship gave way to a modern democracy. In the meantime, foreign visitors to Turkey find that people are usually sociable, kind and helpful.

The religious functionaries of the state stress the value of religion as a system of social control in times of rapid change. 'You can't ensure good behaviour by detailing a policeman to follow every single citizen,' said Mehmet Nuri Yılmaz, the former head of the department of religious affairs. A parliamentary committee dominated by members of the Justice and Development Party included in its report on corruption the unverifiable claim that 'secular ethics' were a factor in its prevalence. In fact, the defence of religion on the grounds of its social utility is a sign of its secularization in line with the organic secularization of society. Officially inspired sermons in mosques preach social solidarity and self-control. Islam, which developed in tightly packed medieval towns, has always made a virtue of getting on with one's neighbours. Charity is a religious duty: a good Muslim does not go to sleep having eaten his fill, while his neighbour is hungry. Texts and traditions are pressed into service to address modern concerns. Believers are reminded that 'there is no compulsion in Islam', and that people should therefore be allowed to find their own way to the truth.

Controlled by the secular state, and incorporated into its administrative apparatus, official Islam in Turkey is developing a philosophy of religious humanism as an alternative to the secular humanism of the intellectual elite. 'Religion is what makes men human,' said Mehmet Nuri Yılmaz who was an active promoter of inter-faith dialogue during his time in office. Turkish Islam is emerging from decades of intellectual stagnation to meet the modern world on its own terms. But, as in other social institutions, change is gradual. Official control, scarcity of means and, at times, official and unofficial discouragement had made Turkish Islam inward-looking and defensively ritualistic. The official religious establishment had concentrated on fighting banned brotherhoods of dervishes and expressions of folk religion. In recent years, *imams* newly appointed to villages have tended to behave like evangelical clergymen in Victorian England, suppressing dancing, singing and drinking, confining women to their 'proper place' in the home, and threatening deviants with hellfire. Now, with thousands of graduates pouring out of university faculties of theology, where comparative religion and sociology are taught, Turkish Islam is beginning to accommodate to social change. A few Turks still go to study theology at al-Azhar in Cairo, the best-known religious university in the Muslim world. But the revival of religious thought in Turkey gives grounds for hope that the traffic may change direction, and that Muslims from abroad may start going to Turkey to study theology, as they already do for secular arts and sciences. But in the meantime there is a small, but dangerous traffic the other way.

Investigations into the terrorist attacks on synagogues and British targets in Istanbul in November 2003 revealed that some of the bombers were Turkish citizens who had been indoctrinated and trained in terrorist camps run by religious extremists in Afghanistan and Pakistan. On their return to Turkey, they recruited among pious mosque-goers without themselves going to mosques, which they considered too lax. Turkey has a long tradition of fighting Islamic fanatics and revivalists who want to turn the clock back to the Middle Ages. In the nineteenth century, the Ottoman administration made every effort to suppress the puritanical Wahhabi sect which was to seize control of a large part of the Arabian peninsula after the First World War. 'The Wahhabis are evil men,' declared the Ottoman reforming statesman, Midhat Paşa, when he was governor of Baghdad in 1870. The destruction of tombs and shrines by the Wahhabi Saudi government when it established itself in Mecca and Medina in the 1920s shocked Turkish Muslims. Demands for the integral implementation of the Muslim *sharia* (*şeriat*) law were resisted by Ottoman rulers long before the establishment of the Turkish republic. It was easy to fight fanatics when they were poor backwoodsmen. It became more difficult when the vast oil revenues of the Saudi government began to trickle down to them. Turkish authorities at first underestimated the danger. In the 1970s they were eager to attract Arab investment; in the '80s the Turkish military government even allowed Turkish clergy in Europe to be paid out of Saudi funds. It was thought that the Turks were immune to fanatical backward-looking interpretations of Islam. Most of them were, but particularly among the Kurds religious fanaticism provided an outlet for a tradition of violence endemic in Kurdish society.

The President of Religious Affairs, who is responsible to the prime minister through a minister of state, controls a network of nearly 77,000 mosques. As some 6,000 of them are surplus to requirements, the department has asked believers to refrain from adding to their number and to devote their donations to the building of schools.[27] The department has on its payroll a staff of 80,000 *imams* and other mosque staff, most of whom are poorly paid as junior civil servants. In 2003 there were protests in the secularist press at an attempt by the department of religious affairs to add another 15,000 employees to its establishment. The department claimed that these were needed to replace unqualified, unofficial prayer-leaders, some of whom, it implied, might hold subversive views. Official mosque personnel are tightly controlled by regional muftis (*müftü*), who keep an eye on sermons and circulate centrally prepared texts. As their title implies, they – and, of course, the president of religious affairs in the capital – have the right to issue rulings (*fetva*) in response to questions put to them by believers. Usually, these questions have less to do with elevated matters of faith or morals than with details of ritual and practice. 'If one of the canonical prayers is interrupted, should one start from the beginning?' 'Can a woman deputize for a man in the pilgrimage to Mecca' (which every able-bodied Muslim is meant to perform at least once in his lifetime)? 'Would one break the fast of Ramazan if one swallowed inadvertently a piece of bread lodged between one's teeth?' Some of these questions are dealt with in textbooks used in general schools, where 'religious culture' is taught but prayers are not allowed. The emphasis in school as in the mosque is on ethics, social solidarity and national unity.

In addition to supplying staff to mosques throughout Turkey, the department sends prayer-leaders to serve Turkish workers abroad. It has also built mosques in the Turkic republics of the former Soviet Union, and trained religious functionaries there. But it has been less active than a Turkish religious brotherhood, the congregation of Fethullah Gülen. The *Fethullahçıs* (Fethullah-ites) are an offshoot of the *Nurcus* ('Congregation of the Light'), founded by the Kurdish sheikh Said-i Nursi who died in 1960. Considered by some as Islamic modernizers, they have been compared with Protestants and with the Catholic Opus Dei, as members of a congregation which seeks to convert contemporary society by the example of its good works. Supported by generous donations from pious businessmen, the Fethullahçıs run a large network of secondary schools in Turkey and abroad, private universities and a quality newspaper as well as a television channel. The schools are well regarded, particularly in the Balkans and the former Soviet Union, where they are patronized by rising middle-class families. The Fethullahçıs insist that they do not proselytize, but provide a sound modern education in an ethical framework. They have won over some Turkish secularists, but most secularists, particularly in the armed forces, fear them and would like to have them banned. Turkish politicians – Demirel, Özal and others – have visited their schools in the former Soviet republics and praised them as outposts of Turkish culture. Local authorities, particularly in Russia, remain suspicious and have accused Fethullah's schools of spreading an Islam-based Pan-Turkic nationalism.

Whether dissemblers or modernizers, the Fethullahçıs (like the Nurcus) are a product of a Turkish Islam which has learned to live within a secular state in a society where secular values prevail. Other brotherhoods have also achieved an accommodation with a republic which has theoretically banned them all. While Demirel contributed to Nurcu publications, Turgut Özal was close to the more traditional, pietistic Nakşibendi brotherhood, which was involved in the development of all the Islamic political parties, sometimes as a sponsor, at other times as a critic of the performance of Islamist politicians. Another old-established brotherhood, the Mevlevis (or Whirling Dervishes), is tolerated as the guardian of an artistic heritage of music and dance, and also as a tourist attraction.

All these brotherhoods are part of orthodox Sunni Islam, within which they perpetuate the Sufi tradition going back to the early Middle Ages. While their practices vary, they are all based on the authority of individual sheikhs (şeyh) who guide their followers (mürit) to a deeper understanding of the truth. The office of sheikh is often hereditary, but new spiritual leaders arise periodically, giving their name to separate congregations within the same brotherhood. The authority which the sheikhs exercise over their followers is feared and criticized by mainstream Sunni Muslims and, of course, by secularized Turks.

One old-established brotherhood, the Bektashis, has become synonymous with the heterodox Alevi community, which sees the secular regime as its protector from oppression by the majority Sunnis. Sunnis accuse the Bektashis (and the Alevis) of being lax, if not antinomian, in their interpretation of Islam. On the other hand, secular Turks appreciate the Alevis for their non-dogmatic approach to life, while Turkish nationalists like to see in them the heirs to the shamanistic faith of their distant ancestors in central Asia. Alevi folklore is certainly expressed in the simple Turkish spoken in Anatolian rural communities. It is more accurate to speak of an Alevi way of life than of a fixed body of beliefs. They resort to hereditary elders (dede) for the solution of their conflicts; they allow women to take part in their rituals; they do not challenge, but do not observe, the Muslim obligations to fast during Ramazan, pray five times a day, go on pilgrimage to Mecca, and abstain from alcoholic drink. ('To pray five times a day is to bore God stiff,' an Alevi driver once said to me.) Instead of mosques, Alevis have meeting-houses (cemevi), which are now often called 'cultural centres'. Alevi ethics are expressed in the simple precept, 'Be in control of your hand, your tongue and your loins.' The Alevis have survived for centuries in the Anatolian countryside, where they lived usually in their own villages, which were often poorer than those of their Sunni neighbours. These villages are now being emptied by migration to metropolitan centres in Turkey and abroad, where the Alevi community is reinventing itself as the focus of a distinctively Turkish humanist Islam open to modernity. But as poor migrants, they are in danger of becoming an underclass. Some young Alevis are attracted by violent extremist organizations of Marxist inspiration, while others stress their affinity with Iranian Shiites with whom they share a special reverence for Muhammad's son-in-law, Ali.

The annual celebration at the shrine in central Anatolia of Hacı Bektaş Veli, the thirteenth-century founder of the Bektashi brotherhood, is usually attended by leading politicians who wish to endear themselves to Alevi voters, said to represent a fifth of the electorate. In 2004, the department of religious affairs decided to include for the first time information on the Alevis in the textbooks of religious instruction (theoretically 'religious culture') which it prepares for use in schools. The Alevis resent the fact that the state subsidizes Sunnis by paying the salaries of the staff of their mosques, while leaving the Alevis to fend for themselves. On the other hand, they do not want to be subject to the kind of control which the state exercises over its salaried Sunni clergy. Theoretically, a fully secular state should neither subsidize nor control any religious body. But the tradition that the provision of basic (Sunni) religious services is the responsibility of the state, on the one hand, and the fear felt by the state, on the other, that Sunni Islam has to be kept in line with republican modernity, cannot be abandoned easily or quickly. The total separation of religion from the state will take time.

Turkey, Atatürk declared, cannot be a country of sheikhs and their acolytes. It is not such a country today in the sense that sheikhs and their acolytes do not dominate it, but many of them have found a comfortable niche in it. They can influence politicians, but it is the politicians who have the last word. The Islamic extremists who are inspired, aided and often financed by parent organizations in Iran, the Arab world, Pakistan and elsewhere, are seen as alien by the great majority of Turkish Muslims, as agents of foreign fanatics, of 'our uncivilized Muslim brothers', whose retrograde mentality Turkey has long outgrown. The bomb blasts in Istanbul in November 2003 dealt a blow to the complacency into which the authorities seemed to have lapsed after the main terrorist organizations of religious fanatics were dismantled, following the defeat of the secular Kurdish nationalists in 1999. Islam, the minister of justice, Cemil Çiçek, said a few days after the blasts, must condemn terrorism without any 'ifs' or 'buts'.[28]

Religious observance is widespread in Turkey. In the latest survey conducted in 1999,[29] 92 per cent of respondents said that they kept the Ramazan fast, 46 per cent that they performed the five daily canonical prayers, 62 per cent that they attended Friday prayers regularly, and 7 per cent that they had performed the pilgrimage to Mecca, while 71 per cent meant to do so. Of the respondents 68 per cent claimed to have sacrificed a sheep on the Feast of the Sacrifices (which marks the beginning of the pilgrimage to Mecca). Every year, the Turkish media complain that this holiday is marred by 'uncivilized' spectacles as sheep are butchered in full public view. 'Again, a lake of blood in our towns' runs a typical headline. Another recurrent complaint is that the hides of sheep are not donated, as the law requires, to the Turkish Aviation Board, set up by Atatürk to train pilots and popularize flying. Instead, traditionalist Muslims give the hides to religious foundations which, the critics claim, use the proceeds to finance 'reactionary activities'.

As far as folk Islam is concerned, 53 per cent of the sample had visited shrines of holy men, and 12 per cent had acquired amulets.[30] Respondents probably exaggerated their observance of the five daily prayers and possibly of the Ramazan fast. But it is safe to say that the majority of men go to the mosque for prayers on Fridays and religious holidays, and observe the 28-day-long Ramazan fast from dawn to dusk, at least most of the time. However, only 21 per cent of respondents said that they wanted the Turkish state to be founded on the *sharia* and, as the authors of the survey point out, many of them had little idea of what the *sharia* meant, given that only 1 per cent approved of the canonical punishment (stoning) for adultery that the sacred law prescribes.[31] Similarly, 80 per cent of men and 91 per cent of women disapproved of polygamy, and 79 per cent of men and 84 per cent of women disapproved of the *sharia* rule that male heirs should have a larger share of the inheritance than female heirs.[32] The authors of the survey estimate that the proportion of genuine supporters of the *sharia* is around 10 per cent, a conclusion in line with other estimates. Of the sample 77 per cent agreed with the statement that Turkey had moved forward as a result of the reforms introduced under the republic.[33]

The relatively low proportion of Islamic fundamentalists revealed by social surveys has not stilled the fears of defenders of secularism or reduced the vigilance of the armed forces, which see themselves, and are seen by society, as the ultimate guarantors of the modern, secular republic. Nearly a year after the election victory of the Justice and Development Party, the commander of the gendarmerie declared: 'Reactionaries whose aim it is to establish a theocratic state are using all the avenues opened to them by democracy and have not given up their efforts to destroy the existing constitutional order and to replace it by an Islamic state based on the provisions of the *sharia*.'[34] The gendarmerie, he added, had detained 1,000 suspected reactionaries, and investigated nearly 6,000 state officials, some 3,500 of whom were disciplined for reactionary activities.

The armed forces, which include the gendarmerie, take great care to expel from their ranks officers and NCOs who have links with Islamic brotherhoods or political Islam. Liberals and, of course, Islamist politicians claim that the army exaggerates the danger of an ill-defined 'reaction', and make common cause with European critics who demand that the Turkish armed forces should disengage from politics and be subordinated to the country's elected government. Yet this criticism has had little effect on the esteem in which the army is held by a public accustomed to see it as 'the nation in arms' and the only guarantee of its security. 'We have no other army,' said Süleyman Demirel, who has often been at the receiving end of military interventions. Likewise, when a questioner tried to goad him into criticizing the military, Recep Tayyip Erdoğan replied, 'It is *our* army.' A poll published in August 2003 showed that in the eyes of 88 per cent of the sample, the armed forces were the most trustworthy institution in the country. It was the highest rating for any army in countries seeking membership of the European Union.[35] The same month, parliament in Ankara amended the constitution to reduce the role of the National Security Council, which became, in theory, a purely advisory body. 'It will make little difference in practice,' a Turkish senior civil servant said in private. 'Commanders come to the National Security Council with clear briefs and solid files of evidence. Politicians, used to shooting off their mouths, do not measure up to them.'

Certainly, the efficiency of the armed forces has profited from their immunity to the political interference that has damaged the integrity of the civil service. It is true that since the establishment of the republic, the armed forces have not been tested in a full-scale war.

The Turkish brigade performed well in the Korean War, but under overall US command and with US logistical support. The military intervention in Cyprus was a comparatively minor operation in which Turkey had overwhelming strategic superiority. On the other hand, the Kurdish troubles have sharpened the army's skills and gained it considerable experience in counter-insurgency operations. All the while, the Turkish armed forces have kept in touch with the latest military thinking in the United States and other NATO countries. Organization and training are under constant review, as is the role of the military in society.

Officers and NCOs are trained for a long career in the armed forces. Enlisted men are conscripts. In July 2003, the length of compulsory military service was reduced to fifteen months, while graduates entitled to train as reserve officers serve for twelve months. Almost the entire male population has personal experience of military life, and, although some resent the interruption in their careers, this experience does not seem to dent trust in the officer corps. There is some talk of creating a smaller, fully professional army, which would certainly not lack recruits at a time of high civilian unemployment. But the traditional identification of the nation with the army, expressed in the description of the Turks as 'a nation that is an army' (*ordu millet*), provides an argument for retaining conscription.

Most officers in the army and navy begin their education in four-year military boarding schools. There are three such *lycées* for the army and one for the navy. Tuition, which is free, includes English lessons and is in line with the national curriculum. Successful students then go on to the infantry college in Ankara, the naval college in Istanbul or the airforce college also in Istanbul, where they receive a four-year university-level education. Women were first admitted to military colleges in 1992, and there were 150 women students in 2002–3. Women officers are employed in non-combat duties. There are no women in non-commissioned ranks.

Military colleges pride themselves on their technical courses: systems engineering, electronics and computer sciences. Some military students are sent to civilian universities for specialist training. Army doctors are trained at the Gülhane Military Medical Academy in Ankara, which has one of the best hospitals in the country. Students who are commissioned when they graduate from the military colleges can receive postgraduate training in one of four military academies, which train staff officers. The academies often invite university professors to lecture on subjects such as management, international relations and security studies.[36] Turkish military schools and colleges accept foreign students, who come mainly from the Balkans and the former Soviet republics, while many Turkish officers receive training in the United States, Britain and NATO colleges elsewhere.

Set apart by their disciplined schooling from their early teens, Turkish officers aspire to be the best and bravest in society. They live apart in officers' housing estates, have their own clubs (known as *orduevi*, army houses), shops and holiday camps. The army mutual fund (OYAK) is a considerable institutional investor and runs its own bank, but it does not have the dominant position in the economy that some conspiracy theorists claim. Nor are the military a separate caste: the children of officers do not usually follow their fathers into the army, which draws most of its recruits from ambitious lower middle-class families too poor to buy their children a good education. Many a Turkish diplomat, academic or journalist can boast of a father who was an officer, but hardly any will send their children to a military school.

The moment he retires from the army, an officer has to fend for himself in civil society. Generals, known colloquially by the Ottoman title of Pasha, can hope for directorships and other senior management positions in the private or public sectors, but this is by no means guaranteed. There are opportunities for specialist officers in Turkey's growing defence industry. Turkish Airlines relies largely on retired military pilots. A military background is an asset in civilian life, but so too is a degree from a good university.

In the last half-century, the Turkish military have ruled the country only by default. They have intervened in politics only when they felt that this was expected of them by majority educated opinion, which had despaired of elected politicians. Liberals criticize military forays into politics on the grounds that they have delayed the development of democratic institutions. But they or their predecessors had often incited the generals to take over and had applauded them when they called the politicians to order. Nevertheless, there is force in the argument that military involvement in politics has prevented civil society from learning from its mistakes. In 2003, the chief of the general staff, General Hilmi Özkök, wondered aloud whether past military interventions had achieved any lasting results. The evidence suggests that they have at least imposed limits to civil strife and allowed the country to develop in peace. But times are changing and the thinking of the top brass is changing with them. The generals take note of educated opinion which, at the turn of the millennium, is predominantly liberal and pro-European. Some commanders, it is true, are disinclined to give up the influential role in society which they acquired in the 1990s when the country was ruled by weak coalitions. But usually they give vent to their opinions and their frustration only when they retire. As long as they are part of the command structure, their main concern is to safeguard the unity of the armed forces. The chief of the general staff is the voice of a military consensus which tends to be prudent, wary of involvement in the designs of politicians, civilian pressure groups and, above all, foreigners.

The fear that the Turkish military might block liberal reforms has so far proved groundless. But there are at least three areas in which the generals are wary of change. When they defend the secular character of the state, as established by Atatürk, they are being loyal to the constitution which entrenches secularism as a principle that may not be amended. The second main concern of the military is to uphold 'the indivisibility of the country and nation'. This principle has been used to ban any expression of Kurdish culture. However, constitutional amendments in 2002, which allow the Kurds to be taught, to publish and to broadcast in their own language, have not been blocked by the generals, however much they may have disapproved of them. Just as in Spain where it was thought at one time that the army would never tolerate autonomy for the Basques and the Catalans, but where the 'regime of autonomies' was then accepted, so too in Turkey the military tend to fall in line with majority educated opinion. Concern for the integrity of the Turkish nation state is also evident in the attitude of the military to events in Syria, Iraq and Iran, countries with Kurdish minorities which Kurdish nationalists can use as a base. Turkish policy regarding these countries has always been concerted between ruling politicians, the military and senior civil servants.

Personalities often determine which party wields the most influence. Cyprus is the third area where the military do not wish to give away the fruits of their victory. But here again they will not challenge the educated consensus.

As in most Western countries, the Turkish military bring their security concerns to public notice. Having done so, they accommodate themselves to the public mood. They have thus accepted parliamentary control of their finances which in the past were largely shielded from public scrutiny. The knowledge that they are trusted by the public encourages the generals to be flexible in their dealings with elected politicians, for the same public which wants the military to keep out of civil life in quiet times, would expect them to intervene if the civil power proved incapable of maintaining law and order. Throughout modern Turkish history the army has been in the vanguard of modernization. Modernization has led to the establishment and then to the widening of the democratic regime. The armed forces can claim part at least of the credit for this achievement. They see themselves not as the enemy, but as the guardians of democracy, as defined by the constitution which was originally drafted at their behest. They are worried when the text is amended, but provided the principles of the republic's founding father are respected, they accept the change if it brings Turkey nearer to the level of 'contemporary civilization'.

Looking back on modern Turkish history, the names one remembers are those of statesmen and politicians, only two of whom – Atatürk and İnönü – started their careers in the army. After them, it has been civilians – Celal Bayar, Adnan Menderes, Süleyman Demirel, Bülent Ecevit, Turgut Özal and Recep Tayyip Erdoğan – who determined the policies which have transformed the country. Civilians acted, while the generals reacted when change threatened to get out of hand. The biographies of the country's civilian leaders throw light on Turkey's transformation. Those of the generals are dull in comparison: military school, followed by promotion in a peacetime army, with perhaps an indication here and there of restraint or the lack of it in promoting a vision of a disciplined, modern society. The generals have provided the ballast in Turkey's ship of state, whose captains have been civilians, and in so doing they have kept in mind the changing norms of developed countries. They are as aware of the inevitability of change as they are of its dangers. If the leaders of the Justice and Development Party are 'conservative democrats', as they claim to be, then the generals are conservative modernizers. The need to catch up with best practice – specifically in the West – does not have to be explained to the Turkish military. Like the rest of society, they are constantly trying to adapt that best practice to local conditions.

The military institution remains an important pressure group, whose power derives from the support extended to it by society rather than from legal arrangements. The Turkish military serve the state, and their service is appreciated by the public.

6

Economic Surprises

A FEW YEARS AGO, scholars began noticing the changing life of Turkey's prosperous middle class. Writing about newly built executive estates (known in Turkish as *site*, from the French *cité*) on the outskirts of Ankara, the sociologist Sencer Ayata noted:

> The inhabitants of the *site*, among whom cultural cleavages are claimed to be almost negligible, are defined by mutual self-respect and respect for other people's privacy. Although not shared by everyone, the perception of the *site* population as a community of select and civilized people finds wide approval. The community is also defined by what it excludes, city life and its vulgar mix of the lower classes, the new rich and the Islamists . . . Marks of distinction are manifested in the details of dress, cars and house decorations as expressions of familial taste and identity. In this respect, consumption is the major dynamic in suburbia.[1]

Rıfat Bali, a private scholar, described the same phenomenon in Istanbul:

> Another important characteristic stressed in publicity for the modern *site* is that what is bought is not just a residence or a villa but a lifestyle. Residents acquire not just a home but an added value which can be described as an intangible and invisible world of privilege. For businessmen and managers who are short of time, the *site* is a self-sufficient miniature town, a clean and select environment with a fitness centre where every sport can be practised and a social centre which contains a cinema, a restaurant and a night-club where they can enjoy their leisure.[2]

By the time the two books were published, Turkey was hit by a major economic crisis, and the inhabitants of the *site*, whose lives they chronicled, were lucky to have kept their jobs. The choice of a life-style was the least of their concerns. Hastily written additions made it clear that the studies turned out to be an epitaph on transient pros-perity. Economic and social forecasts are tricky everywhere; in Turkey they are doubly so. Over the past half-century, spurts of rapid growth have been repeatedly interrupted by crises. Although signs of troubles to come can usually be discerned, the severity and duration of these crises can seldom be determined beforehand.

What will Turkey be like and how will it compare with the rest of the world in the year 2023 when the republic will celebrate its first centenary? The question was put to an international conference in Istanbul in March 2002. The speaker at the closing dinner was Willy Kiekens, the executive director of the International Monetary Fund. His assessment was sober, not to say sombre. The income per person in Turkey, measured on the basis of the purchasing value of the cur-rency, he said, was a quarter of the European Union average, exclud-ing Greece, Portugal and Spain, and a third of the average of these three countries. Kiekens assumed that the three countries would con-tinue to grow at 3 per cent a year for the next twenty years. Taking into account Turkey's much higher population growth, he calculated that the Turkish economy would have to grow by 9 per cent a year to catch up with them. Just to prevent the gap in income per head from widening, growth in Turkey would have to be 4 per cent a year. Kiekens then looked at Turkey's growth record. In the 1980s, it aver-aged 4.8 per cent a year (2.3 per cent per head), and in the 1990s 3.1 per cent a year (a meagre 1.3 per cent per head). The conclusion was inescapable: by the time the Turkish republic was a hundred years old, Turkey would almost certainly still be way behind southern Europe.

The mathematics of the IMF director were unexceptionable. But soon after he spoke, growth in the European Union dropped below 2 per cent a year. As for Turkey, how accurate are the figures for the growth of the economy? Turkey has a good statistical service, but much economic activity is unrecorded. In August 2003, Sinan Aygün, the chairman of the Ankara chamber of commerce, estimated that this unrecorded economy – also known as the grey or black economy – amounted to as much as two thirds of the total and that, therefore, two thirds of tax revenue were lost. The amount of black money circulating, he claimed, varied between 50 and 100 billion dollars. Forty per cent of buildings were, he said, illegal; 23.5 per cent of electricity was stolen from the grid; one third of investments was spent on bribes; one out of three CDs, four out of ten books and 58 out of 100 computer programmes were pirated. The government itself broke accounting rules by spending large sums outside its budget.[3]

These figures may well be exaggerated. One can only guess at what is not recorded. Nevertheless, they suggest that records describe only a part of the picture. However, some data can be estimated more or less accurately. Sampling techniques produce credible figures for farming output. The capacity of power stations and the amount of energy they generate are known. In foreign trade statistics, some allowance must be made for over-recording of exports to maximize tax rebates, and for smuggling which is, by definition, unrecorded. But changes in recorded totals provide a good indication of the country's performance. The extra revenue earned by the treasury in 2003, when it wrote off penalties on tax arrears, provided the principal was paid, gives some idea of past evasion. But even when one allows for such errors and omissions, the corrected totals almost certainly underestimate the size of the economy. It is generally accepted that the black economy costs the state large amounts in unpaid tax. But it is also a factor in the resilience of the economy as a whole, which has bounced back with remarkable speed after successive crises. Undeclared earnings reduce the impact of official austerity.

These old customs are under attack as the country tries to satisfy the IMF, the World Bank and the European Union. But they are not confined to Turkey. An American anthropologist has argued, for example, that life in Italy is based on the amorality of small family units which make up the backbone of the country's economy.[4] In Turkey the extent and persistence of unorthodox practices make it hard to predict economic development. Forecasts based on large arrays of official figures are habitually falsified by events before their ink is dry. Of course, the black economy is not alone in leading forecasters astray. Politics inside and outside Turkey are unpredictable. So too are changes in the world economy into which Turkey has become progressively integrated since the 1980s. In the 1970s, the two sudden increases in the price of oil were responsible for a large part of Turkey's economic troubles. Later, Turkey was relatively untouched by the crisis which interrupted the growth of the 'Asian tigers', but was hit hard by the Russian default in 1998 which almost wiped out the profitable 'suitcase trade' – the unrecorded sale of Turkish consumer goods to travellers from countries of the former Soviet Union.

Left-wing economists argue that, like other developing countries, Turkey did not have a sufficiently strong economy to withstand the effect of the liberalization of capital markets. It is true that since Turgut Özal allowed capital to move freely in and out of the country in 1989, economic difficulties have been aggravated by sudden large outflows of capital. Much of the hot money which moves in and out of Turkey is in fact owned by so-called 'foreigners with moustaches', in other words by Turks who have legally transferred their money abroad and bring it back periodically to earn the risk premium on government borrowing. Similarly, it is argued that Turkey acted too precipitately in entering a customs union with the European Union in 1996, and that a free trade agreement which would have allowed it to set its own tariffs with third countries would have suited it better. On the other hand, competition for capital worldwide and competition with European industry have sharpened the skills of Turkish business.

The extent of Turkey's integration in the world economy is shown by the fact that in 2002 its foreign trade amounted to roughly half its gross national product. The proportion rose the following year: exports which were below 5 billion dollars in 1981 approached 50 billion dollars in 2003, while imports rose from below 14 billion dollars to nearly 70 billion dollars. Most of the trade is in manufactured goods. Turkey exports consumer goods: textiles, clothing, domestic electrical appliances and ceramics, and imports machinery and equipment, some consumer goods and oil. Recently Turkey has become a net exporter of automotive products, mainly motor vehicle parts, produced by factories set up by foreign companies and their Turkish partners. Such joint ventures are now increasingly common as Turkish industrialists rely on their foreign partners for the technology they use and often for capital to apply it. Foreign firms usually prefer to work with Turkish partners rather than own their own factories in Turkey. This is one reason why direct foreign investment in

Turkey remains low. But the main reason is that Turkey has not banished the fear of political and economic instability.

As in Italy, the Turkish economy is dominated by family firms. Some have grown into large conglomerates engaged in manufacturing, banking, insurance, marketing and a variety of services brought together under umbrella holding companies. They sometimes trade a small part of their equity, but the founding families almost always retain control. Where there are no suitable direct descendants to run the business, in-laws are enlisted, marriages being arranged with an eye to managerial talent. The two largest conglomerates – Koç and Sabancı – are major patrons of cultural activities; they have set up their own universities, they endow schools and think-tanks. Eczacıbaşı Holding, the largest indigenous pharmaceutical company, is the major force behind the Istanbul Cultural Foundation, which organizes music, arts and film festivals. Borusan, which produces industrial pipes, pays for a symphony orchestra and sponsors art books. Banks, some of which are owned by the big conglomerates, run picture galleries and publish prestige books.

Outside the ranks of big business, there are thousands of small family firms all over the country. They dominate the industrial estates which have been built outside most provincial cities. Bursa in the west of the country, a city once known for its towels (and hot springs), has become the centre of the motor car industry. Kayseri in central Anatolia produces beds and other furniture, much of it for export. Textiles and clothing come from factories in the Aegean region, round İzmir, and the Çukurova (Cilician) plain, centred on Adana. The gradual implementation of GAP – the development project for southeastern Anatolia – has accelerated the industrial development of Gaziantep.

Turkish manufacturers have won market share largely on price. The biggest challenge they now face is from producers with lower costs – China, in the first place, but also India. To survive they must move up-market as well as become more efficient. It is not only industry which is threatened by cheaper competition. Exports of Turkish tomato paste, cheaper than its Italian rivals, are now threatened by even cheaper Chinese exports. Cheap imports can threaten Turkey's own home market, to which the European common tariff applies and, with it, such preferential treatment as Europe gives to developing countries.

The state has played a leading part in the development of the Turkish economy. As there was little capital in private hands, the first factories built in the 1930s were owned and operated by the state. So too were mines, utilities and railways. Most banks were also state-owned. Since 1950, almost all Turkish governments have promised to reduce the stake of the state in the economy. Indeed, private initiative was encouraged, but it fed off the state, on which it relied for cheap finance and for a part of its profits, while the state continued to own and operate many factories and to provide a wide range of services. The public sector was overmanned; it was starved of investments; its efficiency was impaired by political interference; its accounting was slack. But it was part and parcel of the country's life, distributing benefits at public expense to the needy and the not so needy according to priorities set by politicians. When the state was short of funds, it ordered the banks it owned to grant credits to farmers, small trades-men, private investors, exporters and others, often without regard to the borrowers' ability or even willingness to repay. The resulting losses, which the treasury could not fund out of the government budget, were known as 'duty losses' – in other words, losses incurred by public institutions in discharging duties imposed on them by the state. In 2001 they were a major factor in the worst financial crisis which the Turkish republic had experienced in its history.

Turkey was saved from default by the IMF, which imposed reforms, such as tighter regulation of the banks, an end to political interference in the management of public assets and operations, and privatization which had been proceeding at snail's pace for half a century. In 2002 the public sector still employed more than 3 million people, account-ing for 15 per cent of total employment in the country. What is more, in spite of efforts to privatize state enterprises, employment in the public sector had increased by more than 5 per cent compared with the previous year.[5] In its effects, however, privatization resembles the dissolution of the monasteries by Henry VIII: it is unpopular because it ends outdoor relief and because robber barons profit from it before the public does. State-owned sugar mills, their managers used to say, do not only produce sugar, which used to be imported, they also bring civilization to the countryside. So do uneconomic railway lines, underused provincial airfields, energy transmission lines, tapped by indigent citizens, and a host of other services. Spreading civilization is unlikely to be a high priority for private owners, even if one makes allowance for the existence of wealthy benefactors. Moreover, state subsidies persist in rich developed countries which ask poorer ones to cut them.

Agriculture is a prime example. Throughout most of its existence, Turkey has enjoyed the advantage of being able to feed itself and have a surplus of farm produce for export. The state pioneered the production of new crops such as sugar beet and tea. It was either the main purchaser or the purchaser of last resort of farm produce at guaranteed intervention prices. The system sometimes produced unfortunate results. Subsidized tobacco, which the market did not want, had to be burned. Political interference forced managers of state-owned tea factories to buy low-quality leaf which then had to be dumped. But overall living standards rose in the countryside, and modern techniques were introduced as farmers bought tractors with state credits and used subsidized fuel and fertilizer. Now, at the insistence of international financial institutions, crop subsidies are being replaced by income subsidies, which officialdom finds it hard to calculate, and total aid is being reduced. Turkish agriculture, the farmers claim, is being starved of funds. The cuts in subsidies have certainly been drastic, having been reduced by four fifths between 1999 and 2002, when total state support for agriculture, including rural development, represented only 1.3 per cent of the state budget.[6]

Throughout history Turkey has been renowned for its cereals, particularly hard wheat, the perfect material for Italian pasta. Both the area sown (approximately 18 million hectares) and the production of cereals (some 14 million tons a year) have remained steady for the last decade. Bread is the staple of the Turkish diet. Traditionally, food was divided into two categories: bread and what is eaten with bread (*katık*, literally 'supplement'). The price and weight of loaves are a matter of prime concern for the mass of the people. Town councils often try to regulate the market by operating or subsidizing 'people's bakeries' or distributing free bread. Nevertheless, complaints are often heard that much of the bread is wasted or that farmers feed subsidized bread to their animals. Some cereals (mainly soft wheat) are now imported, but imports and exports of cereals are roughly equal in value (both amounted to 3.6 billion dollars over the eight years 1994 to 2001). Overall, Turkey has been a net exporter of food: agricultural exports were worth 19 billion dollars and imports 14 billion dollars during the same period. However, in 2003 fears arose that, largely as a result of the cut in farm support, the country was becoming a net importer of food.

Fruit and vegetables account for the bulk of farm exports. Turkey is a major producer of hazelnuts. Much of the crop, which averages half a million tons a year, is exported. The cultivation of hazelnuts is concentrated along the central Black Sea coast and the growers' association (*Fiskobirlik*) is a powerful pressure group courted by politicians. The hazelnut capital is the Black Sea coastal town of Giresun, as placards put up by the local town council proudly proclaim.

Now as trade liberalization forces the state to abandon its long-held policy of self-sufficiency in farm produce, and as subsidies are reduced and remodelled, Turkish agriculture is learning to adapt to the market. It is developing new lines, such as out-of-season fruit and vegetables and flowers for export. Inevitably, it is also shedding labour: in 1993, 8 million out of a total labour force of 19 million were employed in agriculture and fisheries; in the year 2000, the figure had fallen to 7 million out of 21 million.

Contrary to widely held opinion, Turkish farmers are and have always been open to innovation. In previous centuries they were quick to introduce new crops, such as potatoes and tobacco; more recently, they embraced enthusiastically new techniques in irrigation, fertilizers, tractors and improved varieties of seed, while they often lacked the knowledge to apply them to the best advantage. The state has helped with model farms and training in agriculture, but agricultural extension services have been inadequate. These are now being improved, particularly in the showcase South-East Anatolian Development Project (GAP). The main problem today is the high cost of inputs (fertilizer, fuel for tractors, pesticides), the new limits set on farm credits, and, above all, the paucity of alternative employment for surplus labour. In terms of the importance of agriculture in the economy and of surplus labour on the land, Turkey is roughly at the same level as Romania, which the EU hopes to admit as a full member in 2007. In Turkey in the year 2001, agriculture which employed 33 per cent of the total labour force produced 11.5 per cent of gross value added in the economy; in Romania the figures were 38 per cent and 13 per cent respectively.[7] In both cases, the peasants are eager to leave the land, where their labour is often not needed and is almost always poorly rewarded.

There is a long tradition of peasants looking for work outside their villages. These migrant labourers (known as *gurbetçi*, 'workers in foreign parts') met seasonal demand, helping to bring in the harvest in richer areas. In his stirring romantic novel *İnce Mehmet* (translated as *Mehmet My Hawk*), the Turkish novelist Yaşar Kemal describes the hardships of families of seasonal workers from the Anatolian plateau who trek down to the Çukurova plain to pick cotton. Now peasants migrate further afield – to towns in Turkey and abroad. Sometimes villages specialize in a particular trade. Thus the British anthropologist Paul Stirling noted that migrants from the village which he studied on the Anatolian plateau developed a special skill in tiling and other building work, which often took them to Saudi Arabia. Many of the Turkish workers in Germany have come from the great pool of labour in central and eastern Anatolia. Migration has left its mark on many villages, sometimes in the shape of little concrete villas built with the earnings of workers in Germany (known as *Alamancı*). Another British anthropologist, David Shankland, noticed that acquaintance with pews in Christian churches had influenced seating arrangements at ceremonies in the village households of the heterodox Alevi community in inland Anatolia. But, he said, the influence of Istanbul customs was stronger still.

Seasonal work, available originally mainly on farms at harvest time and in the building trade during the construction season, now attracts the rural unemployed to holiday resorts along the Aegean and Mediterranean coasts. Tourism is a labour-intensive industry providing work in hotels, restaurants, cafés and shops. Much of it requires training, and schools for staff serving tourists have been set up in sufficient numbers. But there is work also for willing unskilled hands from the rural hinterland, for women employed as cleaners, for male gardeners and porters. Tourism widens the mental horizon of hosts as well as of guests. It is one of the channels through which the standards of developed countries penetrate rural Turkey.

Turkey was slow to develop its immense tourist potential. Until the 1980s, when Turgut Özal opened up the country to the outside world, it used to be said that there were more tourist beds on the Greek island of Rhodes than in the whole of Turkey. The late start has meant that Turkey's hotel stock is newer than that of its older-established Mediterranean competitors. The number of tourist beds has increased fourfold in the last ten years to over 310,000 in 2003. Current investment will add another 225,000 in the near future.[8] The number of foreign visitors has more than trebled from under 3 million in 1987 to more than 10 million in 2001, while receipts increased from under 3 billion to over 7 billion dollars. Germany tops the list of countries sending holidaymakers to Turkey and accounts for close on a third of tourist arrivals. The countries of the former Soviet Union, above all Russia, are in second place with some one and a half million of their nationals spending their holidays in Turkey. Lands where the lemon tree blooms have long attracted sun-starved northerners. The Russian new rich flock to the south of France; intellectuals long to follow Gogol and Dostoevsky to Italy. Rank-and-file tourists go to Turkey and Cyprus in their hundreds of thousands. Russia, newly liberated from Communism, is followed by the United Kingdom which sends up to one million tourists to Turkey a year. There are clear national preferences in the choice of Turkish resorts: Germans and Russians prefer the Mediterranean coast round Antalya, Britons congregate on the Aegean, in and around Bodrum and Marmaris.

In the 1970s when tourism began to be taken seriously, left-wing economists criticized reliance on it, arguing that it was always at the mercy of political and economic crises in the world. Economic downturns and wars or rumours of war do, of course, affect tourism but, so far at least, they have not stopped the upward trend in Turkey's tourist receipts, which recover quickly after temporary setbacks. In the year 2003, for example, the Iraq war made only a brief impression, and by September tourist revenue was one fifth up on the previous year. The terrorist outrages in Istanbul in November then compromised the prospects of the ensuing season.

As in the export of manufactures, Turkish tourism competes

mainly on price. Many five-star hotels have been built, but mass tourism still dominates the industry, and Turkish hoteliers complain that much of the profit is creamed off by package-tour operators. Although there is enough entertainment for young tourists, Turkey has a good reputation as a destination for family holidays. No Turkish resort has acquired the notoriety of places such as Phaliraki on the island of Rhodes, Aya Napa in Greek Cyprus or Ibiza in Spain. The no-nonsense reputation of the Turkish police and the conservative standards of Turkish society have helped prevent the excesses of lager louts.

Turkey has more than 8,000 kilometres of coast, and marinas have been built in Mediterranean and Aegean resorts which can accommodate more than 12,000 yachts. Sailing holidays, pioneered by Turkish intellectuals under the name of 'blue travel', are increasingly popular. In the 1970s and '80s, the government designated the Aegean and the Mediterranean as priority areas for Turkish tourism. In addition, Cappadocia in central Anatolia, with its spectacular landscape of 'fairy chimneys' – the product of the erosion of volcanic tufa – and its unique heritage of abandoned churches and chapels carved out of tufa above and below ground, is now firmly placed on the tourist map. Adventurous travellers go further afield – to see the mountain-top Hellenistic statues of Nemrut Dağ in south-eastern Turkey, the abandoned Georgian and Armenian churches of the north-east and east, and monuments of Seljuk architecture throughout the Anatolian plateau. Turkish metropolitan cognoscenti, many of whom have holiday homes on the warm Aegean and Mediterranean coasts, take second holidays exploring the wooded mountains which line the Black Sea coast. Tourist agencies offer walking holidays, the exploration of Turkey's rich flora, visits to places of religious interest (among them the presumed last home of the Virgin Mary in Ephesus, or retracing the Anatolian journeys of St Paul), and promote conference tourism which helps fill five-star hotels in the off-season.

Tourism depends on good communications. In 2003, Turkey had thirty-eight airports of which fourteen were open both for domestic and international flights. The all-weather road network developed since the Second World War, though adequate for initial needs, is being improved to meet the demands of an ever-increasing volume of traffic. Dual carriageways are being extended to reduce the death toll exacted by the 'traffic monster' – the creature conjured up by the accident prevention campaign, which seems all too often to relieve drivers of their responsibility for the mayhem on the roads. However, the task of upgrading the physical infrastructure is never-ending, particularly since recurrent economic crises often interrupt investment programmes.

In the 1980s Turgut Özal pioneered the build-operate-transfer (BOT) model, and called on foreign companies to undertake infrastructure projects at their own expense, which they would then operate, recouping their investment and finally moving into profit before handing over the completed projects to the Turkish state. Theoretically, Turkey offered an ideal environment for this initiative, since there was enough purchasing power to finance current consumption, but not enough to accumulate a large stock of domestic investment capital. There were motorists and transport companies in adequate numbers capable of paying tolls on new motorways, bridges and tunnels. The same was true of consumers who could meet their electricity, gas and water bills. So the foreign operator of newly built facilities could expect a steady stream of revenue. But in practice few foreign companies responded to the invitation. BOT is attractive only when long-term stability is assured, as it takes a long time to implement a major project and recover its cost. Foreign investors sought guarantees from the Turkish treasury. But the Turkish government had promoted the scheme precisely in order to avoid new liabilities in its balance sheet. In some cases where guarantees were given, the government came to regret them.

In retrospect, all governments are guilty of incompetence in the management of major projects. Costs are difficult – and take-up impossible – to forecast. In the 1980s and '90s, the Turkish government secured the construction of pipelines to bring natural gas from Russia and Iran by guaranteeing to buy specific quantities at pre-set prices on a take-or-pay basis, in other words promising payment whether it took the gas or not. It also agreed with a German-led consortium to buy electricity at a specified price from a hydroelectric project on the Euphrates, at Birecik, just north of the Syrian border. But by the time the Iranian pipeline was completed across the east

Anatolian plateau, and the Blue Stream pipeline was built by the Italians deep under the Black Sea, Turkey was hit by an economic crisis and demand dropped. Acrimonious negotiations followed to vary the terms. Similarly, when the Birecik dam began generating electricity, the world price for energy was lower than had been forecast, and Turkish ministers and civil servants who had signed the deal were accused of beggaring the country. Criticism failed to take into account the fact that supply and demand cannot be accurately matched years ahead, and that the drop in demand was temporary. In the case of energy, it was caused not only by the decrease of economic activity at a time of financial crisis, but also by the curtailment of investment elsewhere. Thus at a time when Turkish provincial cities were crying out for clean fuel, surplus supplies of natural gas could not be used because shortage of funds had slowed down the construction of distribution networks. At the beginning of the millennium, piped natural gas was available only in Istanbul and Ankara. Residents and industry in central Anatolian towns, subject to cold winters, would gladly use and pay for natural gas if it were available. These towns will probably be piped for gas quite soon, but the exact date is impossible to forecast. The assumption that Turkey offered not just a transit route but, more importantly, a large market for natural gas from Russia, the Caspian basin and the Middle East was correct. But as effective (in other words, cash) demand at home did not match projections, the Turkish government sought to pass on surplus gas by promoting projects to extend the pipelines to Greece, and through Greece to western Europe. Governments are not uniquely guilty of getting their sums wrong. But when private corporations miscalculate – innocently or with fraudulent intent – the government may have to pick up the bill. The Turkish financial services sector offered a striking proof of this in the 1990s.

High inflation with which Turkey had to live for some thirty years from the 1970s onwards, as governments propitiated the electorate with unearned benefits, created a perfect environment for crony capitalism. While state banks incurred huge losses handing out government subsidies, private banks grew rich underwriting the public debt by buying treasury bills and pocketing the risk premium. An attempt by prime minister Tansu Çiller to cut the rate of interest triggered a financial crisis in 1994. In order to prevent the collapse of the banking sector, her government guaranteed all deposits. This gave rise to a textbook example of moral hazard, the term used by economists for immoral behaviour. As depositors were shielded from risk, unscrupulous bankers could attract money by offering unrealistic returns, and use the deposits to finance speculative ventures or simply to fill their pockets. Banking supervision was lax, and banks were allowed to invest money in enterprises they controlled. When the ventures failed and banks were threatened with bankruptcy, the state had no option but to take them over together with their debts and pay back the depositors.

As in 1994, the financial crisis in November 2000 followed a drop in the returns on treasury bills, the main source of profits of private banks. A second and more serious crisis three months later finally forced the government to begin reforming the banking sector in accordance with the recipe of the IMF. But stricter supervision did not prevent the collapse and takeover by the state of a major bank – the İmar (or Reconstruction) Bank, owned by the controversial Uzan family. It too had attracted private money by offering high rates of interest, while failing to deliver to investors government bonds it had allegedly bought on their behalf. The Uzan conglomerate relied also on the revenue of two privatized electricity generating companies, which the government then took back, claiming that they had not paid their dues to the state. The Uzans had sought to forestall danger by launching a demagogic political party, the Young Party, which won 7 per cent of the total vote in the 2002 elections. Had it won 10 per cent and achieved representation in parliament, the Uzans would have been shielded by parliamentary immunity.

The vicissitudes of the Turkish banking sector are typical of a developing economy or, to use a term that appeals to investors, an emergent market. In the opening years of the new millennium, as interest rates fell in mature economies, emergent markets offering high returns attracted fund managers. But high returns had to be balanced against high risks. Considering that developed economies and mature markets are themselves not immune either to government bungling or to business fraud, it would be unrealistic to expect the Turkish economy to progress without mishap at an even rate of development towards a radiant future of civilized prosperity. But lessons are being learned and skills developed. Turkish companies are improving their product design and marketing. Sophisticated techniques of market research are being applied. Business studies attract some of the brightest students, and, as a result, management skills are being raised to international standards. The physical and social infrastructure is improving. The economy is benefiting from better transport facilities, schools, universities and health care, however much critics may decry shortcomings in these areas. True, Turkey is lagging far behind developed countries in the use of information technology. At the beginning of the millennium, when in the European Union there were 215 computers per thousand inhabitants, in Turkey there were only 20.[9] But Turkey is catching up fast. Internet journalism is highly developed in Turkey where most national newspapers and television news services can be accessed free. Statistics and other official data are available on-line on a larger scale than, say, in Greece. The 1980s witnessed a large expansion in fixed telephone lines. This was followed at the beginning of the new millennium by a huge increase in the use of mobile phones. The number of subscriptions to cellular services rose from 23 per thousand inhabitants in 1997 to 284 in 2001.[10] In 2003, the number of mobile phone users was estimated at more than 25 million.

The rank occupied by the Turkish economy in the world table varies from year to year, depending on the rate of exchange and the vicissitudes of growth. In 2001, a bad year for the Turkish economy, the World Bank ranked it twentieth by size. The target of becoming the world's fifteenth largest economy can be achieved if the country perseveres with the reforms in the management of the economy which began to be implemented in 1999. After some thirty years when annual inflation oscillated between 60 and 100 per cent or more, the rise in consumer prices fell below 20 per cent in 2003. The prospect of single-digit inflation has allowed the Turkish government to prepare for the introduction of the new lira, shedding six noughts from the devalued currency which the country has been using. The new lira will be the symbol of a rationally managed expanding economy, capable of adapting to the euro if and when Turkey joins the European Union.

Setbacks have sharpened the Turkish spirit of enterprise. While the record of the state in the management of the economy has been, at best, mixed, successive Turkish governments have avoided the large-scale waste of resources occasioned by war and foreign adventures. As a result, the Turkish economy has exceeded the average rate of growth of the members of the OECD, the club of rich countries which Turkey entered by way of the Marshall Plan after the Second World War. No one can forecast when Turkey will achieve the OECD average level of economic development or the level of the European Union. But on past form, it will be this century. If Turkey is lucky, it may even be in the first half of the century. Given the size of the country and of its population, Turkey would then become an economic giant by European standards. The fact that this prospect can already be discussed seriously shows how far Turkey has travelled in the eighty years of its republican history.

7

Education and Culture

ATATÜRK'S AMBITION WAS to educate Turkey. Education was the means by which the country would catch up with contemporary civilization and then go forward with it. Yet when Atatürk died in 1938, three quarters of a population, which then stood at 17 million, were illiterate. He had emancipated women and encouraged women's education. But nine out of ten women could not read or write when he died.[1] What Atatürk did was to establish a uniform system of education and to define the culture it inculcated.

The state had an almost total monopoly of education. The only exception was a handful of foreign schools and schools for the small surviving communities of local Christians and Jews. But these schools too were controlled by the ministry of education, which appointed some of their staff. Primary education was compulsory for five years between the ages of 7 and 12. Turkish citizens could attend foreign schools only after they had graduated from a state primary school. After the age of 12, children could go on to a three-year middle school, and then to a three-year high school. The high schools, named after the French *lycées*, and modelled on them, were divided into general and vocational. Finally, there was the university in Istanbul, which Atatürk had reorganized, and the new university in Ankara. All education was free. But above the primary level it was available only in the towns, and few villagers could afford the expense of boarding their children away from home, even if they could spare their labour. True, the state did provide scholarships and there was a limited number of free boarders in civilian secondary schools. A few military schools, which provided free board and lodging, as well as tuition, offered the prospect of social advancement to children of parents of modest means. There was no religious education.

Like some other Turkish reformers, Atatürk had been influenced by the theories of the American educational pioneer John Dewey who stressed practical education in skills. In 1936 the first steps were taken to train village boys as rural instructors who were then to disseminate both practical knowledge and general culture in the countryside. In 1940, a reforming minister of education, Hasan-Âli Yücel, implemented the project by founding a network of Village Institutes, which had their own farms and workshops as well as classrooms for formal tuition. Practical education for girls was provided in the main towns by Girls' Institutes.

In spite of all these efforts, only a small minority benefited from secondary education. In 1938 there were only 228 middle schools with 84,000 students in the whole country, 75 general and 81 vocational high schools with a total enrolment of 37,000, and only 10,000 university students. The Turkish educational system was not a pyramid; it looked like a minaret rising above a wide base.

The culture of Kemalist schools was positivist, secularist and nationalist. As in France, the main source of Kemalist inspiration, learning was by rote. All textbooks were published by the state: the teacher read and explained them; the student memorized them for his examinations. The main local ingredient was nationalist history which taught the glorious past of the Turks from their origins in central Asia, the decadence of the Ottomans and the radiant future promised by the republic. But Atatürk's theories about the Turkish origins of all civilization were implicitly contradicted by the Western origin of the rest of the curriculum. This was true not only of the positive sciences – mathematics, physics, chemistry and the rest – but also of philosophy which, again as in France, was a compulsory subject in general *lycées*. Musa Anter, a village boy who was to become a leading Kurdish nationalist, tells in his memoirs how he was influenced by the ideas of the French philosopher Henri Bergson, when he was a free boarder at the Adana *lycée* in the 1930s. A few years later, another village boy, Yaşar Kemal, who was to achieve international fame as a novelist, discovered socialism in the same school. The Village Institutes bred not nationalists, but social radicals. This caused their downfall soon after the end of the Second World War when the conservative opposition was allowed a voice. The transformation of the Village Institutes into routine teacher training schools and then their liquidation in 1954 were the first fruits of democracy.

Democracy brought out into the open the bitter antagonism between self-styled nationalists and progressives in Turkish education. Later, Islamists distinguished themselves from secular nationalists, while progressives split into radicals and liberals. Conservatives were more often than not in power after the first free elections in 1950, and this allowed right-wing ministers to appoint and promote nationalist, and later Islamist, staff in the state educational system. But even before 1950, in a vain attempt to stave off electoral defeat, the government of the secularist Republican People's Party introduced religious education in school curricula. First, lessons on religion were allowed only in primary schools and parents had to opt in. Later, parents had to opt out if they did not want their children to receive religious instruction. Few did so.

At the same time there was a phenomenal growth in Muslim religious schools. In order to preserve the fiction of a uniform state education system, religious schools were disguised as vocational colleges for the training of prayer-leaders and preachers. But the fact that girls who could not perform either function in mosques were allowed to enrol contradicted the fiction. At first, religious schools were allowed only at *lycée* level; then religious middle schools were introduced. Students were taught the Arabic alphabet, elementary Arabic and Muslim religious subjects. Koran courses, in which children memorized the holy book of Islam, sprang up throughout the country. Theoretically, they all had to be licensed, but unlicensed courses abounded. At university level, the first faculty of theology was opened in Ankara before 1950. Other universities followed suit. By 1998, enrolment in religious middle schools approached 320,000; in religious high schools there were 193,000 students, while in universities 66,000 students read 'humanities, religion and theology'.

The military at first favoured at least some religious instruction as an antidote to communism, and after the coup of 12 September 1980, instruction in 'religious culture' – a euphemism for Sunni Islam – was made compulsory in schools. But when the Islamist Welfare Party emerged as the single strongest party in the 1995 elections and its leader Necmettin Erbakan became prime minister, the military were alarmed. After engineering the fall of his government in 1997, they insisted on the closure of religious middle schools. This was done by doing away with middle schools altogether, and extending compulsory primary education to eight years, between the ages of 7 and 15. At the same time, the vocational character of *lycées* for prayer-leaders and preachers was asserted, and enrolment in these schools limited to the staffing needs of mosques. It was made more difficult for children to attend Koran courses and the licensing requirement was strictly enforced.

However, in other ways education became more liberal. The state relinquished its monopoly of publishing textbooks and schools were allowed some freedom of choice. As the state education system found it increasingly difficult to meet demand, fee-paying private schools were set up for middle-class children. At university level, a number of private academies, some of questionable quality, sprang up as commercial ventures. In the 1970s, the government of Bülent Ecevit integrated them into the public university system. One by-product of this decision was the closure of the Greek Orthodox seminary on the island of Heybeli, near Istanbul, which could not be attached to any university.

Through all these changes, there was a steady expansion in the provision of education. By the year 2000, literacy among males above the age of 15 had risen to 93.5 per cent; among females it stood at 76.5 per cent.[2] In 1990, there were 24 million graduates of primary schools, 4 million graduates of middle schools, 4 million graduates of high schools and 1.5 million university graduates in the country.[3] While these figures suggest that the skill base has become much more extensive, the pressure for the allocation of greater resources to education has not abated. Critics point out that the share of education in public expenditure declined from 18 per cent in 1990 to 10 per cent in 2000. According to the UN human development report published in 2002, expenditure on education between 1995 and 1997 averaged 2.2 per cent of gross national product, a lower proportion than in many developing countries. But the demand for more money for education begs a number of questions.

First, are available resources used to best effect? Between 1995 and 1997, 35 per cent of educational budget was spent on higher education, 22 per cent on secondary and 43 per cent on primary education. In the year 2000, some 500,000 young people graduated from general and vocational *lycées* and over 200,000 from universities and colleges of higher education. But in 2002, nearly a third of the country's 2.4 million unemployed (representing some 10 per cent of the labour force) were graduates of *lycées* and universities. At least during the economic downturn at the beginning of the millennium, the output of secondary schools and colleges appeared to be adding to the army of unemployed. No one denies the relationship between educational attainment and economic development, but the relationship is not direct. Development does not depend simply on the number of graduates, but on the quality of the education they have received and the relevance of subjects they have studied.

The seventy or so general *lycées* which were in existence in 1938, some of which could trace their history to the reign of Abdülhamit II (1876–1909), were prestige establishments. University admission departments complained that the 2,600 general *lycées* which functioned in the public sector in 2000 were less successful. They were starved of resources; teachers were often demoralized; there were reports of drugs and alcohol abuse among the pupils.[4] As university admission was centralized and a system of points introduced in the competition for a limited number of places, parents who could afford it enrolled their children in private high schools or had recourse to crammers. By 1999 there were over 400 private high schools teaching nearly 60,000 students. Some schools straddled the public and private sectors. This was the case with the chain of Anatolian *lycées* (*Anadolu liseleri*), where some subjects were taught in English. In any case, fees and parental contributions crept into the state system. Governments had little choice: the resources of the ministry of education could not satisfy demand.

This was particularly true of higher education. In the 1980s and '90s dozens of new universities were founded in the public sector. At the same time, private charitable foundations were allowed to set up fee-paying universities. By 1999 there were over 400 faculties in more than seventy universities (state and private), with another 140 four-year and 360 two-year colleges of higher education. Even so, hundreds of thousands of applicants for university places were disappointed every year. A few unsuccessful applicants with private means went to study in the six universities set up in northern Cyprus where English was used as a medium of instruction. Others went abroad. In the year 2000, the authorities knew of 19,000 Turkish students (14,000 undergraduate and 5,000 postgraduate) in foreign universities (including those in northern Cyprus). According to official statistics, which underestimate true numbers, the United States attracted some 2,000 undergraduate and a similar number of postgraduate Turkish students. The sixty or so Turkish students, which official statistics recorded in 'Africa', were almost certainly at the Islamic university of al-Azhar in Cairo. The Turkish authorities view them with suspicion.

Private universities award a limited number of scholarships to promising students. Otherwise, only the richest families can afford to send their children to them. Fees at the three best-known private universities in Istanbul vary between 7,000 and 12,000 dollars a year. Given that the majority of students have to spend a year learning English before embarking on their four-year degree course, the total cost, including board and lodging and books, can amount to 100,000 dollars. Education in a university in the West is even more expensive. In 2003, the cost to parents was estimated at 35,000 dollars a year. That year, the starting salary for English-speaking new graduates of good universities in Turkey stood at around 1,000 dollars a month.[5] This did not deter rich parents from making a long-term investment in their children's future. But their number was limited. In 1999–2000, out of 1.4 million university students in the country, less than 30,000 were enrolled in private universities.

Two state universities (the Middle East Technical University in Ankara and Boğaziçi/Bosphorus University in Istanbul) use English as a medium of instruction. So do the most prestigious private universities, such as Bilkent in Ankara and Bilgi, Koç and Sabancı in Istanbul. English is popular with both parents and students, who see it as the key to success in the wider world. But teaching in English is controversial, particularly in state schools and universities. Few dispute the fact that knowledge of English is essential in order to keep abreast of technical literature. But it is admittedly unnatural for Turkish teachers, often with an imperfect command of English, to use English to instruct fellow Turks. One solution is to restrict

English to tuition in technical subjects. The large Marmara University, a state establishment in Istanbul, has English-speaking as well as French-speaking faculties, in addition to the Turkish-language mainstream. The French government is subsidizing French-speaking faculties in the new Galatasaray University. This public-sector university extends to higher education the tradition of Galatasaray *lycée*, which taught French to the Ottoman and then the republican elite in Istanbul. Tuition in English does not need subsidies from foreign governments. But English-medium universities have links with universities in the United States and, to a lesser extent, in Britain. Here a key role was played by Turkey's most prominent academic manager and politician, Professor İhsan Doğramacı.

A paediatrician by profession, Professor Doğramacı achieved international recognition by establishing a children's hospital which then grew into Hacettepe hospital and later into Hacettepe University in Ankara. When a military regime came to power in 1980, and decided to cure the radical unrest that had paralysed higher education in the 1970s, it subjected all universities to the control of a Higher Education Council (YÖK). Professor Doğramacı became its first chairman. Undeterred by the criticism which he attracted by being associated with the purge of left-wing academics, Professor Doğramacı secured official backing for his own private university, which he named Bilkent ('Knowledge-town', a term reminiscent of the Soviet *akademgorodok* in Siberia). Judicious investment, purchases of what was to become prime building land outside the capital, and state support gave Bilkent a sound financial base. Investment income and high fees allowed the university to expand its facilities, while deflecting criticism by granting a large number of scholarships. Comparatively high salaries attracted some of the best teaching talent in Turkey as well as good foreign academics. With its auditorium, philharmonic orchestra, sports centre, streets of residences for staff and students, a high-class hotel and restaurant, Bilkent now rivals the older Middle East Technical University (ODTÜ), into which the state has poured large resources and which stands proud in a well-wooded park on what was once a bare hillside outside Ankara.

Some of the new provincial universities also have large attractive campuses. As civic pride demands a local university (and also a local airport) as a symbol of city status, and as politicians lobby vigorously to satisfy their constituents, the state has made large investments, scattering impressive concrete (rather than redbrick) structures for higher education throughout the country. Some campuses now have their own neo-Ottoman mosques, which, university administrators argue, follow English and American precedents of university churches and chapels. But it has been easier to put up buildings than to find adequate teachers. When university expansion started, some provincial universities had to rely on 'flying professors' – academics who flew in from Istanbul and Ankara, gave their lectures and then returned home. Some came from older universities which sponsored the new foundations. Thus Istanbul Technical University helped set up the Black Sea Technical University at Trabzon, and the Middle East Technical University did the same for the university in Gaziantep, in southeastern Turkey. But there is still a large gap in standards between the best universities in Istanbul and Ankara and provincial establishments. However, a common factor is the determination of students to achieve good results.

At the top end of the scale, the medical schools of Istanbul University have had an excellent reputation for over a century. The Istanbul Technical University, which German academics helped to fashion, trains graduates who can then proceed successfully to doctoral work abroad. It counts among its alumni some of Turkey's most prominent politicians – Süleyman Demirel, Turgut Özal and Necmettin Erbakan. They had a common tendency to measure progress by the amount of building that went on in the country – the building of dams and factories, roads and bridges, apartment houses and hotels. The more the better, whatever the cost. Their training had made them highly numerate, but their promises on the election trail and their performance in office rested on the most optimistic, not to say unrealistic, assumptions about the resources available to the state. It took the electorate some time to realize that politics and engineering are subject to different rules.

First degrees in science from the Middle East Technical University and Bilkent in Ankara can stand international comparison. Economics and business studies, popular in a country dreaming of riches, are well taught in prestige universities. The humanities are less suited to the surviving tradition of teaching by rote. Political passions and prejudice also affect teaching.

There are many liberal academics in Turkey, particularly in the new prestige universities. There are also strongholds of nationalist feeling. Istanbul and Ankara universities are jealous guardians of Kemalist orthodoxy. Their secularist and nationalist ethos shades into distrust of the outside world, seen as a source of plots against Turkey. This affects the attitudes of civil servants and judges trained in the Ankara faculty of political science and the Ankara and Istanbul law schools. Although, in theory, academics are supposed to be proficient in at least one foreign language, some lack linguistic skills and, as a result, their thinking has narrow – nativist – horizons.

Since its foundation in the 1980s, the Higher Education Council has been battling against Islamist tendencies, which have come to the fore particularly in some new provincial universities. The authorities have also tried to stop Islamist foundations from setting up private universities. Defenders of academic freedom have been critical of the Higher Education Council and of the power of the president of the republic to make a final choice among candidates chosen by faculties for the post of university rector. The right of the universities to run their own affairs has been increasingly recognized. But while administrative arrangements change, the state retains the duty of maintaining standards and allocating resources. Moreover, as long as academic staff in state universities are treated as civil servants, their salaries are bound to lag behind those of their colleagues in the private sector. Some academics combine their work in state universities with part-time lecturing in private establishments or with consultancy and other forms of private practice. Others move to private universities after retiring from public service. Competition may raise standards all round, but it also makes it more difficult for state universities to retain the best people, particularly in the humanities. In science, the laboratories and other technical facilities of state universities cannot be matched in the private sector. In medicine, university clinics set up by state universities operate like private hospitals and can attract the best available talent.

The Turks have a passion for education, and children are under intense pressure to perform well. Secular education has benefited from the importance given in Islamic culture to the transmission and acquisition of religious knowledge. Education has always been deemed an act of piety; now it is also a patriotic duty. Primary schools have a weekly flag ceremony, at which the children chant in unison:

I am a Turk. I am honest. I work hard. I have a principle – to protect my juniors, to respect my seniors, to love my country and my nation more than myself. I have an ideal – to rise and go forward. Great Atatürk! I swear to march without stopping on the road you have opened to the end you have chosen. May my existence be a gift to the [common] existence of the Turks. Happy is he/she who calls himself/herself a Turk.[6]

To pay for the education of a poor child has always ranked high in the hierarchy of meritorious acts. Wealthy Turks acquire merit in the eyes of their fellow citizens by building schools. The highest state dignitaries, from the president of the republic downwards, attend inaugural ceremonies when these new buildings are taken over by the state educational system. Long before they founded their own universities, the largest Turkish industrial conglomerates donated primary and secondary schools to the state. The private Turkish Education Foundation is financed by donations sent in lieu of flowers at middle-class funerals.

In the teaching profession, high social esteem compensates for low pay. Teachers' Day is celebrated every year, when Atatürk is commemorated as the country's first and quintessential teacher. There is no lack of motivation in Turkish education. But there is not enough dialogue and creativity. Another defect is the tendency of ministers of education to make frequent, and often arbitrary, changes in the curriculum and teaching methods.

Turkey has progressed a long way from the state of ignorance which Atatürk decried. It trains qualified staff – doctors, engineers, architects and other professionals – in sufficient numbers to meet the country's needs. It even exports qualified staff to the West. But the brain drain is not a major problem, as the place of emigrants is quickly filled by new graduates. New ideas still come from the West. Turkey has some way to go before it becomes a centre of original thinking.

By and large, the same is true of high culture. Until after the

Second World War, French influence was dominant in literature and painting, German influence in architecture and serious music. America is now the main source of inspiration in both high and popular culture. Foreign films – Hollywood productions, in the main – are released almost instantaneously. Western – again, mainly American – television shows and local imitations fill the schedules of Turkish channels. Western best-sellers are quickly translated (not always well) and published in Istanbul. Yet a distinctive Turkish style, a Turkish voice can be discerned. The concerns of Turkish creative artists are more social, and therefore political, than is the case generally in the West.

The first generation of Turkish republican writers was preoccupied with cultural change from patriarchal Ottoman life and Islamic culture, however attenuated, to new, as yet undefined, Western ways. Characters in novels tended to be two-dimensional embodiments of simple ideas – corrupt conservatives versus young progressive idealists. Nevertheless, there was a certain sadness in the heroes, as the new life failed to measure up to expectations. The literature of social protest gathered strength in the 1930s and swept all before it as censorship was relaxed after the Second World War. In 1950, the year of the first free elections in the history of the republic, the country was shocked into awareness of village poverty by the publication of *Bizim Köy* (*Our Village*), the fictionalized experiences of Mahmut Makal, a young graduate of the Village Institutes. Five years later, another village boy, Yaşar Kemal, broke all best-seller records with his novel *İnce Mehmet* (*Mehmet My Hawk*), a romantic story of a rebel against the oppression of landlords in southern Turkey. Yaşar Kemal was the first Turkish novelist to achieve international fame, and most of his many novels and short stories have been translated into English, French and other languages. But the hope of his many admirers, not to mention millions of patriotic Turks, that he would be awarded the Nobel Prize has so far been disappointed. Like many other writers and artists, Yaşar Kemal was for a time an active member of the socialist Turkish Workers Party (TİP).

Later, feminism became a prominent theme in literature, as women writers, some from poor backgrounds, made their appearance. All the while, the life and trials of the educated middle class in Istanbul, from which the majority of writers still came, continued to be treated in imaginative literature. As the wave of socialist romanticism subsided, this Istanbul tradition inspired Turkey's latest literary star, the novelist Orhan Pamuk. His novel *Yeni Hayat* (*The New Life*), an allegorical quest for authenticity in Turkish culture, has achieved sales second only to Yaşar Kemal's *Mehmet My Hawk*. The success of the English translations of Orhan Pamuk's novels has, once again, inspired the hope that he would be the first Turkish writer to receive the Nobel Prize for literature. In culture, as in other fields of endeavour, Turkey is forever seeking the seal of international approval as it tries to move to centre stage.

Modern Turkish poetry is dominated by the work of the romantic Communist, Nazım Hikmet (1902–63), who was imprisoned between 1938 and 1950 on a trumped up charge, and became on his release a star turn in the Soviet-backed World Peace Movement. He started as a Turkish Mayakovsky and ended as a Turkish Pablo Neruda, an icon of committed Marxist literature. But he had strong local roots; his concern for social justice was genuine; and his eloquent command of his native tongue has earned him a position analogous to that of Pushkin in Russian literature, as the begetter of modern Turkish poetry. Nazım Hikmet is the only Turkish poet known outside the country. But there are many others, some combining skilfully the advocacy of social causes with the urbane tradition of the Ottoman gentleman. If Nazım Hikmet's thundering declamations are one aspect of Turkish poetry, an equally characteristic voice is that of writers who seek solace where they can, as they survey the scene with a sad, amused eye.

Melancholy and humour are also the prevailing sentiments in Turkish short stories – the first, illustrated by the work of Sait Faik (1906–54), the second by that of Aziz Nesin (1915–95). Sait Faik is the Turkish Chekhov, the compassionate observer of 'little people' in the Istanbul of the 1930s and '40s. Aziz Nesin, a product of an indigenous satirical tradition, is known for his deflation of the bureaucrats of the republic. An outspoken atheist, he was buried secretly in an unmarked grave. Both writers have been translated into English and are appreciated by connoisseurs of Turkish life. They deserve a wider audience.

Turkish commentators tend to complain that their compatriots are not great readers of books. Nevertheless, nearly 10,000 titles were published in 1999. True, the print runs are small. But, as Yaşar Kemal and Orhan Pamuk have proved, works of literary merit can sell in their hundreds of thousands. Books are usually published in paperback. Production standards, which were very low until after the Second World War, have risen gradually, and most books are now handsomely produced.

A common characteristic of Turkish writers today is their awareness of the Western literary canon. They know the world classics better than many Western writers, and they follow new work that attracts attention abroad. The same can be said of music and the visual arts. In music, Turkey has produced good performers and interpreters, but composition tends to be an exercise in foreign fashions – whether atonal serious music or pop for Turkish clubbers. However, in pop the mixture of Turkish folk tunes, Western instrumentation and Arab plaintiveness can produce a specifically Turkish sound, which is immensely popular with the young and which is occasionally noticed abroad.

Rich Turks pay high prices for the work of the best-known local painters, such as the expressionist Fikret Muallâ (1903–67), who spent much of his life in France, Bedri Rahmi Eyüboğlu (1911–75), another French-trained artist who introduced Anatolian motifs into his cubist compositions, and the socialist realist Nuri İyem (1915–), the Turkish Diego Rivera. Abstract painting became popular in the 1960s. Later, the Istanbul Biennale introduced conceptual art.

Italian and French teachers have shaped the tradition of the Academy of Fine Arts, founded in Ottoman times. It is now the nucleus of Mimar Sinan University in Istanbul, and continues to give sound training in the visual arts. In the absence of an indigenous tradition of representational sculpture, which fell under the Islamic ban on figurative art, most of the early monuments of the republic were produced by Italian and German artists. Later, Turkish sculptors took naturally to an abstract style.

In late Ottoman times architecture was the preserve of local Armenians and foreigners (mostly Italians). The first notable Turkish architect under the republic, Kemalettin Bey (1870–1927), was trained in Germany. In Turkey, he developed what was called a national style, producing traditional work, like the elegant small mosque on the waterfront at Bebek in Istanbul (1913), as well as public buildings resembling Orientalist European colonial constructions. The British mandatory administration in Palestine employed him to repair the Dome of the Rock mosque in Jerusalem. A more modern style, incorporating local features, was developed by Sedat Hakkı Eldem (1908–88), who began by working alongside the Italian architect Giulio Mongeri (whose work includes the Catholic neo-Gothic church of St Anthony of Padua, built in Istanbul in 1913). Other practitioners of various modern fashions followed, like Emin Onat and Orhan Arda, who built the Atatürk mausoleum in Ankara in a Germanic monumental style (completed in 1953). There is little local distinctiveness in the many skyscrapers built by Turkish architects in recent years. Elsewhere local features are introduced: eaves, protruding upper storeys, restatements of Ottoman domes or Seljuk conical roofs. Modern mosques, which have arisen in their thousands since the end of the Second World War, are almost invariably undistinguished copies of Ottoman prototypes, built with reinforced concrete and other modern materials. Inevitably, since Turkey has been a comparatively poor country throughout the republican period, shoddy construction predominates in the vast majority of new buildings.

Native public entertainment, like the *Karagöz* shadow plays in which a puppeteer manipulates leather cut-outs, is dying out. Theatrical performances in the Western style were first staged in Istanbul in the nineteenth century. Many of the first impresarios and actors were indigenous Armenians, who played an important part in the transmission of Western culture to Muslim Turks. After the proclamation of the republic, the Istanbul City Theatre, under its German-trained director Muhsin Ertuğrul (1892–1979), became the centre of dramatic art in Turkey. His repertoire included Western classics as well as local work, such as comedies satirizing old Ottoman ways. In 1936 a state conservatoire was established in Ankara under a refugee German director, Karl Ebert (later of Glyndebourne fame). Directors and actors trained by Ebert brought a modern natural style to the network of state theatres established in the 1950s. After working in state theatres, some of Ebert's students became actor-managers of their own private theatres. The best-known and most enduring was the Kenter Theatre run by the talented actress Yıldız Kenter, who brought many modern Western plays to the attention of the Turkish public. Local plays reflected contemporary social concerns, above all the hardships of village life, as the theatre became an important voice of the radicalism which swept the country in the 1970s. The prominence of the theatre in Turkey's intellectual life then gradually decreased with the spread of television. Nevertheless, in 1999, there were one hundred theatres active in Turkey, a third of them in private hands. They staged some 400 original Turkish plays, watched by some two million spectators, and 130 translated works which attracted an audience of some 800,000.

The first modern Turkish opera was composed by Ahmet Adnan Saygun in 1934, at Atatürk's behest, for the entertainment of the visiting Shah of Iran. Then in the 1940s, the State Opera House began staging regular productions. The guiding hand was once again that of Karl Ebert. After the Second World War, Dame Ninette de Valois laid the foundations of the Turkish state ballet. In 1999, there were 24 productions of local and 56 of foreign operas and ballets, staged in six halls and watched by an audience of 250,000 (most of whom chose foreign works). As elsewhere, opera and ballet are a minority taste, and need public support to survive. Standards are quite high, and guest foreign directors and artists are often employed. Public subsidies to the arts are resented by philistines and also by Islamic conservatives. At the turn of the millennium, their archetypal representative was the mayor of Ankara, Melih Gökçek, who declared famously that ballet was 'below-the-waist stuff'.

Turkish film-making survived the advent of television, which provided a new outlet for the low-budget melodramas and slapstick comedies in which the local cinema industry specialized. But there has also been more ambitious work, usually inspired by social realism. Its best-known exponent, and the only Turkish film-maker known outside the country, was Yılmaz Güney (1937–84), a colourful provincial from southern Turkey, who was imprisoned for his political convictions and then again for murdering a public prosecutor in a brawl, and died in exile in France, where he was acclaimed as a Kurdish socialist. As with other arts, the Turkish cinema is strongly influenced by foreign art films, the best of which are shown in the annual Istanbul film festival. In 2000, there were just over 600 cinemas in Turkey. They attracted 14 million spectators for foreign films, and only three million for local productions.

People with a serious interest in the arts – inevitably, largely from the well-to-do middle class, but also the aspiring young – are well served in Istanbul, Ankara and, to a lesser extent, İzmir, with their orchestras, concert halls, cinemas, galleries, bookshops, and literary and arts journals. The foreign visitor moving in these circles has to take care of his cultural credentials. But for the vast majority of Turks – dwellers of low-rent metropolitan estates or provincials, outside university campuses – culture and entertainment are synonymous with television, radio and the daily press. Television, in particular, with its five public-service and twenty or so private national channels listed in 2002, provides the country's common discourse, and football the common passion.

Football began to be played in Turkey at the beginning of the twentieth century, when the first three clubs were founded in Istanbul. These clubs – Galatasaray, Fenerbahçe and Beşiktaş – continue to dominate the game to this day. All three were originally made up of amateurs. Galatasaray (known affectionately – and for no known reason – as *Cim-Bom*; colours: red and yellow) was the sports club of the imperial *lycée* of the same name. It was founded 'to play the ball-game as a team, like the English, and to beat foreigners'. Although it is now fully professional like the other two, it retains an aura of gentility. Its successes in the year 2000, when it won both the UEFA Champions Cup and the Super Cup, raised the nation's morale in the midst of an economic crisis. Fenerbahçe (colours: blue and yellow) was originally the local club of a well-to-do suburb on the Asian shore. Beşiktaş (colours: black and white) started as a gym club in a modest neighbourhood behind Dolmabahçe palace on the Bosphorus, a fact which still attracts well-to-do fans with a social conscience. The three clubs began by playing in the Friday and Sunday leagues in the Ottoman capital, where work stopped both on Muslim and on Christian days of rest. A national federation and a national team were formed in 1923, the year in which the republic was proclaimed. The game spread gradually to Anatolia, starting with İzmir. League football turned professional in 1951. Football grounds were extended and modernized to accommodate a mass following, as money poured in from advertising and television rights. In the provinces, businessmen, sometimes of dubious probity, became patrons of local clubs. In the year 2002, the press published reports that the game had been penetrated by mafiosi, who fixed matches, organized betting in order to launder their illicit gains, and even encouraged gangs of hooligans. Certainly, what was originally a pastime of Istanbul gentlemen now gives rise to popular passions which sometimes erupt in riots. Referees have a hard time, in spite of the fact that many of them are on loan from the army, the most trusted and respected institution in the republic.

Turkish football acquired an unfortunate reputation in the year 2000, when two British fans were stabbed to death in Istanbul on the eve of a match between Galatasaray and Leeds United. But local pride was satisfied when Turkish professional football teams, which have long employed foreign players, began to sell players to prestigious European sides, and particularly when the Turkish national team achieved third place in the World Cup in South Korea in 2002. Devotion to Turkish football is supposed to link Turks, Kurds and citizens of the Turkic republics of the former Soviet Union. The military and civil authorities fighting Kurdish separatism in southeastern Turkey have tried to foster this link by supporting football teams in cities such as Van and Diyarbakır, and encouraging them to do well in the national league. Whether this has furthered national integration or, on the contrary, added to local animosities is hard to determine.

While football has swept all before it, wrestling, once considered the Turkish national sport, has declined steadily since its high point in 1948 when the Turkish team won six gold medals at the London Olympic Games. So-called 'greasy wrestling' – in which the contestants, who wear tight-fitting long leather breeches, are smeared in olive oil – attracts tens of thousands of spectators at the annual championship at Kırkpınar, outside Edirne in Turkish Thrace. As wrestling declined, Turkey won Olympic gold medals for the record-breaking performance of a refugee from Bulgaria, the weightlifter Naim

Süleymanoğlu (originally, Suleymanov), who became a national hero at the height of the Cold War.

The Turks have been celebrated for their horsemanship through-out history. Atatürk sought to preserve the tradition, and had a race-track built outside Ankara, which doubled as a parade ground for national holidays. In recent years horse races have declined in popu-larity, as betting has switched to football pools and lotteries of various kinds. Racing has also been harmed by accusations of fixing and cheating, which led on one occasion to spectators setting fire to the stands of the Istanbul racetrack.

Atatürk's efforts to encourage sport and physical fitness have been taken up by his successors, in spite of opposition by conservative Muslims who object to what they consider as displays of nudity in sporting contests and, particularly, in the parade held annually on 19 May, the anniversary of Atatürk's landing in Anatolia at the start of the War of Independence. However, even the Islamist politician Recep Tayyip Erdoğan was a keen and talented football player in his youth. He was to acknowledge later that he had committed a sin by wearing football shorts in violation of the Islamic taboo on uncovering the male body between the waist and the calves. But the sight of running shorts did not prevent Ali Müfit Gürtuna, Erdoğan's successor as mayor of Istanbul, from giving the starting signal in the annual Istanbul marathon from Europe to Asia across the Bosphorus bridge.

Scouting started in Turkey on the eve of the First World War. The republic sought to shield it from foreign influences, but international contacts have been gradually established in recent years. Sea sports – swimming, sailing, fishing, diving – were late in coming to Turkey. Atatürk was an enthusiastic swimmer and sponsored sailing regattas. In recent years, the growth of a prosperous middle class with holiday homes on the Aegean and Mediterranean coasts has done much to promote the allure and glamour of the sea.

It is no longer tradition or religion, but lack of resources which limits active participation in sports in Turkey. With space at a premium in overcrowded cities, the accent is on games, such as bas-ketball or netball, which can be played in small playgrounds or sports halls. The Turkish sports scene can be expected to become more varied and lively as the country grows richer. There is certainly no lack of interest or of domestic talent. National statistics listed over 5,000 sports clubs and nearly 180,000 'active participants in sports' (presumably members of registered teams) in 1999. Middle-class joggers, sailors and golfers, prominent on the Istanbul social scene, do not figure in this total.

8

Ankara Governs

'ANKARA, ANKARA, BEAUTIFUL Ankara! All victims of misfortune turn to you,' proclaims a patriotic poem which Turkish schoolchildren used to learn by heart. So too do seekers of fortune. As a result, the capital is Turkey's waiting room.

Ankara and government are synonymous. The Turkish republic was organized as a centralized state, and the advent of free elections in 1950 did little to change its character. All important decisions are taken in the capital, which is the seat of parliament and of the government, and the headquarters of the general staff of the armed forces. True, there has been some devolution of power to local government, but Ankara continues to hold the purse strings. Businessmen go to Ankara to deal with the government, sort out difficulties or ask for favours. Petitioners flock there to lobby their members of parliament and seek audiences with politicians and senior civil servants. In 2003 it was estimated that some 10,000 people came to Ankara every day to attend to their business with the government.[1] Foreign embassies form a large diplomatic colony which is at the centre of the capital's social life.

Politics is Ankara's main occupation and preoccupation – the politics of government and the politics of the centralized civil service. The national media which, with the exception of the multi-channel public service broadcasting organization TRT, are centred on Istanbul maintain well-staffed Ankara offices for their political and diplomatic coverage. Business corporations, which again are mainly Istanbul-based, have liaison offices in the capital. But in recent years Ankara has developed a second string, which, however, is also intertwined with the government. The capital has become a major centre of higher education.

In 2000–1, the six universities in Ankara – four public and two private – provided tuition to some 140,000 students (9 per cent of the countrywide total), and employed nearly 16,000 academic staff (23 per cent of the total). The high staff-to-student ratio reflects the higher than average quality of the capital's establishments of higher education, which include some of the best English-medium universities in the country – the Middle East Technical University in the public sector and the private Bilkent University. University hospitals – the hospital which formed the nucleus of Hacettepe University, the Gülhane Military Medical Academy hospital, and the hospital of the new private Başkent University – are among the most advanced and best-equipped in Turkey. Academics, many of whom double as government advisers or move to and fro between universities and government technical services, such as the State Planning Organization and the State Institute of Statistics, have become an important element in the capital's intellectual and social life. Students have introduced youth culture to the neighbourhoods where they congregate – the cafés and bookshops round the Kızılay crossroads in Yenişehir (the New Town, the first modern district to take shape after Atatürk had proclaimed the republic) or the cafés, patisseries and restaurants on the slopes of Kavaklıdere, below the presidential palace of Çankaya.

Atatürk thought of Ankara as the showcase of new Turkey. But when he died in 1938 the showcase was small and largely empty. In 1940, the first census after Atatürk's death, the capital had a population of only 188,000. The German town-planner Hermann Jansen, chosen by Atatürk in 1928 to design the new capital, assumed that its population would reach the level of 300,000 after fifty years. In fact, by 1980 the capital's citizens numbered 2,200,000. By the year 2000, Ankara had become Turkey's second largest city with a population of 3,200,000. But its rate of growth of 2.1 per cent a year between 1990 and 2000 was fairly low by Turkish urban standards. As primarily a provider of central government services, Ankara offers fewer employment opportunities than do economic growth centres like Istanbul, İzmir or Bursa.

Although Jansen's plan was quickly undermined by speculative building at the expense of parks and gardens, Ankara has more green spaces than other Turkish cities. Embassy gardens on the slopes of the hill of Çankaya provide some relief, but, particularly in recent years, the main effort has come from the metropolitan town council which has established parks and gardens round the blocks of flats and high-rise office buildings which dominate the cityscape. The Jansen plan has left its imprint on city development in other ways too. As the plan provided, the long Atatürk boulevard, extending from Ulus square at the foot of the citadel to Çankaya hill in the south, remains the main axis of the city. Jansen's second axis, from east to west, has also guided the city's development, with the western suburbs along the road to Eskişehir attracting new smart middle-class estates. The road to these suburbs is lined with huge new government buildings which complement the complex of ministries (*Bakanlıklar*) placed by Jansen in the New Town at the foot of Çankaya hill. Designed in Atatürk's lifetime by Clemens Holzmeister, the Austrian architect who built the Çankaya presidential palace, but completed under the second president İsmet İnönü, this complex established the heavy interbellic German style of architecture as a feature of the Ankara scene. In the era of the Bauhaus, Germany was at the centre of innovation in architecture and town-planning, and modernity was Atatürk's ideal. The new parliament building near the ministries and the Atatürk mausoleum on a low hill some distance away provide Turkish variants of this German style.

Turkish life and habits have found a home in these Germanic ministry buildings. Their wide corridors are lined with chairs for petitioners. So too are the waiting rooms of the private secretaries of ministers and senior civil servants, all approached through a *chef de cabinet*, who entertains the favoured few and plies them with glasses of tea as they wait to be admitted to the great man's presence. The inner sanctum has armchairs, often in ornate French style, and divans for visitors who are invariably offered more tea as they discuss their business.

Jansen allowed for quiet residential neighbourhoods of villas separated by narrow streets in the vicinity of the capital's administrative centre. As the villas have been replaced by apartment blocks and offices, the narrow streets have become clogged with traffic except where the city fathers have set up pedestrian zones. But the main difficulty faced by traffic is in negotiating the crossings of the main north–south axis of the Atatürk boulevard. Motorcades of official cars with outriders speeding along the boulevard have given it the nick-name of the 'protocol road'. President Ahmet Necdet Sezer, elected in 2000, enhanced his popularity when he dispensed with presidential cortèges and asked his driver to stop at red lights. In recent years underpasses and bridges for pedestrians have eased traffic congestion, without eliminating it.

In the 1990s the city's reliance on road transport was reduced by the construction of a light railway (*Ankaray*) and a metro, which both cross the city from east to west, intersecting at Kızılay square. Thanks to these improvements it is easier to move around Ankara than it is in Istanbul – whether by car or walking on the wide pavements of the boulevard. Ankara, its citizens claim, is quieter and more civilized than its larger rival, Istanbul, the old capital. It is, of course, also less exciting, and at the end of their careers, politicians, civil servants and academics gravitate to Istanbul with all its discomforts. Ankara has one advantage: as a hub of communications and thanks to a new ring road, it offers easy access to the countryside – to skiing slopes in the winter, the forests of Bolu for picnics in the summer, or the coasts of the Aegean and the Mediterranean for longer holidays.

Ankara has moved on from the days of its early development, when the poet Yahya Kemal said, 'The best thing about Ankara is getting out of it.' It was then a one-horse town or, more accurately, a capital with one comfortable hotel (the Ankara Palace, today a government guesthouse), one good restaurant (Karpiç, where Allied and Axis diplomats glared at each other during the Second World War) and one smart night-club (Süreyya's, where visiting foreigners formed romantic attachments). Today its yellow pages bristle with five-star hotels, Turkish and foreign restaurants, and clubs for every age group. Like Madrid, another inland capital, Ankara has the best fish restaurants in the country, supplied from the Black Sea, the Aegean and the Mediterranean. Politicians, academics and media people chew over the problems of the country and exchange political gossip in bars and restaurants which move in and out of fashion periodically. There are health centres for the well-to-do, sports centres for the energetic, ballet schools for middle-class girls. Smartly dressed military cadets walk up and down the boulevard on their days off. But a sadder side of life is evident on working days when long queues of junior civil servants, cleaners and porters wait for a cheap 'people's bus' to take them to and from their jobs.

Built at an altitude of some 3,000 feet on the Anatolian plateau, Ankara has a dry continental climate, which has been somewhat softened by afforestation and the building of dams. Services in the city are comparatively good. The advent of natural gas has dramatically reduced pollution; water and power shortages have been overcome, and the town council keeps the streets reasonably clean.

In 2001, the Ankara metropolitan municipality employed some 18,000 staff, of whom 6,000 were classed as civil servants and the rest as workers. After having been run by the centre-left (or rather establishment) Republican People's Party (CHP) for many years, it passed to the control of the Islamists in 1994. The Islamist mayor, Melih Gökçek, boasted of having invested nearly 720 million dollars in his first seven years in office. Although routinely attacked by secularists, he appears to have served the city well. Parties of various hues control the eight boroughs into which the metropolitan area is divided. Characteristically, Çankaya, the smartest borough, was run at the turn of the millennium by the centre-left CHP.

The presidential palace which used to mark the southern edge of the city has now been left behind by a new wave of development on the crest of the hills which separate the plateau of Ankara from the hollow cradling the small lake of Gölbaşı. Squatters' shacks have been cleared from these southern approaches of the city and have been replaced by estates for civil servants, officers and middle-class private citizens. One development, the garden suburb of Or-an, home for many years of the leading social-democratic statesman Bülent Ecevit, is going the way of similar attempts at creating the framework of comfortable middle-class life – villas are being replaced by blocks of flats, and the original owners are escaping further afield to new suburban estates. The example was set by Ankara's first garden suburb of Bahçelievler, built in the 1930s and '40s, which has been engulfed in the city and covered with concrete blocks.

Old Ankara round the citadel has become a tourist attraction. In addition to its ancient walls and old mosques, it has the best-arranged museum in the country – the Museum of Anatolian Civilization, housed in an Ottoman religious college (*medrese*). Its magnificent collection of pre-classical art – Hittite, Lydian, Phrygian, Carian – has put Ankara on the tourist map, as an essential stop on the way to Cappadocia and its medieval churches carved out of volcanic rock. The old city has excellent restaurants with views over the new city, and numerous shops selling rugs and tourist goods.

The symbol of the new city is by now not Çankaya palace, but the Tower (*Ankara Kulesi*) with its restaurant on a revolving platform, on a ridge not far from the presidential palace. But for the conservative-minded the most significant building is the great Kocatepe mosque, completed in 1987. It is at the heart of a complex which houses the Presidency of Religious Affairs, the department of state which employs and controls all mosque personnel throughout Turkey. A supermarket below the mosque helps finance the religious trust con-trolled by the Presidency. Under Atatürk and İnönü, the mosques of the old city, the most famous being the sanctuary of Hacı Bayram Veli, near the ruins of the temple of Augustus, were adequate for modern-izers, who required the services of religion for funerals and little else. There were no mosques in the new city until 1959 when one was built in the inner suburb of Maltepe. Maltepe mosque has two minarets; Kocatepe four, as befits its central role in the official religious estab-lishment.

A mosque with two minarets and four stars figures on the contested logo adopted by the Islamist mayor of Ankara. Secularists insist on the old logo, the Hittite stag holding the sun-disc between its antlers. The battle of the logo illustrates the conflict between two cultures, which are gradually learning to tolerate each other in Turkish society. After many an inconclusive court battle, secularists and Islamists have been left with their own symbols, free to pursue their different ways of life, often in separate neighbourhoods – the secularists in their smart flats in Çankaya, and tradition-bound rural migrants in modest suburbs on the way to the airport, where right-wing borough councils provide housing, jobs and mosques for their clients.

It is in one of these boroughs, the lower middle-class suburb of Keçiören, that Recep Tayyip Erdoğan, leader of the Justice and Development Party (AKP), decided to have his home when he became prime minister in 2003. Atatürk had stayed briefly in the building of the old Ottoman farm school (now the faculty of agriculture of Ankara University) in Keçiören before moving to Çankaya, which was then in the open country. Erdoğan has moved in the opposite direction from the prime minister's residence in Çankaya, which has become a smart inner-city neighbourhood, in order to demonstrate his determination to stay close to the people from whom he springs. Atatürk had to rely on Ottoman gentlemen from Istanbul and the Balkans when he set up the republican administration in Ankara. Now most of the people who govern Turkey from Ankara come from Anatolia. But while the composition of the political ruling class has changed, the tradition of government harks back to the Ottoman reformers of the nineteenth century who introduced French administrative practices to Turkey. France modernized its administration after the Second World War when it moved towards decentralization, regional government and, slowly and cautiously, to multiculturalism. In Turkey this process has just begun.

Parliament in Ankara still reflects its Jacobin origins. It is a unicameral national assembly – the Turkish Grand National Assembly – meeting as ever under the motto 'Sovereignty belongs unconditionally to the nation'. But the nation's 550 elected representatives enjoy less trust than does the army. Their sovereign authority has been curbed by institutions inspired by American practice – a constitutional court in the tradition of the United States Supreme Court, and the National Security Council which channels military advice to the civil government, advice which weak governments have at times treated as orders. This has led Turkish liberals to complain of the existence of a 'deep state' (a translation of the French concept of *l'état profond*), a presumed occult alliance of generals, senior civil servants, compliant politicians and businessmen using unorthodox methods to keep the country under control. To make the people genuinely, and not just theoretically, sovereign, liberals want Turkey to become a member of the European Union, which they see optimistically as the guardian of democratic values and human rights. As the liberal groundswell swept the country in the opening years of the twenty-first century, political and administrative reforms were introduced with unaccustomed speed. It is too early to judge their effect.

Ever since the days of the reforming sultans in the nineteenth century, Turkish reformers have sought to curb arbitrary government by means of elaborate legislation. But to this day the personal intervention of ministers and their senior officials is needed to secure effective action from a French-style bureaucracy bound by rules and regulations wide open to interpretation. Civil servants enjoy considerable legal protection. If dismissed or denied promotion, they can apply for redress to the council of state, the highest administrative tribunal. They can be tried only under special statute. Nevertheless, many are afraid of taking responsibility. Their tendency to delay action is caricatured by the expression 'Not today. Come back tomorrow!' with which, it is said, they often answer requests from the public. Where Indians rely on the chit to find their way through the bureaucratic maze, Turks have until recently needed a *pusula*, a word derived from the French *boussole*, or compass, by which to steer through the official paperwork. Most documents have to be countersigned, and government offices are full of people in search of the second or third signature needed to give effect to an official document. Countersigning extends to the highest level. Government decrees and bills have to be signed by several ministers, often by all the members of the cabinet. The absence of a single minister, who may not be directly concerned with the matter in hand, can delay action. After collecting all the necessary signatures, decrees and many senior appointments have to be countersigned by the president of the republic. In his last term of office, the social-democratic leader Bülent Ecevit complained that most of his time was taken up signing the promotion papers of junior civil servants.

Although Atatürk held the reins of power in his own hands when he was the first president of the republic, the constitution which he devised vested executive authority in the prime minister and his cabinet who were responsible to parliament. As the titular head of the executive, elected by parliament, the president could, if he wished, take the chair at cabinet meetings, but he was otherwise a figurehead, at least in theory. The powers of the president were extended in the third constitution, devised by the military in 1982, which allowed him to make a number of senior appointments, to refer legislation to the constitutional court or ask parliament to reconsider it; but the form of government in Turkey remains parliamentary rather than presidential. Decisions are taken by parliament, carried out by the cabinet and ratified and promulgated by the president. The system works when the government has a solid majority in parliament, and the president and prime minister are on good terms. But the president's power to delay action can embarrass the government. When, as is often the case, the president and the prime minister come from different backgrounds, they can come to represent different social forces and pressure groups – the military, the bureaucracy, the business community or the wider electorate. At the beginning of the millennium, the president, who was a retired senior judge, often clashed with prime ministers driven by political necessity. In the end, the will of parliament, represented by the government, prevails, but a clash at the highest level of the administration can unsettle the country.

Checks and balances abound. The constitutional court can invalidate laws and regulations. The council of state can invalidate contracts awarded by the government and other administrative decisions. There is a state supervisory council which reports to the president of the republic, and an audit court which checks all government revenues and expenditure. The court of appeal is divided into divisions, and the decision taken in any particular division is itself subject to appeal to the plenum of the court, which after issuing its verdict may allow a final judicial review. Many constitutional provisions have effect only if laws are passed to implement them, and many laws can be enforced only if and when regulations are issued spelling out enforcement procedures. Legal texts can be impenetrable, as Ottoman administrative jargon intermingles with newly minted Turkish terms. Conflict of law occurs as parliament amends specific laws, then amends the amendments, often without considering the effect on other laws which remain unamended. When the higher bureaucracy is not in sympathy with the government, as has often been the case since the first free elections in 1950, it can obstruct it at every turn.

However, the business of government must proceed, and the public expects quick – and favourable – decisions from its elected rulers and their officials. Governments have to respond to this pressure. To do so they often have to cut corners. Every minister who comes to power in Ankara and every senior official he appoints wants to leave his mark. When he became prime minister in the 1980s, Turgut Özal went outside the civil service and recruited high-flyers from the private sector. These 'princes', as they were known, left a mixed legacy. The fact is that the legal framework which he inherited inhibited action, and reforming it was a long and arduous process. That process is now under way. In the meantime, while Turkish liberals point to a lack of democratic accountability, the country suffers from an unpredictable exercise of power by ministers, legislators, administrators and judges, as laws and regulations change and political initiatives follow each other in quick succession.

As in the West, the current fashion in Turkey is to introduce into the administration managers and managerial practices from the private sector. Human resources are to be 'optimized' by retraining in skills. Flexible pay scales, reflecting qualifications and merit, are to replace the *barème*, which Turkey had imported from France, with its rigid classification of functionaries in divisions and subdivisions. In any case, the *barème* has been breached by the employment of contract staff and an arbitrary division between 'functionaries' and 'workers', the latter often better paid. The story of an under-secretary of state who was naturally classed as a 'functionary' and was consequently paid less than his official driver, classed as a worker, is a staple of the debate about the anomalies of the pay structure in the civil service. To complicate matters, functionaries and workers have long had access to different pension and welfare schemes. The management of the civil service certainly cries out for a more rational approach. The problem is not new. When Refik Saydam, who had been a successful minister of health, was appointed prime minister in 1939, he declared famously, 'Everything must be changed from A to Z.' He did not get very far.

While successive governments have proclaimed their intention to 'cut down the state' and streamline the administration, the number of people employed by the central government has continued to grow. In 2003 it was estimated at 2,600,000, of whom 16 per cent were in Ankara. At the beginning of the millennium the central government employed 23,000 inspectors to control the administration and state economic enterprises throughout the country. Corruption resists their efforts. To supplement inadequate salaries and to alleviate hardship in the provinces, the government provided in 2003 official lodgings for nearly a quarter of a million employees, who also had at their disposal some three thousand 'social centres', or clubhouses.[2] That year, the ruling Justice and Development Party promised to reduce the scale of official housing, dispensing for a start with houses for members of parliament. It will not be easy to see the plan through, as the house that goes with the job (known in bureaucratic language as *lojman*, from the French *logement*) has become part of the way of life not only of bureaucrats, but also of academics and other professionals.

Political interference is the bane of the administration. It makes for discontinuity in policies, programmes and personnel, and swells the public sector with the clients of ruling politicians. On taking up office, ministers and senior civil servants often abandon the projects initiated by their predecessors in favour of their own pet schemes. In the year 2001 alone, projects valued at some 4 billion dollars were struck out of the budget.[3] Government projects are implemented in fits and starts as and when budgetary appropriations are available. This results in delays and budgetary over-runs. The malady is not, of course, confined to Turkey. As a rule, the state mirrors society. If Turkey is littered with unfinished official projects, it is also full of unfinished private buildings. Families often move in to the ground floor of a house, from which structural steel and concrete columns stick out awaiting a second and then a third storey that will be built when the owner finds the money to complete the job.

Nevertheless, the administration works in its own way. The state discharges its primary duty of protecting the life and property of its citizens. In the words of Geoffrey Lewis, the doyen of Turkish studies in Britain, Turkey is a country where policemen get paid and, one could add, mail is distributed by postmen. Whatever the deficiencies in legislation and law enforcement, it is, as its constitution proclaims, a state based on law.

At the beginning of the twenty-first century, the republic's fifty-ninth government was steering through its twenty-second parliament amendment after amendment to its fourth constitution. Empowering local government was the fashionable idea. But the quality of local government varied – some councils were efficient and honest, others notoriously corrupt. Clearly, central government had to retain powers of supervision, control and redress. The reforms are proceeding, but Ankara continues to govern.

In the eighty-one provinces (*il*, modelled on the French *départe-ment*) into which the country is divided, the central government is represented by governors (*vali*, similar to the French *préfet*), who oversee the provincial offices of central ministries and also the func-tioning of local government – provincial and town councils. Until recently, the governor was the most important local personage, and his mansion (*vilâyet konağı*, government house) outshone the premises of the local town council. Now, people pay greater heed to the mayor, whose resources exceed those of the governor. Every province is sub-divided into districts (*ilçe*), administered by deputy governors (*kay-makam*), usually young graduates who bring to mind district officers in the British empire. In Turkish literature the *kaymakam* is often por-trayed as a progressive idealist at odds with corrupt local notables who plot his downfall by intriguing with politicians. Social anthropologists Ildikó Bellér-Hann and Chris Hann have seen his role as that of a fixer, whose telephone word is necessary and sufficient to unblock bottlenecks in official as well as private business.

As the elevation of districts to the status of province brings gov-ernment jobs and funds, politicians have curried popular favour by carving out new provinces. This has increased the need for regional coordination. Unfortunately, regional divisions vary from one gov-ernment department to the next. The statistical service, the highways department and the hydraulic service all use different regional bound-aries. So too does local government when unions of municipalities are set up. Turkey has noted the fashion for regions in the European Union, and there has been talk of following the European model of regional self-government. But apart from the fact that European prac-tice often duplicates services and is therefore expensive, the fear of divisive local patriotism inhibits any move which might imperil the unitary structure of the Turkish republic. At the beginning of the mil-lennium, the government of the Justice and Development Party is trying to devolve services to the level of provincial and town coun-cils. But whether as a direct provider or as a regulator, a strong central government will continue to rule Turkey.

9

Istanbul Lives

ISTANBUL ASPIRES TO the title of a world city. It wants to be classed
with New York, London, Paris, Rome. With its 9 million
inhabitants at the beginning of the millennium, it has size on its
side. It also has history and the monuments to prove it. Its Byzantine
walls and churches, Ottoman mosques and palaces, and modern
skyscrapers bear witness to its importance since 330 AD, when
Constantine the Great chose it as the capital of the Roman empire.
Its setting at the junction of Europe and Asia is incomparable. For
Turks, 'the pearl of the Bosphorus' is a symbol of their glorious
imperial past and the embodiment of their present vigour. The past
is in the skyline of the old city, dominated by the minarets of the
mosques which bear the names of Ottoman sultans; the present is
pictured in the two bridges spanning the Bosphorus strait and the
skyscrapers of the new business district. In Turkish speech, Istanbul
stands for what is best in the country. Istanbul manners, Istanbul
ladies and gentlemen, Istanbul accent, Istanbul fashions – used as an
adjective, the name of the city denotes excellence.

'I'm a true lover of Istanbul,' Recep Tayyip Erdoğan declared when
he became the first Islamist mayor of the city in 1994. 'I was born and
grew up here. It is here that I caught sight of the wider horizon . . . It
is an act of worship to serve a city that won the praise of our beloved
Prophet.'[1] Muslim tradition has it that the Prophet Muhammad made
this promise to his followers: 'You shall conquer Constantinople. Peace
be upon the prince and the army to whom this shall be granted.' It was
granted in 1453 to another Muhammad, Mehmet the Conqueror,
whose name is commemorated by the mosque which he commissioned, the district in the old city in which it is situated, and by the
second Bosphorus bridge, called the Bridge of the Conqueror (*Fatih*

Köprüsü). By the time that bridge was built, the republic had rediscovered its Ottoman heritage, and the city which used to celebrate only the departure of the last Allied occupation troops at the end of the Turkish War of Independence in 1922, added to its official calendar the anniversary of the conquest on 29 May. On that day the Janissary band, dressed in ancient Ottoman uniforms, marches out of the military museum, next to the old Ottoman war college, and processes through the city to the sound of drums and pipes. The Janissary style of marching – two steps forward, one step back – reflects the fortunes of the city, which has picked itself up and moved on after every setback in its colourful history. It is today, as its promoters say, throbbing with activity in commerce, the media, culture high and low. It accounts for 13 per cent of the country's total population, 21 per cent of its urban population, 11 per cent of its workers, 30 per cent of its industrial investments, 40 per cent of its trade and 21 per cent of its gross national product.[2]

Istanbul is without doubt a great metropolis. It is also more Turkish and, therefore, more representative of the country as a whole than ever before. True, it is ahead of the country whose best talent it attracts. When the republic was established, earnest reformers decried Istanbul as 'the Byzantine whore', and accused it of sucking the resources of poor but honest Anatolia. Today, the citizens of Istanbul complain that they are being held back by Ankara with its self-serving politicians and bureaucrats. But the distinction is artificial. The citizens of Istanbul are part of Turkish society, and share both its virtues and its vices. Istanbul will join the first league of world cities when Turkey realizes its potential and becomes a rich country.

Istanbul ceased to be the capital of Turkey in 1923. But it had become provincial long before that, depending on the West for money, ideas, fashions. When Atatürk died in November 1938, in the sultans' nineteenth-century rococo palace of Dolmabahçe on the Bosphorus, Istanbul was a modest, quiet, agreeable provincial city. Its population had peaked at some 1,100,000 under Allied occupation in 1922, when it was swollen with Christian refugees from Anatolia and White Russians fleeing from the Bolsheviks. It dropped to little over 690,000 after the departure of the bulk of the refugees and of many indigenous Christians, and then began to climb slowly. In 1935, at the last census before Atatürk's death, it stood at 740,000.[3] Physically, the city had changed little in his lifetime. The list of new buildings was short: Atatürk's summer villa on the beach at Florya (near the modern airport), a few monuments to him and to the republic, and some blocks of flats for the new Turkish middle class.

Otherwise, the city and its infrastructure were as the sultans had left them. But Istanbul was emptier and poorer: there were gaps filled with rubble in the old city, gaps also between the city and suburbs, many of which were self-contained villages, as their names testified: Arnavutköy (the Albanian village), Yeniköy (the new village), Ortaköy (the middle village), Yeşilköy (the green village, formerly Ayastefanos/San Stefano). There were fewer than 5,000 motor cars in the city, which relied for transport on the trams built by foreign concessionaires, on one of the oldest and shortest underground funicular railways in the world, and on Clyde-built ferries purchased by an Ottoman public company.

Today, old-established Istanbul families look back nostalgically to the inter-war years, when there was little money, but ample space for life. Many a Turkish biography opens with memories of childhood behind the high walls of tumbledown Ottoman wooden mansions with their gardens and outbuildings. Ali Neyzi, an Istanbul gentleman (or effendi, in Turkish *Istanbul efendisi*) of good Ottoman stock, writes:

> Two large blocks stand today in the garden of the mansion of Mehmet Ali Aynî Bey, where I spent my childhood. If I am not mistaken, there are twelve flats in each block. This means that the blocks house twenty-four families. Given that there are four people in an average family, nearly a hundred people live in our old garden . . . [What is now a road] was a roughly paved lane when I was a child . . . A large wooden gate bore the number 4. When all four wings were opened, the entrance to the garden was four metres wide. The tiled porch looked like a small house. We had great fun climbing up a chestnut tree and then jumping on to the roof of the porch. Next to the gate, there was a long building, also with a tiled roof, which was used as a stable, with room for a carriage and sleeping quarters for the grooms.[4]

This is the stuff of dreams in today's crowded Istanbul. A secluded garden on the Asian shore of the Bosphorus inspired the poet Can Yücel:

As I walked past the walls of seaside mansions at Kanlıca,
A hole in the wall caught my eye.
I pressed my eye against the hole:
A garden,
Not a garden, but a pool,
Not a pool, but a garden
Dissected by water lilies.
They came with their dark-green leaves,
Their white-yellow flowers.
Who knows how much they fancied their prettiness
For human eyes, perhaps?
But in the garden, there was no one, no master, no landlord.
They enclosed it with walls on all four sides
To stop us entering paradise.[5]

In 1936, two years before Atatürk died, the French architect and town planner Henri Prost was invited to draw up a master plan for Istanbul. He assumed that the population of the city would stabilize at around 800,000. For a few years the plan was respected. This was made easier by the fact that growth was arrested by the Second World War. A few refugees were admitted; many were turned away. The foreign embassies, now officially consulates, filled with intelligence officers. In 1942–3, a wealth tax, directed theoretically at war profiteers, deprived local Christians and Jews of much of their property. Alienated and insecure, many left the country as soon as the war ended. Their places were taken by new arrivals from Anatolia and by Muslim refugees from the Balkans.

The 1950s witnessed the beginning of rapid growth. Poor migrants from the countryside built shacks on the periphery, and sought work in workshops and factories, some in the heart of the city, on the banks of the Golden Horn, which Henri Prost had unwisely designated an industrial area. The shacks were called *gecekondu*, literally 'put up by night', as their owners made sure that their building had a roof of sorts within twenty-four hours. This prevented the authorities from pulling it down without recourse to the courts. Politicians eager for the votes of the migrants then proceeded to issue title deeds to the new settlers and to provide basic amenities, such as water and electricity. Corrupt networks known as 'the building-site mafia' developed, selling to the migrants publicly owned land, which the state was unable to guard, as local politicians looked the other way.

Latife Tekin, a village girl who moved to Istanbul with her family, describes the scene:

> One winter night, on top of a hill where huge metal containers tipped the city's rubbish by day, eight shacks appeared in the light of lanterns, a little distance from the heaps of refuse. These eight shacks made of pitch-covered cardboard obtained on credit, of building timber, of breeze-block brought in horse-carts, were seen first by men who came to sort out the rubbish. They all ran to the shacks without dropping the baskets and the bags they carried on their backs. They began chatting with the builders of the shacks. A harsh strong wind cut through their conversation. The hunters in the rubbish said that the crooked walls and ramshackle roofs would not stand up to the wind. The builders decided to fix ropes to the roofs and to prop up the walls.[6]

The population of the city rose to nearly 1,500,000 in 1960, finally exceeding the 1922 peak figure. As the number of private motor cars multiplied, the prime minister Adnan Menderes launched the first major scheme to improve roads. Two avenues were carved through the old walled city to the south of the Golden Horn, and coastal roads were widened. But congestion was little eased, particularly as tram tracks were torn up and the ferry service in the Bosphorus was scaled down. The motor car came to rule the city and its demands could never be met. Menderes was later accused of violating property rights and allowing the destruction of historic buildings, but without his drive the city would have seized up. New landmark buildings arose on the slope overlooking the Bosphorus above Dolmabahçe palace: the Hilton, the first major hotel built since Ottoman times, and, near it, a broadcasting house (*Radyoevi*), an exhibition centre, a football stadium. Their siting followed the guidelines of the Prost master plan, which was twice amended in the 1950s and finally became a dead letter.

Unplanned growth gathered pace through the politically troubled 1970s, when there was little improvement in infrastructure. One notable exception was the first bridge across the Bosphorus, which was designed by the British architects, Freeman, Fox and Partners, and built by a British-German consortium. It was completed in 1973. Decried at first by left-wing politicians as a waste of public money, it soon became the symbol of Istanbul. More importantly, it led to the rapid development of the suburbs on the Asian shore, which came to house one third of the city's population. On both shores, old picturesque suburbs and villages, where the rich had their summer houses, became incorporated in the city and engulfed in the wave of concrete apartment blocks.

Urban development initiated by Menderes was pushed forward when Turgut Özal became prime minister in 1983. An energetic mayor, Bedrettin Dalan, removed workshops from the banks of the Golden Horn and began the huge task of cleaning up this polluted inlet, improved waste disposal, and widened coastal roads by building new embankments. A second bridge rose to the north of the first Bosphorus bridge, and was linked to a modern motorway which was gradually pushed to Edirne in the west and Ankara in the east. Bedrettin Dalan was accused of favouring political clients, but he left his mark on the city. His successor, the Social Democrat Nurettin Sözen, had an even more troubled time, as his director of waterworks was gaoled for corruption. But he did start work on the metro, the underground railway, the first section of which, from Taksim square (the Piccadilly Circus of Istanbul) to the northern suburb of Levent, was opened in 1999.

By that time the city council had passed to the control of the Islamists. The new mayor, Recep Tayyip Erdoğan, was widely feared by the secularized middle class. However, his party's pet project of building a grand new mosque, which would have dwarfed the monument to the republic and the Atatürk cultural centre on Taksim square, was shelved, and his party's aversion to alcohol made itself felt only in municipal receptions and in cafés operated by the municipality. An attempt to ban drinkers from pavement cafés failed in the colourful flower and fish market at the heart of old Beyoğlu. The market lies outside the gate of the British consulate, originally the British embassy, built in 1845 in the style of an Italian Renaissance palazzo by Sir Charles Barry, the architect of the Houses of Parliament. Badly damaged by fire in the 1990s, it suffered again in November 2003 when a suicide bomber drove up in a car full of explosives and set it off outside the main gate. This attack and a simultaneous explosion outside the London-based HSBC bank in the new business centre of

Levent, in the northern suburbs, together with explosions outside two synagogues a few days earlier, killed sixty people, including the British consul general, Roger Short. It was the worst act of terrorism in the modern history of Istanbul.

Erdoğan's performance as mayor allowed him to launch himself as a national politician after he had been ousted from the town hall and sent to gaol for a few months for offences against secularism. His successor, Ali Müfit Gürtuna, was also credited even by his opponents with being an energetic improver of public amenities.

Turgut Özal's reform of local government in 1984 opened the way to the establishment of the Istanbul Metropolitan City Council to which thirty-two borough (district, *ilçe*) councils are now subordinated. At a lower level, the traditional neighbourhood headman (*muhtar*) still functions, issuing and certifying documents and keeping an eye on the indigent, and his (rarely her) poorly remunerated post is often hotly contested. In the year 2000, the number of people living in the metropolitan area approached 9 million. It had increased by more than 3 per cent a year over the previous ten years, when the net rate of increase for the whole country was 1.8 per cent. Even so, the growth of the Istanbul population had dropped from a peak of over 5 per cent a year in the 1950s and early 1970s. It will probably stabilize at around 10 million, as industry moves away.

The economy of Istanbul now relies largely on services. It hosts the headquarters of banks and of industrial companies. But the factories are elsewhere: along the shores of the gulf of İzmit, to the east, the scene of a devastating earthquake in 1999, in Thrace on the northern shores of the sea of Marmara or inland towards the Bulgarian frontier, or again in distant Anatolia. True, there are still scores of workshops within the municipal area, but the evil-smelling tanneries outside the city walls at Yedi Kule (Seven Towers) have finally been moved to the city's Asian hinterland. Inevitably, the departure of industry has aggravated unemployment in the city's poorer suburbs.

As in other cities throughout the world, the local grocer has given way to supermarkets, some of which are associated with international retailing companies (such as Migros and Carrefour). But it is still often possible to ring up the local shop and ask for groceries to be delivered by a boy. In blocks of flats, where most middle-class families live, this service is sometimes provided by the ubiquitous concierge (*kapıcı*/doorman), usually a migrant from Anatolia, who lives with his family in a small basement flat, and looks after common services, such as central heating. The doorkeeper's wife can add to the family income by working as a maid for the tenants.[7]

The Metropolitan Municipality is in charge of the metro, of buses and so-called rapid sea-buses (but not of the old ferries), of water supply and waste disposal, and of the sale of natural gas. The city was piped in the 1990s for the distribution of natural gas, which came from Russia via the Balkans. Although fuel oil and coal are still used for heating, the arrival of natural gas did much to clean the Istanbul air. The exhausts of the one and a half million motor cars and half a million buses, vans and lorries registered in the city in the year 2000 are now the major source of pollution.[8]

The Metropolitan Municipality had that year a budget of just over 3 billion dollars, of which it earmarked one billion for investment[9] in projects such as the extension of the metro, which is to link up with the new light tram network in the old city. Most of the revenue of the Metropolitan Municipality is derived from central government. But while Istanbul province produced 34 per cent of total government revenue in 1999, it received less than 6 per cent of budget allocations.[10] Even so, amenities are visibly improving. Recreation areas are opening up in the concrete jungle of the suburbs. Water supply became more secure when streams in the mountains in Thrace near the Bulgarian frontier were tapped. The city is cleaner as a result of more efficient rubbish collections and waste disposal. But its physical configuration makes some neighbourhoods liable to flooding after heavy rain.

Istanbul is built on hills – the seven hills of the old walled city, a number chosen to emphasize its claim to be the New Rome, and the hills on either side of the Bosphorus. As the city expanded, buildings filled also the hollows between and behind the hills, while others perched precariously on steep slopes. The rich live in houses with a view – over the sea of Marmara, Istanbul harbour and the Bosphorus. The poor live inland. There are still settlements of shacks. But these re-creations of village cottages with their small plots compare favourably with the dense, charmless estates of ill-built apartment houses where most migrants now live. The well-to-do refer to them as *varoş* (suburbs, a word which has a derogatory connotation similar to that of the old *banlieue* of Paris). The *varoş* has yet to produce its literature.

Migrants from specific areas stick together. Thus the poor district of Gaziosmanpaşa, inland from the Golden Horn, which had some 750,000 inhabitants in 2000, has a concentration of heterodox Alevis from central and eastern Anatolia. On the Asian shore, another poor district, Ümraniye with a population of 620,000, is known for its Sunni fundamentalists, whose spiritual home is, however, in the old walled city in the district of Fatih.

There are areas of acute deprivation in some of the suburbs peopled by rural migrants. Research conducted in 2002 in a densely populated neighbourhood of the suburb of Bağcılar revealed that the chief earner in two thirds of households had only primary education, that in 18 per cent of households children did not attend school, that in a quarter of households at least one child died in infancy, that one fifth of the children suffered from a physical handicap, and that 7 per cent of the 40,000 inhabitants of the neighbourhood did not figure in the population register. Not surprisingly, there was not a single woman university graduate. Nearly half of the people in the neighbourhood had come from the east and south-east of Turkey – the country's poorest and most backward regions – and another third from the Black Sea area.[11]

The existence of backward villages-within-towns is common to many developing countries. In Istanbul, the record suggests that it is a transient phenomenon. In the meantime, poverty is widespread. Research conducted by the Istanbul Municipality in 2002 showed that half of the households in Greater Istanbul had a monthly income of less than 250 dollars.[12] In 1994, when the average national income per person in Istanbul was 3,100 dollars, 60 per cent of the citizens had between them only 20 per cent of the total income of the province of Istanbul.[13]

Poor rural migrants bring to Istanbul the problems of the country-side – the resentment and alienation of minority communities, like the Kurds and Alevis. Terrorists find safe houses in the poor suburbs; criminals and smugglers can hide in them; juvenile delinquents emerge from them to mug pedestrians in the city centre. Nevertheless, the spectacular terrorist outrages of November 2003 do not alter the fact that Istanbul is still a comparatively safe city. At the beginning of the millennium, the police force, which was 10,000 under strength, numbered just over 30,000 officers (or one for 300 inhabitants). Road traffic cries out for better regulation. In 2002, nearly 200 people were killed and 5,000 injured in some 120,000 accidents.[14]

In Turkey, road traffic accounts for 95 per cent of passenger movements. Three quarters of these passengers are carried by some 10,000 intercity coaches. Istanbul is the hub of this traffic. In 2002, the main Istanbul coach station, to the south of the Golden Horn, registered 80,000 passenger movements a day. Coaches link Istanbul not only with all the main cities in the country, but also with the Balkans, Russia and other republics of the former Soviet Union, Europe and the Middle East. Domestic tourism accounts for much of this traffic, with nearly 20 million passengers carried during the summer season of 2002.[15]

Soon after the end of the Second World War, work started on the first new large mosque to be built in Istanbul since the proclamation of the republic. Designed in the classical Ottoman style in what was then the smart northern neighbourhood of Şişli, it was a sign of the greater visibility of Islam in a society given more freedom to determine its way of life. No important central mosques have been built since then, as the old neighbourhoods had been well endowed with places of worship in Ottoman times. But new mosques have proliferated on the periphery in a development reminiscent of the boom in suburban church building in Victorian England. The architectural style of the new mosques is unadventurous. They are usually standard-issue adaptations of Ottoman models, built in concrete, often with unstable minarets liable to come down in gales. By the year 2000, Istanbul province had more than 2,500 mosques, or one for every 4,000 inhabitants. It is not an excessive number. But with the exodus of the Christians, there is an over-supply of churches. As the Greek population decreased from a peak of over 300,000 on the eve of the First World War to a few thousands today, most Greek churches stand empty. In the year 2000, the Armenian community had thirty-five churches, more than one for every thousand members. There are also sixteen synagogues serving a Jewish community estimated at some 25,000 people. The most important, near the Genoese-built tower of

Galata, which overlooks the harbour, has been attacked twice – once by Palestinian terrorists, then in 2003 by Turkish (or rather Kurdish) suicide bombers in the service of the Islamist terror international.

The old centre of Beyoğlu, once the European district, and the harbour district of Galata are being gradually gentrified. However, many well-off families, typically of young executives, have moved much further afield, to new suburban estates on the edges of the Belgrade forest in the west, or in what was once open country behind the hills lining the Asian shore of the Bosphorus, in the east. Good motor roads bring these modern office-workers quickly to the edges of the main built-up area; then they get stuck in slow-moving traffic.

The main business centre has moved from Galata and Beyoğlu to the hill of Maslak overlooking the middle stretches of the Bosphorus. In the 1990s Maslak was crowned with skyscrapers, housing the headquarters of banks and business conglomerates. This is Turkey's Manhattan, and after the economic crisis of 2000–1, it stands as a monument to the inflationary era in which Turkey rushed forward without counting the cost. But, as the Turkish proverb has it, the devil took a hand in hurried work. The skyscrapers float on a sea of debt.

Transport is the main problem, earthquakes the main fear of the citizens of Istanbul. Road congestion has bred solutions such as the *dolmuş*, the shared taxi or now, more frequently, minibus, plying along fixed routes, and the *servis*, private minibuses taking children to school or employees to their offices or factories. The two Bosphorus bridges, their approach roads and the coastal road on the European shore of the Bosphorus are clogged with traffic most of the time. A decision has been taken to build a train tunnel under the harbour. A third bridge may follow. But even these major projects will not provide a solution so long as the city relies almost exclusively on surface motor transport. The best hope lies in the extension of the metro and wider use of sea transport.

The earthquake in August 1999 which caused 17,000 deaths and destroyed a wide swath of new housing and industrial estates on the Asian approaches to Istanbul shook the city's psyche. It is widely believed that Istanbul is hit by a major earthquake once every century. 'August 1999 was not the big one,' people say in ominous tones. The 1999 earthquake caused death and destruction in the outer suburb of

Avcılar, beyond the Atatürk airport, where the Anatolian fault line emerges from under the sea of Marmara, but spared the rest of the city. Local government, which had been notoriously lax, when it was not corrupt, in issuing building licences, appears to have heeded the warning. Building controls are now more effective. But the stock of sub-standard and badly sited buildings is immense, and the fear of a catastrophe will not be easily exorcized.

With all its problems and fears, Istanbul radiates energy. In 1999 it had twenty universities with over 160,000 students (11 per cent of the country's total) and nearly 12,000 teaching staff (almost a fifth of the total for Turkey). Most are in state universities. Istanbul University which, rhetorically, traces its origin to 1453, the year of the Conquest, but was in fact founded in 1863 and reformed in 1933, heads the list with some 3,500 staff and nearly 60,000 students. Next in size is Marmara University, with its main campus on the Asian shore. The state university which provides the most attractive environment is Boğaziçi (the University of the Bosphorus) set in the compound of the old Robert College, established by American missionaries a century and a half ago above the fortress of Rumelihisarı on the Bosphorus.

The numerous private universities founded in recent years are essentially liberal arts colleges. One exception is Yeditepe (Seven Hills) University, founded by former mayor Bedrettin Dalan. Its central campus dominates the Asian suburbs from the hill of Kayışdağ, and boasts a huge glass portal, built in the central Anatolian Seljuk style. A university hospital and a dental hospital, said to be the best in the country, lie some distance away from the central campus. The two family holding companies which control much of the Turkish economy – Koç and Sabancı – have both founded small, well-endowed universities on the outskirts of the city. Koç chose a spectacular site – a wooded hill overlooking the northern entrance to the Bosphorus and the Black Sea. Built in a style inspired by the traditional architecture of old Ankara, where Vehbi Koç, the founder of the dynasty, had his first grocer's shop, its campus is one of the best examples of successful modern development in and around the city. In contrast, the founders of the private Bilgi (Knowledge) University used a converted multi-storey car park in a run-down neighbourhood for their main building. But by attracting some of the country's top academics, they made a success of their project of a non-residential city university.

'Media academics' are a feature of modern Turkish life. They write newspaper columns, appear on TV programmes and in public discussion panels, and write reports which set the agenda of the political debate. Istanbul is the centre of Turkish media – the national press, commercial television and radio, advertising agencies and public relations companies. In recent years many of these enterprises have established links with global concerns. So too has Turkish big business which is centred on Istanbul.

The national press, based on Istanbul, is lively and well produced. It has become a capital-intensive industry, dominated by powerful conglomerates. At the turn of the millennium, by far the largest was the Doğan Media group. Its stable included the country's best-selling newspaper (*Hürriyet*), and a number of other dailies which ranged from popular providers of trivia about domestic and foreign celebrities to serious newspapers, like *Radikal*, the favourite reading matter of young left-wing liberals. The group controlled also two national television channels, published books and magazines, and owned marketing and other commercial companies. Top circulations hovered around the million mark when they were propped up by expensive promotion campaigns. These have now been cut back and circulations have fallen in spite of the decrease in the cover price.

For Doğan Media, newspapers are a commercial enterprise. In other cases, the owners' main purpose is to influence – some would say to blackmail – politicians and other public figures. As a perceptive observer has remarked, newspaper columnists (many of whom double as television pundits) have become the country's new aristocracy.[16] The proliferation of TV channels, most of which appear to be run at a loss, also owes much to the quest for power and influence. Istanbul is the base of three of the country's four all-news television channels, which include the Turkish affiliates of CNN and NBC. Turks, as well, of course, as foreigners, can supplement the offerings of local media by watching foreign television, available on cable in middle-class residential neighbourhoods. In Istanbul and Ankara there is a wider choice of international public-service channels than one can find on cable in London and many other Western cities.

This concentration of the rich, the articulate and the well-travelled makes for a lively social life. The Istanbul cultured class is much more open to foreigners, whether residents or visitors, than is the European bourgeoisie. But hospitality and the resolve to enjoy life spread beyond the confines of rich society. Even in the midst of the economic crisis in 2001, the citizens of Istanbul enjoyed themselves as best they could. While the city's golden youth rush around in sports cars, students of modest means fill the seaside cafés of Ortaköy, at the European foot of the Bosphorus bridge. In and around the taverns (*meyhane*) of Beyoğlu young people will sing and dance – Turkish pop and country dances – spontaneously and unselfconsciously. It is because life for the poor is hard that no occasion for fun is missed. But even the better off and the well-educated do not find it easy to live in the style to which they aspire. The main earner in a middle-class household often has two jobs and a working spouse. Few such families have more than two children. But throughout society, the extended family survives as a support network. One way of overcoming the difficulties of transport is for parents, grown-up children and relatives to occupy separate flats in the same block.

In spite of the dominant work ethic fed by the fear of unemployment, Istanbul, like all large cities, has to cope with the antisocial behaviour of a small minority of young men who rebel against the traditional seriousness of Turkish life. Known as *maganda*, the name given to a repulsive cartoon character, they drew attention to themselves during the boom years of the 1980s and '90s, when the media popularized Western lifestyles.[17] They add to the noise in and around places of entertainment, and the pushing and shoving on busy pavements. Unlike the earlier exemplars of city toughs (known as *külhanbeyi*), the *maganda* lack a code of honour. They are a portent of the drawbacks of cultural transformation through which Istanbul is passing.

In the 1930s when sources of income dried up, Istanbul became noted for its wheeler-dealers, known by the French term *affairiste*. Inflationary development from 1950 onwards bred a more flamboyant type of entrepreneur adept at obtaining credit, often through political connections, and expert in cutting corners. Istanbul attracted also provincial *nouveaux riches* (known in Turkish as *hacı ağa*, the boss who has been on a pilgrimage to Mecca). Old-established Istanbul residents turned up their noses at them. They deplored also the influx of the rural poor. Istanbul, one heard repeatedly, was no longer a city of gentlefolk, but a huge conglomeration of peasants. The complaint was overdone. But, just as in Italy the pizza of the poor Mezzogiorno invaded the prosperous north, so too the smell of provincial kebab houses and of *lâhmacun*, an Anatolian pizza with a filling of mince-meat, assails delicate nostrils in Istanbul. In restaurants and clubs, the Turkish tango and the Viennese waltz have been replaced by raucous *arabesque* pop sung by scantily clothed artificial blondes.

As Anatolia invades formerly smart venues, Turks who share the Western way of life move elsewhere. They too enjoy national culture, but they choose different ingredients. Even at the height of the reforms, the Kemalists' dislike of the Orient did not extend to 'authentic' Turkish folk music or to Ottoman court music. Now the republican elite has rediscovered the splendours (sometimes exaggerated) of Ottoman life in many of its aspects. The old capital is the natural centre of Ottomania. Çırağan, a nineteenth-century Ottoman palace on the Bosphorus, and a converted Ottoman prison in the old city are among the city's smartest hotels. Old Ottoman wooden houses have been rescued and are used as hotels and pensions. Every effort is made to preserve the dwindling number of *yalı*, wooden seaside mansions on the Bosphorus. The gardens and pavilions of Sultan Abdülhamit's Yıldız palace and of the Emirgân forest have been restored and thrown open to the public. The old Ottoman mint and dockyard have been refurbished as venues for meetings and exhibitions. A cultural centre is taking shape among the merchants' villas on the Princes islands, an hour or so away by ferry in the sea of Marmara.

Spearheaded by the Turkish Automobile Touring Club, under its former president Çelik Gülersoy, this work of salvaging the Ottoman heritage relies on the initiative of voluntary organizations, such as the History Foundation (*Tarih Vakfı*). The difficulty of establishing a partnership between the state and private enterprise is illustrated by the slow progress of a cultural centre being built round an imperial hunting lodge in a valley behind Maslak. Sponsored by the private Istanbul Cultural Foundation (*İstanbul Kültür Vakfı*), this complex will include a theatre, a concert hall and exhibition galleries. But the release of state funds needed for the construction has been fitful. Official projects are often less successful than purely private initiatives, as witness the film-set effect of the restoration of parts of the walls of Istanbul. But although mistakes are made, the tide of uglification appears to have been turned, just in time.

A law has been passed to preserve the beauties of the Bosphorus. True, it has been breached in places where new estates rise above the preserved shoreline. Nevertheless, a drive up and down the hills overlooking the strait yields vistas which can stand comparison with views of Rome from the Pincio. The urban panorama in Istanbul is more haphazard, but the Bosphorus is more impressive than the Tiber. As it twists and turns, ships appear and disappear from view; there are still trees in plenty and a few open spaces; the bridges rise delicately high above the strait. The taste of the citizens of Istanbul may be less sure than that of the Romans, but lapses are compensated by the lively charm of seaside markets with their profusion of fishermen's stalls and heaped displays of fruit and vegetables, by the quality and variety of restaurants, and by throngs of passers-by who love their city, warts and all.

The classic Turkish cuisine developed in Istanbul, in and around the Ottoman palace. It was a multi-ethnic achievement as, until recent times, many of the most celebrated cooks and restaurateurs were Greeks who gave of their best when cooking for Turks. The most sought after Turkish cooks came to Istanbul from one particular district – Mengen, in the province of Bolu, between Istanbul and Ankara. The Istanbul cuisine relies heavily on fish, vegetables and olive oil (which became plentiful after the Ottoman conquest of Crete in the seventeenth century). It has little in common with the Turkish kebab houses, which have proliferated in the West.

For the foreign visitor or resident, who turns his eyes away from the suburban estates, which, in any case, he has little need to visit, Istanbul is an enchanted city. The hotel stock is new, and included twenty-two five-star hotels in the year 2000. Outside international hotels, life is cheap for the Westerner, as prices reflect the comparatively low cost of labour. Some 17,000 'yellow' taxis cruise the streets in search of passengers. The drivers are usually helpful and honest, even if their knowledge of the city's geography is sometimes rudimentary, as many of them are new migrants from the provinces. There are international schools and hospitals, good doctors and dentists. The paucity of craftsmen and mechanics, which developed after the departure of most indigenous Christians, has been largely remedied. But, like many businessmen, the *usta* or master craftsman is sometimes better at cutting corners than providing lasting solutions.

Expatriate executives and backpacking young foreigners are welcomed into their Turkish peer groups. For the foreign executive, Istanbul provides a full range of business services: legal advisers, accountants, conference organizers, public relations experts, researchers, secretaries, translators. Knowledge of English is widespread, particularly among educated young people, as many schools and universities use English as a medium of instruction. Cable television carries all the major international and foreign channels. It is easy to travel inside and outside Turkey. The Atatürk airport in Istanbul now has one of the best terminals in Europe, and is easily accessible from the city centre.

Istanbul was until recently a self-contained world. Its rich citizens hardly ever went abroad; they went to Anatolia under compulsion only; their travelling was limited largely to the annual move from the city centre to the summer house on the Bosphorus or the shores of the sea of Marmara. As the waters round Istanbul became polluted, middle-class summer houses have moved away to the coasts of the Aegean and the Mediterranean. Holidays see an exodus to these distant shores. The roads in and out of Istanbul fill up with queues of motor cars. Impatient and inexperienced drivers contribute to the high toll of road accidents. But the itch to travel, to discover the country and the world, to enjoy sea, sun and sand is not easily restrained.

Weather in Istanbul depends on the direction of the wind. When it blows from the north, the climate resembles that of southern Russia. A southerly wind brings the Mediterranean to the city. Known as *lodos*, this wind from the Mediterranean is supposed to have an unsettling effect, rather like that of the *Föhn* in Bavaria, and is blamed for a variety of ailments. In the winter the city can be cold, wet and windy. Sea mist and exhaust fumes can cover it as with a grey blanket. In January the average temperature can be as low as 3°C and rainfall as high as 100 mm. In the holiday months of July and August, the average temperature is in the range of 22° to 25°C, and rainfall varies from less than 1 mm to 80 mm.

Istanbul has its drawbacks. Its infrastructure does not match its size. As in the rest of the country, official bureaucracy can infuriate. The service citizens enjoy too often depends on connections. Networking is the key to social life. Its very vitality makes Istanbul a tiring city. Early European travellers admired its calm. Now lethargy has moved its home from the Orient to the rich countries of the West. It will be a long time before the citizen or resident of Istanbul can share the Frenchman's right to a 35-hour week and five or more weeks of paid holiday a year. It will be a long time too before he enjoys the amenities found in Western capitals.

Istanbul's dream is to be chosen as the site of the Olympic Games. It could happen this century. The immediate aim is to become the centre of a region stretching from the Balkans to central Asia. Already some companies active in the southern republics of the former Soviet Union find in Istanbul a convenient base for their operations. Expatriates working in central Asia, the Caucasus or the Middle East enjoy a break in the city. Although the Istanbul business community is strongly in favour of membership of the European Union, their city can gain a competitive edge from the absence of EU rules and regulations. But services need to be improved and the, admittedly exaggerated, fear of insecurity banished, if it is to develop its potential as the main regional business centre. Istanbul has gathered many laurels, but it cannot rest on them.

IO

Eastern Approaches

ASTERN TURKEY IS beautiful in the spring. As the snows covering the high plateau melt, the meadows and hillsides come alive with wild flowers. Later, tractors start ploughing the land for crops of wheat, barley and sugar beet. The plateau is edged by high mountains. Beyond them, to the east, at the foot of Ağrıdağ (Mount Ararat), lies the Aras valley, warm and wet enough to allow the cultivation of rice. To the south, Lake Van, at the centre of an inland basin, reflects the blue sky. Further south, the piedmont of upper Mesopotamia is cut by the deep valleys of the Euphrates and the Tigris, where swaths of green mark the cotton plantations irrigated by newly built dams. Pistachio and almond trees dot the hillsides.

Towns as old as history have burst out of their medieval confines. The new neighbourhoods are not picturesque, but their wide avenues, apartment houses and four- and even five-star hotels bear witness to recently acquired wealth. Every town of note has a new university set in a large campus of concrete buildings. There are more airports than airlines willing to use them. Communications by road and air are good, condemning to idleness the rail network built in the first years of the republic. Local civil society is vigorous: mayors respond to the demands of their electors; there are well-supported chambers of commerce, often in impressive new premises.

Nevertheless, the Third World has not been banished. It survives in some dilapidated city centres, where girls are kept indoors, while bands of boys find enjoyment in stoning cars. It is to be found in untidy villages of roughly built peasant houses, separated by unpaved tracks. Tens of thousands of rural migrants, many displaced by the insurgency of Kurdish nationalists, are huddled in shacks on city out-skirts. Unemployed youths while away their time in coffee-houses, dreaming of finding a job or actively planning to move westwards, perhaps even to Europe. The casual traveller staying in a modern hotel or looking at well-stocked shops in the new neighbourhoods can easily overlook the poverty which laps round the islands of modest competence. Although there are rich landowners, some owning entire villages, there is little evidence of great wealth, for the rich migrate to the west where they spend the revenue of their eastern estates and enterprises. Some of the money invested by the government similarly trickles out.

Eastern Turkey is changing; it is integrated in the national economy; it is developing. But it has a long way to go before it catches up with the west and its coastlands. Geography and history make for harshness. Conditioned by centuries of border wars and of intertribal fighting, by clashes with the encroaching centralized modern state, by too little employment and too much resentment, the east offers fertile ground for blood feuds, and for religious and political fanaticism. As western Turkey becomes more relaxed, and sometimes indifferent, in its practice of Islam, it is the east which supplies the country with religious leaders, official and unofficial. Roadside service stations, advertising their mosques and prayer halls, can be picked out by their minarets, often painted a hideous green – a sight uncommon in western Turkey.

The provinces grouped in the eastern and south-eastern regions are Turkey's Middle East – the poorer, more backward part of the country. Of the country's population, 12.7 million people, or 19 per cent of the total, lived in the two regions in October 2000. But they accounted for only 8.4 per cent of gross domestic product. When expenditure on household consumption was calculated in 1994, the monthly figure for the Marmara region, which includes Istanbul, amounted to just under 1,200 dollars. In eastern Anatolia it was only 177 dollars, and in the south-east it was as low as 153 dollars. The two regions are home to most Turkish citizens of Kurdish origin. But ethnic origin is not the most important factor in their underdevelopment.

Throughout recorded history the Kurds have lived in the mountains lying between the Anatolian plateau and the Mesopotamian plain in the south, and between Anatolia and the plateau and plains of Iran in the east. Before the fall of the Ottoman empire, the Kurds came under the rule of two sovereigns: the sultan in Istanbul and the shah in Teheran. As Kurdish is an Indo-European language akin to Persian, which many Kurds used as their literary language, the dividing line between Kurds and Persians was blurred in Iran. But there is a religious difference, as most Kurds are Sunni Muslims, while Persians are Shiites. In the Ottoman empire, the split between Sunnis and Alevis (a heterodox Shiite sect) straddled the ethnic divide, which was manifest in language and, to some extent, in customs. After the First World War, three million or more Ottoman Kurds found themselves in Iraq and a few hundred thousand in Syria – two new Arab states which were placed under British and French mandates respectively before gaining their independence. Kurds in the southern Caucasus, who had come under Russian rule in the nineteenth century, became citizens of the independent republics of Azerbaijan and Armenia when the Soviet Union disintegrated. As a result, the Kurdish population is now divided among six countries. But the largest concentration is in Turkey.

Kurdish nationalists believe that their people descend from the ancient Medes, who were related to the Persians. There are at least four Kurdish languages, which Kurdish nationalists prefer to call dialects, although some are mutually incomprehensible. In Turkey most Kurds are born to various dialects of the Kirmanji (Kırmancı) language, while a minority, in the west of the Kurdish-speaking region, speak a language which they call Dımılî and which outsiders call Zaza. Both Kırmancı and Zaza have by now been more or less standardized. In Turkey they are written in the Latin alphabet, using Turkish orthographic conventions with the addition of extra letters (x, w and q). In Iraq, Kurds speak Kirmanji south of the Turkish border, and a language called Surani (or simply Kurdi), further east and south, and use the Arabic alphabet to write them. A meeting of Kurdish intellectuals from several countries held in 2003 in the Turkish city of Diyarbakır issued its statement in three languages: Kirmanji, Zaza and Surani.

The Kurds, who were originally Zoroastrians like the Persians, were converted to Islam gradually after the Arab conquest in the seventh century. In Turkey, Iraq and Syria, there is still a small number of Yezidi Kurds, who now call themselves Zoroastrians, while their detractors describe them as devil-worshippers. Muslim brotherhoods have a firm foothold among Kurds in Turkey, the most prevalent being the strictly orthodox Nakşibendî brotherhood, which originated in central Asia, and its offshoot, known as Kadirî.

Until recent times the Kurds have been a tribal, nomadic people. There were hardly any Kurdish towns. Towns such as Diyarbakır, Mardin and Siirt in south-eastern Turkey had a population of Ottoman officials, Arabic-speaking townspeople, and Turkish-speaking Armenians. Kurdish chieftains had their mansions in these towns, where Kurdish tribesmen went to trade their produce and buy necessities. The settlement of Kurds in Turkish towns is a recent phenomenon, accelerated by the expulsion of the Armenians during and immediately after the First World War. Not only did Kurds occupy abandoned Armenian houses; they also began practising some of the trades which had been an Armenian preserve.

The organization of the Kurds was tribal. Single tribes formed confederations which sustained autonomous principalities. Until the nineteenth century, the Ottomans exercised indirect rule over their Kurdish subjects. But when European-style centralization was imposed, Kurdish principalities were suppressed, and leadership in Kurdish society passed to tribal chieftains and to religious leaders, usually heads of brotherhoods. Often, the religious leader or sheikh (*şeyh*) was also the landlord (*ağa*). At the end of the nineteenth century, Sultan Abdülhamit II formed Kurdish cavalry regiments under the command of their tribal leaders. Called after the sultan's name, and modelled on the Cossacks, the Hamidiye survived under a different name when the Young Turks took over. Their final disbandment under the republic was a factor in Kurdish disaffection. This was fed also by the disestablishment of Islam, which had served as a bond between Ottoman rulers and their Kurdish subjects, and, as ever, by resentment at increasing central control manifesting itself in taxation and conscription. The extortion of protection money and brigandage also dried up as sources of revenue for the Kurds. However, the frontiers drawn at the end of the First World War opened new possibilities for smugglers.

Kurdish society was always violent. Now, even where tribal structures have broken down, feuds rooted in them persist. When nomadic tribes were settled on the land, this was usually registered as the private property of its chieftain who often became an absentee landlord. Along with family feuds, opposition to the landlords and to the central government fed violence, which found justification in religious or secular political ideologies. Kurdish Islam and Kurdish Marxism are distinctly less sophisticated and more bloodthirsty than their Turkish varieties. True, most Turkish citizens of Kurdish origin want nothing better than an opportunity to escape from poverty. Fanatics are always a minority, but there are proportionately more of them in the Kurdish-speaking region than elsewhere. The tradition of violence dies hard, and modern education does not always banish it.

There are, of course, many people of non-Kurdish origin in eastern and south-eastern Turkey. In popular reckoning, the Kurdish area lies east of the Euphrates, and also south of the headwaters of the river. Erzincan and Erzurum in eastern Turkey and Gaziantep in the south-east are predominantly Turkish towns. But, particularly in recent years, millions of Kurds have moved from their villages and hamlets into local towns and beyond. In eastern Turkey, while the rural population decreased by 6 per cent between 1990 and 2000, that in towns increased by 14 per cent; in the south-east, the number of town dwellers rose by a quarter, while the village population increased by only 7 per cent.

Ethnic origin is not specified in statistics of population, migration or fertility. Nor can it be, since intermarriages are widespread, and since Kurds who move outside their original homeland are gradually assimilated into Turkish society. Nevertheless, the number of Turkish citizens who identify as Kurds runs into millions – according to a recent survey, they constitute 13 per cent of the population. However, only 5 per cent believed that being Kurdish was the most important thing in their lives.[1] This corresponds roughly to the proportion of people (6.3 per cent) who cast their votes in the 2002 parliamentary elections for DEHAP (the Democratic People's Party), which speaks for Kurdish nationalism. The DEHAP vote was, naturally, strongest in the south-east, where the party controls the main town councils. DEHAP increased by 1.5 per cent the share of the poll won by its predecessor (HADEP/People's Democracy Party) in the 1999 elections, but then suffered a setback in local government elections in March 2004.

In 1938, when Atatürk died, it was forbidden to speak of Kurds, and in towns the authorities could fine people who spoke Kurdish in public. The government had just put down the last important Kurdish rising in the mountains of Dersim (renamed Tunceli), south of Erzincan. The assimilation of linguistic minorities was official policy. It was assisted by an improvement in communications which linked formerly inaccessible areas with the rest of the country. In 1935, the railway network reached Diyarbakır, the chief city in the south-east. Erzurum, in the east, had to wait for a railway connection until 1939, a year after Atatürk's death. Railways and the establishment of law and order in an area where strongmen had made the law and brigandage was widespread, were the main achievements of Atatürk's republic in the eastern parts of the country. In the economy, education and health care, progress was at first barely noticeable. The Second World War stopped it altogether.

The post-war era brought both rapid progress and problems. First came the construction of modern all-weather metalled roads which ended the isolation of an area divided by high mountain ranges. Long-distance coaches, linking every provincial town with the metropolitan areas in the west, made it easier for easterners to migrate in search of a better life. As in the rest of the country, tractors reduced the demand for farm labour, while better medical services reduced the death rate, particularly among children, allowing the population to increase rapidly. At the same time, more and better schools raised popular expectations.

Even before the first free elections of 1950, the ruling Republican People's Party had co-opted Kurdish tribal notables into the ranks of its unopposed members of parliament. The Democrat Party which took over in 1950 did the same during its ten-year rule. So did its successors. Rival parties recruited rival notables who could deliver solid blocks of votes. They often changed sides as this party leader or that offered better terms: jobs for retainers, subsidies, sometimes ministries. While tribal and religious notables played the system, many young Kurds, often from poor backgrounds, made use of the educational opportunities provided by the state to carve out careers in politics, the administration or business. Kâmuran İnan, a staunch defender of Turkish national interests, first as a diplomat and then a right-wing politician in the 1970s and '80s, came from a prominent family of religious leaders in the eastern province of Bitlis. Hikmet Çetin, leader of the Republican People's Party and foreign minister in the 1990s, rose from a modest background in a township near Diyarbakır. Ferit Melen, a native of Van, made a career in the civil service before becoming a minister and, for nearly a year, prime minister in the 1970s. His compatriot, Yalım Erez, rose to prominence as chairman of the union of chambers of commerce, before becoming a right-wing minister in the 1990s. The families both of İsmet İnönü, Turkey's second president, and of Turgut Özal, prime minister and then president in the 1980s and early '90s, came from the mixed Turkish-Kurdish town of Malatya. İnönü was accused by his opponents of being Kurdish, Özal made no secret of his partly Kurdish origin. Some other careers were more dubious. Inhabiting a frontier region, the Kurds had a tradition of smuggling. In recent years, some have turned their attention to drug smuggling, where the Kurdish mafia now has pride of place. 'The Kurds are savages,' many Turks will say in private. 'Rough easterners [that is, Kurds] are bringing crime to our cities' is a remark one hears not only in Istanbul, but from Trabzon in the north to Mersin in the south, and Kayseri in the centre to İzmir in the west. Kurdish nationalism is, at least in part, a response to this attitude.

Kurdish nationalism first arose among notables at the end of the nineteenth and the beginning of the twentieth centuries, notables who had clashed with state authorities or lost out in conflicts with rivals. But by the time Atatürk died, it had few adherents in Turkey, where the republic had suppressed risings which had combined Islamic with some nationalist demands. A handful of Kurdish nationalist leaders were active abroad, mainly in Syria, but they posed little threat to the republic. The threat increased after the end of the Second World War. While Turkish Kurds remained quiescent and were largely content to work through the electoral system, the Soviets sponsored a short-lived Kurdish republic in Iran. In Iraq, where the Kurds had been promised a degree of autonomy under the British mandate, a tribal leader, Molla Mustafa Barzani, rose against the central government in Baghdad. This inspired some Kurdish nationalist activity in Turkey, which the Democrat Party government suppressed without difficulty in the 1950s.

The military junta which seized power in 1960 exiled a number of prominent Kurdish notables. The officers believed that the survival of feudalism was at the root of disaffection in the east, and that local people would join the Turkish mainstream once feudal lords were removed. But danger lay elsewhere. The liberal constitution of 1961 allowed the formation of the socialist Turkish Workers Party, which attracted a number of educated Kurds. They were active also in the left-wing university debating societies, known as Thought Clubs which formed a nationwide federation (FKF). Before long, young Kurdish socialists disagreed with their Turkish colleagues and formed their own Eastern Hearths of Culture. Becoming further radicalized, they renamed themselves in 1969 as Eastern Revolutionary Hearths of Culture (DDKO). After the 'coup by memorandum' of March 1971, the Turkish Workers Party and the revolutionary student clubs were dissolved. But radicals of the left and right, Turkish and Kurdish, resumed their activities and started fighting each other when the army withdrew into the background. On the left, the radical student organization Devgenç (Revolutionary Youth) spawned a more militant breakaway group, Devsol (Revolutionary Left). Within this radical ferment of the 1970s and the bloody confrontations to which it gave rise, the most violent of all Kurdish nationalist organizations was born. It called itself PKK (Partiya Karkeren Kurdistan/Kurdistan Workers Party).

If violence is a way of life in the east, the PKK leader Abdullah Öcalan embodied it. Öcalan was born in 1948 into a poor family in a village situated between Urfa and Gaziantep in a linguistically mixed area.[2] He grew up speaking Turkish, and his espousal of Kurdish separatism appears fortuitous. At secondary school he felt socially disadvantaged. This made him truculent in the pursuit of advancement. Applying for a place in an airforce training school, he was turned down because he was past the age of entry. He then secured a place in the vocational school for state surveyors and land registry officials, and on graduating was appointed to Diyarbakır, where he took bribes to finance his ambition. He was accepted into the law school of Istanbul University, but a scholarship from the finance ministry allowed him to transfer in 1971 to the faculty of political science in Ankara, the seedbed of senior bureaucrats.

The limited military intervention in March that year, when the armed forces imposed on the country a civilian government of their choice, had led to a short-lived, and therefore ineffectual, repression of student militancy. Öcalan fell in with the Marxists who ruled the roost in the student body. He was arrested in April 1972 along with some other students for distributing an illegal proclamation. The seven months he spent in a military prison in Ankara turned him into a professional revolutionary. The previous decade, the Marxist Turkish Workers Party (TİP), banned in 1971, had opened a public debate on Kurdish disaffection which many of its members sought to resolve on the lines of the Soviet nationalities policy. Moscow, which pretended to solve the national question by establishing federal republics 'national in form, but socialist in content' – that is, totally subject to rule by the All-Union Communist Party – was not the only source of inspiration. The inclination to violence, strong throughout rural Turkey and particularly so in the backward eastern provinces, found theoretical justification in the theory and practice of anti-imperialism. The Vietnamese Communist commander, General Giap, Che Guevara in Latin America, and the theoretician of rural guerrilla resistance, the Brazilian Carlos Marighela, were the heroes of militant left-wing students everywhere. But while in the West, revolutionary militancy was easily contained by a prosperous law-abiding society, it found fertile ground in the discontents of young people whose ambitions were frustrated by the authoritarian methods used to police poverty in developing countries. As in the West, Turkish revolutionaries split into factions which fought each other as fiercely as they fought the 'class enemy'. Personalities, differences in tactics and ethnic affiliation determined the divisions.

After serving his apprenticeship in several revolutionary groups, Öcalan decided to form his own organization. It came into being at a meeting in Ankara in 1975. Öcalan remained in the capital, while the small band of his supporters travelled to the east to 'take the revolution to the people' and form local nuclei. In November 1978, Öcalan left Ankara to head a meeting in a village in the province of Diyarbakır, where his organization, which until then had borne the vague title of 'revolutionaries of Kurdistan', was reorganized as the Kurdistan Workers Party (PKK).

The PKK had two initial advantages. At a time when the tribal structure of Kurdish society was breaking down in line with urbanization, the party relied on detribalized Kurds, mostly from poor backgrounds, who had received enough education to see themselves as modernizers. Secondly, by force of Öcalan's personality, it was the most violent in an array of violent Kurdish groups. Of the twenty-two participants in the inaugural meeting of PKK, twelve were subsequently denounced as traitors by Öcalan. They included a woman, Kesire Yıldırım, whom Öcalan married, but who then broke with him and succeeded in surviving in Europe, while seven of the 'traitors' were murdered at Öcalan's orders.[3]

The PKK directed its initial activity against enemies in the southeast, in particular members and supporters of the Bucak clan, feudal landowners in the province of Şanlıurfa. A total of 354 of these 'fascist agents and local reactionaries' were murdered and 366 injured in the two-year period up to 12 September 1980, when the military assumed direct power in Turkey. By then Öcalan had left the country for Syria, securing for the PKK the third advantage which allowed it to sustain a bloody insurgency in south-eastern Turkey for fifteen years. It is almost impossible for a terrorist organization to survive without foreign bases. In turn, foreign bases need at least foreign toleration to serve their purpose. Toleration can shade into complicity which, in some cases, can amount to discreet help by foreign authorities. Öcalan escaped to Syria in July 1979. He was to stay there for twenty years under the protection of the main Syrian intelligence service (*Mukhabarat*).

Kurdish tribes had for centuries used and been used in regional power politics as they fought each other and their overlords. They enlisted Tsarist Russia against the Ottomans, and vice versa, in the First World War. In the aftermath, some played the British card against the Ankara government, while others supported Turkish nationalists. Öcalan followed the same tradition. But first he had to prove that he had a force at his disposal.

The regime of Hafez al-Asad in Damascus gave him a chance to assemble it in the camps set up by Palestinian militants in Lebanon. The Syrian ruler saw Turkey as an enemy. Turkey was a member of NATO; he was a Soviet protégé. He could not reconcile himself to the cession to Turkey in 1939 of the province of Hatay, which, as the *sancak* of İskenderun, had been part of French-mandated Syria, and where the Alawite community, to which he belonged, had a considerable presence. He wanted to stop Turkey from using for irrigation water from the Euphrates, of which Syria and Iraq had been virtually the sole users. Already in the early 1970s, Hafez al-Asad had discreetly directed to Palestinian camps Turkish Marxist revolutionaries, radicalized by the student unrest which had swept the West. A few years later, many of these 'sixty-eighters' (*soixante-huitards*, named after the Paris riots in 1968) returned to Turkey, benefiting from an amnesty. The more violent stayed behind, and were joined by new desperadoes, such as Öcalan.

The Syrian dictator was too prudent to allow large-scale incursions into Turkey from his territory. Öcalan found a way through by forming a tactical alliance with the Barzani faction which used its stronghold in northern Iraq to fight Hafez al-Asad's Arab rival, the Iraqi dictator Saddam Hussein. Later, when Barzani was enlisted by the Shah of Iran, America's regional ally, Öcalan took up with Barzani's rival, Jalal Talabani, whose bailiwick lay to the south-east of Barzani territory and who was supported by Syria and, indirectly, by the Soviets. The fall of the Shah in 1979 opened up new possibilities for the PKK. The new Islamic regime in Teheran became quickly embroiled in a struggle with its own Kurdish citizens. The PKK came in handy to divide the Kurds and to weaken Turkey, an ally of the American 'Great Satan'. As Teheran and Damascus formed a common front, PKK fighters were infiltrated into northern Iraq through Iranian territory.

From northern Iraq the PKK launched its first attack on Turkish security forces north of the frontier on 15 August 1984. It was the start of a long guerrilla campaign, directed by Öcalan from Damascus, relying on arms and money procured outside Turkey, but supported by cells which the PKK had formed inside the country and which assembled fighting men in the mountains of eastern Turkey. As the Turkish government recruited village guards to fend off attacks by PKK insurgents, the rebels fought on two fronts – against Turkish security forces and also against rival Kurds. The rural population of south-eastern Turkey was caught in the middle. Turkish authorities forcibly evacuated villages they could not control; the PKK attacked those that had sided with the Turkish government and killed village guards together with their women and children. Öcalan passed a 'military service law' under which young Kurds were press-ganged into the PKK. His men killed teachers, mosque personnel and even distributors of Turkish national newspapers. They destroyed some 2,000 public buildings, including 250 schools and fifty health centres, and wrecked industrial machinery. Widespread devastation, compounded by the response of Turkish security forces, was meant to radicalize the local population.

The situation worsened after the failure of the Kurdish rebellion in northern Iraq, following the defeat of Saddam Hussein in the 1991 Gulf War. To prevent an influx of hundreds of thousands of fleeing Iraqi Kurds, the Turkish government took a lead in setting up a Kurdish safe haven in northern Iraq, protected by Allied aircraft operating from Turkey. It did not take the PKK long to establish itself inside the safe haven and use it to extend its operations in Turkey. In Ankara, the government formed by Süleyman Demirel after the 1991 elections was uncertain how to respond. In December that year Demirel, visiting Diyarbakır in the company of the deputy prime minister, the Social Democrat Erdal İnönü, declared that he recognized 'the Kurdish reality'. The declaration had no practical consequences. In 1992, when Erdal İnönü refused his supporters permission to attend a meeting of Kurdish nationalists in Paris, eighteen Kurdish nationalist MPs who had been elected on the ticket of his party (SHP) reverted to the purely Kurdish, People's Party of Toil (HEP), to which they had originally belonged. As PKK attacks intensified, President Turgut Özal established indirect contact with Öcalan and with the Iraqi Kurdish leader Jalal Talabani, who persuaded Öcalan to declare a unilateral truce in March 1993. But in May, PKK terrorists, acting, it was claimed, in defiance of Öcalan, murdered thirty-one unarmed Turkish soldiers and four civilians in an ambush. Tansu Çiller, who succeeded Demirel as prime minister a few days later, decided to end the insurgency by fair means or foul and allowed the security forces to deal with the rebels in their own way.

One way was to turn a blind eye to the activities of death squads recruited among the local enemies of the PKK – Kurdish Islamic terrorists, whom the media called Hizbullah, after their counterparts in southern Lebanon. Unorthodox methods stored up trouble for the government, while doing little to end the PKK insurgency. Finally, after they had engineered the fall from power of the Islamist-led coalition, in which Tansu Çiller was deputy prime minister, the military took the bit between their teeth and warned Syria that it would have to expel Öcalan and end its support for anti-Turkish terrorists or face the consequences. Squeezed between Turkey and Israel and with Russia on the sidelines after the dissolution of the Soviet Union, Hafez al-Asad capitulated.

Forced to leave Syria, Öcalan travelled the world in search of refuge. Russia turned him down; Italy packed him off, while refusing to extradite him to Turkey; Greece procured for him a Cypriot passport and gave him temporary shelter on Greek diplomatic premises in Kenya. Alerted by friendly intelligence services, a Turkish commando team snatched him from Nairobi in January 1999. Put on trial, Öcalan cut a poor figure in the dock. He called off the armed struggle and asked to be allowed to play a part in the task of democratic reconciliation. He was nevertheless sentenced to death, with a stay of execution pending the hearing of an appeal to the European Court of Human Rights and, perhaps more to the point, pending a change in the public and political mood in Turkey. At first, many, if not most ethnic Turks wanted to see Öcalan hanged. Nearly 5,000 members of the security forces had been killed, and 11,000 injured during the insurgency.[4] The cost to Turkey's defence budget has been put at 15 billion dollars.[5] But, natural as it was, the desire for revenge gradually subsided. The PKK and its sympathizers had also, of course, suffered heavy losses. They made up the bulk of the 35,000 or more people killed between 1984 and 2001. In August 2002, the Turkish parliament amended the constitution, abolishing the death penalty. In October Öcalan's death sentence was commuted to life imprisonment.

The capture of Öcalan practically ended the PKK rebellion, although sporadic incidents and mopping up operations continued. In April 2002, the PKK, meeting in Brussels, dissolved itself and re-formed as the Congress for Freedom and Democracy in Kurdistan (KADEK), where, it hoped, it would be flanked by like-minded organizations of Iranian, Iraqi and Syrian Kurds. The following month, the European Union put the PKK on its list of banned terrorist organizations. A few hundred PKK militants remained in Turkey, a few thousand in northern Iraq and in Iran, and many sympathizers in western Europe. In December 2002, KADEK declared that it was ending its unilateral ceasefire in Turkey. There was little noticeable difference on the ground, and in November 2003 KADEK dissolved itself, or rather changed its name to Kurdish People's Congress (KONGRA-GEL), which, it declared, would fight for Kurdish rights by democratic means. However, it added, it would keep 'self-defence forces'. The threat of Kurdish separatist terrorism persists.

Ethnic Kurds had arrived in Europe in the ranks of Turkish migrant workers. At first they were strangers to the politics of identity. But the discomforts of life in an alien environment fosters self-definition. Refugee militants came along to proselytize the migrants. When West European countries suspended the recruitment of foreign workers after the 1973 oil crisis, economic migrants found that they could come in only in the guise of asylum seekers. Extremist organizations were there to help them formulate their claims. Once admitted, these new migrants were beholden to the extremists who demanded their support and subjected them to 'revolutionary taxes' and other forms of extortion. The intellectual leaders of Kurdish nationalism first established themselves in Sweden. They sought recruits mainly among the two and a half million Turkish citizens or ex-citizens in Germany, a fifth of whom are said to be of Kurdish ethnic origin. There are now Kurdish political and cultural organizations in Sweden, Germany, France, the Low Countries, Britain and the United States. Kurdish nationalism has thus acquired a base in the West from which it will continue to propagate its political ideology.

Another difficulty facing the Turkish authorities as they grapple with the Kurdish question is that political developments among the Kurds of Iraq, Iran and Syria are bound to affect Kurds in Turkey too. Kurdish nationalism is a many-headed hydra, and it will survive somewhere, if not everywhere. The defeat of the PKK insurgency has given Turkish public opinion an opportunity to debate how Kurdish nationalism can be accommodated within the Turkish republic. In view of the persistence of this nationalism, assimilation, historically the preferred policy of Turkish authorities, can never be fully realized, even though organic assimilation goes on as Kurds move into a Turkish environment. While the image (and the fact) of Kurdish backwardness persists among Turks, there is little ethnic animosity between Turks and Kurds. Realizing that few Kurds want their own separate state, which is bound to be poor and unruly, Kurdish nationalists now confine themselves to demands for cultural rights, such as instruction and broadcasting in Kurdish. Some of them dream of a binational Turkish and Kurdish state, which might be extended to include Kurds in adjacent countries. Most Turks believe that this would simply add to their problems.

The overthrow of the regime of Saddam Hussein in Iraq by the force of American and British arms in the spring of 2003 has added to the urgency of the Kurdish problem facing Turkey. When the Turkish parliament refused to allow US troops to cross Turkish territory in order to open a northern front against Saddam Hussein, the small number of Americans airlifted to northern Iraq relied on the militias of Barzani and Talabani, the two Kurdish leaders who had established autonomous administrations after the end of the First Gulf War in 1991. As Saddam's regime crumbled, Kurdish militias entered the towns of Mosul and Kirkuk, which have a mixed population of Arabs, Kurds and Turkomans. Barzani and Talabani played the time-honoured game of using outside powers – now represented by the Americans – in order to carve out their own autonomous region and include within it the oilfields of Kirkuk. The two leaders, who had earlier enlisted Saddam Hussein's help in their bitter internecine feuds, presented a common front in 2003. But their rivalry will persist, if only because it is based on linguistic difference: Barzani leads Kirmanji-speakers, and Talabani Surani-speaking Kurds. Abdullah Öcalan's brother, Osman, who had long represented the PKK in Teheran, and who then moved into northern Iraq to lead the remnant of PKK militants, also tried to ingratiate himself with the Americans, but was rebuffed.

The ethnic strife which developed in northern Iraq after the fall of Saddam Hussein, and which pitted Kurds against Arabs and Turkomans, highlighted the danger of a similar situation arising in

Turkey if the grip of the central government were relaxed. Preserving law and order is the primary task of the Turkish, as of any other government. Beyond that, liberals in and out of Turkey argue that the best way to preserve Turkey's multi-ethnic society is to allow it to become multicultural. But many Turks fear that far from satisfying Kurdish nationalism, multiculturalism would whet its appetite and encourage separatist ambitions. In August 2003, the Turkish constitution was amended and citizens were given the right to publish, broadcast and receive instruction in 'regional dialects'. The authorities did not rush to allow the Kurds to exercise these rights in practice. Whether the government could or should move faster in granting cultural rights to the Kurds is the subject of a lively debate inside Turkey. Turkey's south-eastern provinces breathed a sigh of relief when the PKK insurgency ended in 1999. With law and order re-established, emergency rule was gradually reduced and finally lifted in November 2002. But the fear of renewed disorder will not be banished quickly or easily.

Abdullah Öcalan was captured by Turkish commandos on 15 February 1999. A year later, on 17 January 2000, the leader of Hizbullah, Hüseyin Velioğlu, was killed when security forces raided his safe house in an Istanbul suburb.[6] The police then uncovered a string of safe houses throughout the country. In many of them they found the remains of men and women, who had been tortured and then murdered. These revelations caused a wave of revulsion, particularly after a TV channel broadcast a video shot by Hizbullah showing the torture and murder of one of its victims.

Hizbullah had come into existence in the Kurdish area (in Diyarbakır) in 1980,[7] and although it spread throughout the country, its militants were, by and large, of Kurdish origin. Like the PKK, these political Islamists spent much of their time murdering each other. But their victims included also some of Turkey's most prominent secularists – the investigative journalist Uğur Mumcu, the academic Professor Ahmet Taner Kışlalı, the newspaper editor Çetin Emeç, and others. As in the case of the PKK, Hizbullah needed and received foreign help, which came from shadowy authorities in the Islamic republic of Iran.[8] These authorities may well have commissioned the murders of intellectual leaders of Turkish secularism.

There is little doubt that some members of the security forces originally turned a blind eye to the activities of Hizbullah, seeing it as a counterweight to PKK.[9] But after the defeat of the PKK, the state made every effort to root out Kurdish Islamist extremists. More than 3,500 alleged members of Hizbullah were arrested and charged between 1991 and 2001. If there was original complicity, the state paid a high price for it: on 18 January 2001, members of Hizbullah in police uniforms murdered Gaffar Okkan, the energetic and popular police chief of Diyarbakır. The murderers were later apprehended. Worse was to follow. Fanatics, mainly from the Kurdish areas, slipped out to Pakistan for military training and then fought in Afghanistan, Chechnya and elsewhere as 'jihadis' (fighters in the Holy War). Returning to Turkey, they carried out a series of deadly suicide bombings in Istanbul in November 2003, killing sixty people. The authorities were unprepared. They believed that the organization set up by Velioğlu and his fellow conspirators had been dismantled. But the fanaticism which inspired them had not been eradicated, and provided recruits for foreign instigators of international terrorism.

There are no easy solutions to the Kurdish question – neither liberal democracy nor repression will conjure it away. Experience in other countries suggests that economic development, far from reducing nationalist disaffection, increases it as people whose energies had formerly been taken up by the struggle to survive find time to worry about their identity. But if it cannot be resolved, it can be managed more or less peacefully. This is the task of Turkey's elected legislators, who include ethnic Kurds in fair proportion. After the 1999 local government elections, Kurdish nationalists were reluctantly allowed to administer the main cities in the ethnically Kurdish area. The experiment is promising, even if its results cannot be foretold. By the end of the twentieth century, the Kurdish question had ceased being a taboo subject in Turkey. It will remain on the political agenda for many years to come.

The claim that the Turkish state exploits its Kurdish areas and treats them as a colony is false. As a recent study has shown,[10] public non-military expenditure in the region has always been in excess of public revenue from it, and the gap has widened since the 1980s. The causes of the persistent backwardness of the Kurdish areas have to be sought elsewhere, in geography, topography and, above all, in inadequate human capital – outdated social structures and low average educational attainment. The state still finds it hard to force families to send their girls to school, and harder still to keep them there. The less education there is for women, the higher the birth rate. In 1989, women in eastern and south-eastern Turkey wanted, on average, to have 3.4 children, but had given birth to 5.7; in the west they wanted 2.3 children and had 2.6. Turkey's Middle East will remain backward as long as it is a land of uneducated, ill-treated women.

Terrorists in Turkey are not, of course, all of Kurdish origin, although Kurds predominate among them. Nor is PKK (and its successor) the only Kurdish terrorist organization. The PKK has drawn its support mainly from speakers of the Kirmanji (Kırmancı) Kurdish language and those who profess, or come from the tradition of, Sunni Islam. Kurds who belong to the Alevi community and those who speak the minority Zaza (Dılımî) Kurdish language have tended to form their own underground organizations. Since there are more Turkish than Kurdish Alevis, these organizations straddle the ethnic divide. They have a base in the Tunceli province, the mountainous stronghold of Zaza-speaking Alevis, but they have been active also over a wide area extending west and north to the shores of the Black Sea. While the PKK has had little success among Kurds in Turkey's metropolitan areas, inter-ethnic terrorist organizations inspired by Marxism-Leninism have a strong presence in poor neighbourhoods in Istanbul and elsewhere, particularly among migrants of Kurdish origin.

The two main Marxist-Leninist terrorist organizations comprising both Kurds and Turks are TİKKO (Turkish Worker and Peasant Liberation Army) and DHKP/C (Revolutionary People's Liberation Army/Front). TİKKO is active mainly in the area south of the central Black Sea coast. DHKP/C, whose leadership appears to be in Europe, where the EU entered it on the list of banned terrorist organizations in May 2002, is notorious for its murders of high-profile personalities as well as of rank-and-file policemen, mainly in Istanbul. It carried out more than fifty assassinations in the eight years to 2002. Its victims include the former prime minister Nihat Erim, seven retired generals, a member of the Sabancı business dynasty, and a British insurance manager.[11] The choice of targets reflects the terrorists' hostility to 'international capitalism and its local watchdogs'. DHKP/C, which has links with the Popular Front for the Liberation of Palestine (PFLP), is one of the few surviving members of the family of European terrorist groups which included the Red Brigades in Italy and the Baader-Meinhof gang in Germany. Its fanaticism finds expression in the self-immolation of suicide bombers and hunger strikers. TİKKO and DHKP/C are involved only indirectly in the Kurdish question in Turkey, although both organizations have been accused of cooperating with PKK.

The PKK insurgency has held back the development of eastern and south-eastern Turkey. But, paradoxically, it has moved the region closer to the Turkish mainstream by focusing attention on it. In addition to hundreds of thousands of soldiers and policemen, many politicians and journalists, as well as businessmen who were urged to invest in the region, now have first-hand experience of it. At the same time, large numbers of local people have moved west to escape the fighting. A movement seeking to detach the Kurdish areas from Turkey, totally or partially, has thus helped integrate them with the rest of the country.

Integration will be pushed forward by the South-East Anatolia Development Project (GAP), the largest-ever development programme in the country. This integrated hydroelectric, irrigation and social development project is in the tradition of the British-built Gezira scheme in Sudan and the Tennessee Valley Authority in the United States. The aim of GAP is to harness the Euphrates and Tigris for the development of south-eastern Turkey and of the country as a whole. Both rivers rise in Turkey. The Euphrates flows from Turkey through Syria to Iraq. Further east, the Tigris, after leaving Turkey, briefly marks the boundary between Syria and Iraq and then flows through Iraq, joining the Euphrates in a common delta at the head of the Persian Gulf. The Euphrates does not have any important tributaries south of Turkey's border with Syria. On the other hand, the Tigris is fed by tributaries rising in Iraqi Kurdistan, and these tributaries provide half the flow of the river along its lower course. This means that while both Syria and Iraq depend on Turkey for the use they make of Euphrates water, Turkish control of the headwaters of the Tigris poses little danger to Iraq and none to Syria.

The first concrete dam in Turkey was built in 1936 (two years before Atatürk's death) on the Çubuk stream to supply water to Ankara, the new capital. At roughly the same time, the government started thinking about the development of hydro-power to generate electricity. Economic development was delayed by the Second World War, and it was not until the 1950s that an ambitious dam-building programme was put in hand. The first new dams were built in western, southern and central Anatolia to meet the demand of growing cities for drinking water and electricity. Although some villagers were displaced, the programme was immensely popular, and prime minister Adnan Menderes took the credit for it. The first two important hydroelectric power stations were built in 1956 on the Sakarya river west of Ankara, and the Seyhan, north of the southern city of Adana. Eastern Turkey, with its high mountains and fast-flowing rivers breaking through gorges on their way to the Mesopotamian plain, had to wait for another twenty years. The fact that unlike the rivers of western and southern Turkey, whose course lies entirely within the country, the Euphrates and the Tigris are transnational, crossing Turkey's boundaries on their way to the sea, complicated matters.

Until the 1970s Turkey had made no use of the waters of the two rivers, which flowed unimpeded to Syria and Iraq, carrying all their water to the two countries, and, at times, threatening them with floods. Turkish plans to draw off water were naturally resisted by countries which had been its sole beneficiaries. However, Turkey could not continue to deny itself this important resource. It was ready to settle on the basis of a compromise, provided its ownership of water rising within its territory was recognized. The Turks argued that they had as much right to that water as the Arabs had to their oil.

In 1974 a study sponsored by the World Bank found that if Turkey maintained an average monthly discharge of 500 cubic metres per second, as the Euphrates passes from Turkey to Syria, this would satisfy existing downstream requirements for power generation, irrigation and future growth.[12] The figure of 500 cubic metres per second is equivalent to roughly half the average flow of the Euphrates. Although Turkey promised to abide by the 'rule of 500', Syria wanted a guaranteed greater share. In the absence of an agreement, the first Turkish dam on the Euphrates, at Keban near the town of Elâzığ, was completed in 1975 without the help of the World Bank, which did not wish to be drawn into the controversy. In any case, foreign credits were available from other sources.

The Keban dam, the largest to be built in Turkey until that time, was designed solely for electricity generation and not for irrigation. The same was true of Karakaya dam, downstream from Keban, which entered service in 1987. By regulating the flow of the Euphrates, without subtracting from its flow, both dams benefited Syria, which however continued to demand a say in decisions affecting the management of the river. The dispute became more acrimonious when GAP was set up in 1986 and irrigation was inscribed in its programme alongside power generation. Syria tried unsuccessfully to stop it.

The GAP plan aimed to irrigate 1.6 million hectares in the valleys of the Euphrates and Tigris rivers, and to install 7,500 MW (megawatt) of electrical generating capacity at a total cost of 32 billion dollars, including social welfare projects. The master plan for the fifteen years 1990 to 2005 provided for the expenditure of some 14 billion dollars. Nearly half this sum had been spent by the end of 2001. In the decade to 2001, investment in GAP varied between 5 and 8.5 per cent of all investment in the country.

Although scarce resources have delayed implementation, nearly three quarters of the energy programme had been completed by the end of 2001. In 1999, GAP (excluding Keban) supplied 13 per cent of all electricity generated in Turkey and 43 per cent of all hydroelectricity. In the decade to 2000, the value of electricity supplied by GAP to the national network was estimated at 11 billion dollars.

The Atatürk dam, north of the city of Şanlıurfa (the classical Edessa), the largest single project in GAP, was the first to be used both for power generation and for irrigation. Production of electricity began in 1992. Irrigation had to wait for the completion of the twin tunnels which feed water from the dam to the Harran plain, south of Şanlıurfa. By 1999, after the completion of the first tunnel, water drawn from the Atatürk dam lake and distributed in open concrete-lined ditches irrigated more than 100,000 hectares of the plain. Throughout the GAP area, the implementation of the irrigation programme has been slow: in the year 2000, the irrigated area amounted to 215,000 hectares. The GAP plan provided for a varied list of crops: cereals, fruit, vegetables, as well as cotton. In practice, cotton, which brings the quickest returns to farmers, has been the main crop. There has been criticism of this concentration on the notoriously thirsty crop of cotton. Perhaps market forces will gradually open the way to crop diversification.

The Atatürk dam and the irrigated Harran plain, south of it, are the most eye-catching achievements of GAP. The 170-metre-high rockfill dam containing an artificial lake of 817 square kilometres (the largest in Turkey, and larger than any natural lake, except for Lake Van in the east, and the marshy Salt Lake in central Anatolia) dominates a landscape of hills, whose empty barren slopes are being gradually planted with trees and shrubs. The Harran plain, until recently the colour of brown dust, is now emerald-green. The villages in the plain, and nearby cities, dotted with multi-purpose community centres, schools and industrial estates, are a showcase of GAP-sponsored social and economic initiatives. The lives of the 90,000 villagers in the Harran pilot area have been transformed. They have access to roads, electricity, drinking water, schools and health centres. They live longer, healthier lives.

It is a far cry from the first dams built in the 1950s to serve a purely economic purpose, when the needs of local inhabitants did not enter the planners' minds. Two cities, in particular, have developed rapidly with the help of GAP: Şanlıurfa, where GAP has its regional offices, and Gaziantep, a growing go-ahead industrial city to the west of the GAP area. The argument by some environmentalists that local inhabitants have not benefited from GAP does not stand up to the most cursory examination. Even outside the area earmarked for irrigation, such as the hilly open country between Diyarbakır on the Tigris and Şanlıurfa in the Euphrates basin, cultivation has spread as peasants have learnt how to use groundwater more productively.

In a country like Turkey, where successive civilizations have flourished, it is impossible to carry out large construction projects without disturbing archaeological sites. The Atatürk dam lake covers the remains of Samsat, the ancient Samosata, birthplace of Lucian, the greatest satirist of the Hellenistic age. More care was taken when the Birecik dam, below the Atatürk dam on the Euphrates, threatened the site of Zeugma, an important Greco-Roman staging centre in upper Mesopotamia. Archaeologists uncovered and saved superb mosaics, which were then restored in the regional museum of Gaziantep. The preservation of the archaeological heritage was one of the grounds on which environmentalists objected and, finally, successfully obstructed the building of the Ilısu dam on the Tigris. The dam threatened the lower part of the medieval Muslim fortress of Hasankeyif, endowed with mosques and monuments by local Turkoman and Kurdish tribal chieftains.

An international campaign tried every argument, valid or specious, to stop the development: human rights, the threat to the Kurdish cultural heritage (the Turkish heritage did not interest foreign objectors), the alleged inadequacy of compensation for displaced locals, gaps in environmental impact studies. The fact that the dam would not have been used for irrigation, but only for energy generation, that Syria would hardly be affected (as the Tigris bypasses it), that Iraq can rely on tributaries rising in its own territory, and that Arab agitation against the project had the purely political purpose of embarrassing Turkey, did not deter objectors from claiming that the Ilısu dam threatened the Middle East with water wars. As it happened, the campaign coincided with an economic crisis in Turkey which reduced demand for energy. At the same time, the Blue Stream natural gas pipeline built under the Black Sea to transport Russian gas and a newly completed pipeline from Iran supplied Turkey with more energy than it could consume. There was no harm, therefore, in delaying the Ilısu project – none except to local people, who will continue to scratch a living in an inhospitable environment, and whose attempt to grow trees for the sole purpose of receiving compensation payments when the dam was built will not now yield the expected returns.

Environmentalists have recently turned their attention to pipelines which are decried as sources of atmospheric warming and said to be otherwise dangerous, in case they develop leaks or are sabotaged. Turkey will have to get used to protesters from rich countries who urge it to eradicate poverty without disturbing a leaf or a twig. Of course, development carries a cost. But the electorate demands development in the shape of factories, dams, roads and artificial irrigation; it wants more jobs and a more prosperous life, and the government is bound to respond.

Eventually, Turkey's southern neighbours will also benefit from the development of the south-eastern provinces of Anatolia. People living on both sides of the border suffered when the Ottoman empire was divided at the end of the First World War. South-eastern Anatolia, which had marketed its produce in Aleppo in Syria and Baghdad in Iraq, became a dead end abutting on closed frontiers. Legitimate trade gave way to smuggling. In the 1950s and '60s, the Baghdad Pact, which linked Turkey, Iraq, Iran and Pakistan in a defensive alliance with Britain, and then its successor, the Central Treaty Organization (CENTO), brought some improvement to transit routes from Turkey to Iran and Iraq. A direct rail link was established between Turkey and Iran; some work was done on roads from Trabzon to Iran and from İskenderun to Iraq. But the volume of trade was small. Trade with Iran and Iraq rose considerably when the two countries fought each other in the 1990s and both clamoured for supplies from Turkey. Then during the PKK insurgency, large stretches of Turkey's frontier with Syria were mined; Turkish troops entered the Kurdish areas of northern Iraq in hot pursuit of terrorists. Legitimate commerce suffered. After Saddam Hussein's invasion of Kuwait, the embargo on trade with Iraq hit the economy of Turkey's south-eastern provinces hard. The oil-for-food programme sanctioned by the United Nations and smuggling, which was officially tolerated, did not make good the losses occasioned by the interruption of regular trade.

Diplomatic relations and trade with Syria improved after Turkish pressure forced the Syrian authorities to expel the PKK leader from Damascus in 1998. The Syrian government, which had campaigned for years against Turkey's use of the Euphrates waters, even sent a minister to attend the inaugural ceremony of a GAP project. But Syria is comparatively poor. Iraq, on the other hand, is rich in natural resources. Under a rational government which would use oil revenue to advance the country's prosperity, it could become a major market for Turkish exports and Turkish contractors, a position it occupied briefly during the Iran–Iraq war. At that time, the road from the Turkish Mediterranean port of Mersin to the Habur crossing on the Iraqi border was used by fleets of trucks carrying Turkish and foreign supplies to Iraq, while Iraqi oil flowed through the enlarged pipeline from Kirkuk to Ceyhan (Yumurtalık) in the gulf of İskenderun. By 2002, the road from Mersin had been improved to motorway standard as far as Gaziantep, and the work of extending the motorway to Şanlıurfa, and then through Diyarbakır to Habur was well under way. But traffic did not match increased capacity. The people of southeastern Turkey were waiting with impatience for the day when trade would again begin to flow, making use of improved transit facilities. The overthrow of the regime of Saddam Hussein by the Americans and their coalition partners in 2003 has brought that day nearer.

Turkey has done its best to raise standards in the eastern and southeastern provinces through the GAP programme and through incentives to investors in the area. Development was held back both by the PKK insurgency and by instability south of the border. The defeat of the insurgency in 1998–9 removed one obstacle. But it is only when Turkey's eastern and southern borders become genuinely open to trade that Turkey's Middle East will have a chance of overcoming the handicap of its isolation from the prosperous coastal regions. The advent of rational regimes in Iraq, Iran and Syria could also ease Turkey's problems with Kurdish nationalism. It may take a long time before people of Kurdish origin are integrated, without being necessarily assimilated, as citizens with full rights of the countries which they inhabit. This process, which has already begun in Turkey, offers the best hope for the Kurds and for their rulers – the Turks, Iranians and Arabs in whose midst they live.

The alternative to integration is separation through the creation of an independent Kurdish state. This is the long-term aim of many Kurdish nationalists, and the short-term target of extremists among them. The troubles in Iraq have already led to ethnic cleansing, first by Arabs when Saddam Hussein was in power and then by Kurds after his downfall. The creation of a Kurdish state, be it autonomous or independent, would entail transfers of population on a much larger scale. Nor would the outcome justify the suffering and bloodshed. All the parties to the conflict would be impoverished and the region would become more unstable. Once destroyed, a multi-ethnic society cannot be rebuilt. Turkey deserves support as it tries to resist such a dire prospect.

I I

Red Apple or Sour Grapes

TWO ANCIENT LEGENDS have provided symbols for Turkish nationalists. The first and better known is the legend of the Grey Wolf (*Bozkurt*) which guided the Turkish tribes on their westward migration from their homeland in southern Siberia. In the legend, this homeland is called Ergenekon (a Mongol word meaning a pass through steep mountains), and is described as an inaccessible valley surrounded by high peaks. Only the wolf knew the way out. The grey wolf was probably a tribal animal totem. The second legend represents the ultimate objective of Turkish conquests as the Red Apple (*Kızıl Elma*). It was first located in Constantinople, where, according to one theory, it was the popular name given to the golden orb held aloft by the statue of the emperor Justinian I. After the conquest of the city in 1453, Rome became the Red Apple as the final objective of the Ottomans, and the symbol of the triumph of Islam over Christendom. The dome of St Peter provided a convenient factual counterpart. When the Ottomans failed to reach the capital of Western Christendom, they sought the Red Apple in Vienna, the capital of their main foe, the Habsburgs. Others moved it to Moscow whose Tsars proved to be more formidable adversaries than the Habsburgs. The Ottomans were unable to pluck the Red Apple in any of these cities. But the legend lived on. Today, Turkish nationalists of the left and right – ex-Marxists and ethnic nationalists – who fear that Turkey would disintegrate if it accepted the membership terms of the European Union, call themselves the Red Apple Coalition. It is a perverse use of the legend. For the overwhelming majority of the Turks, it is not opposition to, but membership of Europe, and beyond Europe of the West as a whole, that is the Red Apple, the ultimate objective of their endeavours.

When Recep Tayyip Erdoğan emerged victorious from the elections in November 2002, he decided that his first and most immediate task was to secure a firm date for the beginning of negotiations on accession to the European Union. It was a shrewd move at a time when Turkey's military and civilian establishment looked askance at the origins of Erdoğan's career in political Islam. Europe, where the military were subordinated to the civil power, would get the generals off his back. Moreover, by backing Europe he would get the people on his side. Moderate Islamists wanted EU membership, because they believed it would gain them greater religious freedom, and above all the end of all restrictions on women wearing headscarves in schools, universities, government offices and at official functions. However, in the report it published in October 2003 on Turkey's progress towards membership, the EU Commission made no mention of the ban on headscarves when it listed what it considered to be Turkey's shortcomings. Turkish liberals campaigned for membership in order to achieve the freedoms enjoyed by West Europeans. The army saw membership as the culmination of Atatürk's reforms, of which it considered itself to be the guardian, while insisting that Turkey's security concerns should be taken into account. Turkish business wanted access to European capital and markets, and West European standards of administration at home. Kurdish nationalists were passionate pro-Europeans, because minority rights are recognized in the EU.

Europe is the promised land. In March 2004, Kemal Unakıtan, finance minister in the government of the Justice and Development Party, told the party faithful in Istanbul:

> You must realize that our way leads to Europe. Go to Europe and look around: you'll see there what you want to have in Turkey. That's where we'll take Turkey. Have a good look: people are always smiling there; they are tolerant; their income levels are high; they don't pay too much attention to each other, but they show respect and understanding; no one usurps the rights of others; bank funds are not stolen, resources are not plundered. Turkey's place is in the European Union. We must raise ourselves to their level. There's no other way.[1]

Advocates of Turkish membership point out that the Ottoman empire was always involved in European power politics, as an ally of

France against the Habsburgs, for example, or of Britain against Russia, that even in times of war goods and ideas moved in both directions, and that at the end of the Crimean War in 1856, the Ottoman empire was recognized as a member of the European concert. After the Second World War, Turkey became a member of the Organization of European Cooperation (OEEC) when it began to benefit from the Marshall Plan. It was admitted to the Council of Europe in 1950. It joined South European countries, such as Italy and Greece, in the southern command of NATO, when it entered the alliance in 1952. When Turkey became an associate member of the European Economic Community in 1964, the president of the European Commission, Professor Walter Hallstein, declared:

> Turkey is part of Europe. This is the ultimate meaning of what we are doing today. It confirms in incomparably topical form a truth which is more than the summary expression of a geographical concept or of a historical fact that has held good for several centuries. Turkey is part of Europe: and here we think first and foremost of the stupendous personality of Atatürk whose work meets us at every turn in this country, and of the radical way in which he recast every aspect of life in Turkey along European lines.[2]

Since then the European Union has repeatedly confirmed Turkey's eligibility for membership. In 1996, Turkey became the first country which was not a full member of the EU to have a customs union with it. Then in December 1999, the EU Council of Ministers named Turkey formally as a candidate for full membership. In theory, therefore, Turkey's right to membership has been recognized. This has not stopped the former French president Giscard d'Estaing from saying in 2003 that Turkey's accession would spell the end of the European Union. Giscard was at the time president of the convention which drafted a new European Constitution, a convention in which Turkey was represented. Clearly, the contractual position has not dispelled European misgivings. In the autumn of 2002, a survey conducted by the European Union found that Turkey was the least popular of the candidate countries. At that time, the number of migrants from Turkey (and of their descendants) who had become EU citizens already stood at 1.3 million, a figure higher than the population of

Cyprus and Malta, which were to become full members in 2004. In addition there were 2.5 million holders of Turkish passports resident in the EU. The biggest concentration was in Germany, where there were 2.6 million migrants from Turkey, of whom 700,000 had become German citizens.[3]

European attitudes to Turkey are partly determined by the experience of Turkish migration. Most of the migrants came originally from poor rural areas. They found it difficult to integrate into the society of host countries and lived among themselves. Few learnt the language of the host country; most relied for news and entertainment on Turkish television relayed by satellite or European editions of Turkish papers. The scholastic record of their children was below average. The subordination of women among Turkish migrants shocked their European neighbours. What is more, the alienation of the migrants favoured the spread among them of ethnic nationalism and religious fundamentalism. But even the most xenophobic Europeans did not accuse the Turks of being lazy. On the contrary, they established a reputation for hard work and, gradually, for entrepreneurial skill. There are Turkish businesses now all over Europe, and both their customers and their employees are no longer confined to the migrant community. There are also signs that the third, if not the second, generation is adapting and integrating. Politicians of Turkish origin have been elected to European parliaments. The migrant community has produced writers both in Turkish and in German. Mixed marriages are no longer a rarity. The former German chancellor, Helmut Kohl, whose Christian Democrats are in the forefront of the opposition to Turkey's accession, has a Turkish daughter-in-law.

Turks in Europe are gradually coming to lead European lives. But what about the home country? The biggest difference between the European Union and Turkey lies not in religion, institutions and culture, but in the fact that Turkey is much poorer than Europe. Turkey is incomparably better off than it was in 1923 when Atatürk established the republic. But so is Europe, and the answer Atatürk gave that year to an Austrian journalist who had asked about the compatibility of the East and West, still holds true: 'Think of two men facing you: one is rich and has every means at his disposal, the second poor and with nothing to dispose of. Apart from the absence of means, the spirit of the second man is in no way different from or inferior to that of the first. This is precisely the position of Turkey as it faces Europe.'[4]

True, Atatürk underestimated the lasting effect of historical and social conditioning on people's way of life. He believed that, just as there was a single universal civilization, so too there was a single culture. This may be true of high culture – of the arts and of science. But culture denotes also a whole way of life, and habits of life differ demonstrably from country to country. But here too there is increasing convergence internationally and standardization domestically. A letter posted on a Turkish internet site complained:

> Last week when I visited several towns in the east, I realized that Anatolia is rapidly losing its local colour. There is almost no difference now between Elâzığ and Ankara, between Malatya and Konya. The same architectural models, the same shopping culture, the same taste in food, the same human material. Familiar colours, similar complaints, standard young people. It is as if a skilful hand has put a grey uniform on top of the colourful costumes of distant cities . . . As you drive into any city the car radio picks up the local station playing, not local folk music, but the top of the pops from London, Paris and Istanbul. Young people who want to dress differently in İzmir or in Antalya have all been fitted out by the same mad Italian, and all look not different, but exactly the same. Local workshops weave rugs with a Dalmatian design. In the suburbs of Diyarbakır babies are dressed in T-shirts inscribed AC/DC, and people who do not know what heavy metal is, move around like walking advertisements for hard rock groups they have never heard of . . . Weddings are less like village weddings and more like weddings on television . . . Local dishes are increasingly hard to find, while (or should one say because?) American hamburger and pizza parlours have established themselves in the best locations . . . Houses look as if they have all been made by the same tasteless contractor: multi-storey, impersonal, unlovely, with satellite dishes bunched on balconies. In every city, the same 'no-alternative' shopping streets, and crowds that have no alternative but to shop there. Go to any home in the country and you will see food cooked in pots and pans offered by the same newspaper publicity campaign, served in plates and on a tablecloth which are part of the offer. Encyclopedias distributed in a similar campaign stand like gravestones on empty bookshelves . . . The lively cultural mosaic of which we say we are proud is pasted over mercilessly by the standardized plaster of global culture.[5]

Bingöl, a provincial centre of some 70,000 inhabitants in south-eastern Anatolia, is just such an unlovely town. It attracted worldwide attention when it was discovered that several of the suicide bombers whose explosions destroyed two synagogues, the British consulate and a British bank in Istanbul in November 2003, had come from this one small town. Bingöl was built and given its name by the central government after the suppression of the revolt led in 1925 by Şeyh Sait, a Kurdish sheikh of the Nakşibendi brotherhood, who sought the return of the Islamic caliphate, while being also a primitive Kurdish nationalist. Since his days, secularist Kurdish nationalists have parted company with Kurdish religious fanatics. The civil war between the two factions has perpetuated the local tradition of violence, which finds expression also in mafia-type activities, in smuggling, in feuds between families and the brutal treatment of women within them. Some Turkish commentators complain that the European insistence on minority rights has hit Turkey before it had completed the process of nation-building – that is, before it had assimilated the Kurds. More to the point, Turkey is trying to decentralize before it has completed the work of civilizing its own Middle East. True, the central government had done its best for the mountainous province of Bingöl, where tax revenue covers only 11 per cent of public expenditure, one of the lowest proportions in the country.[6] It had given it a secular high school (*lycée*), where one of the bombers had studied. Another bomber was the best pupil in the *lycée* in the town of Mardin, also in the southeast. Modern education did not suppress, at least among some young people, a violent resentment which found new grievances. The local traditions of religious fanaticism and of violence fed into the Islamic terror international, when the young bombers went to Pakistan and Afghanistan for training and indoctrination.

At the turn of the millennium, Istanbul University, which had a strictly secularist rector, witnessed a procession of bearded young students shouting, 'A curse on all infidels!'[7] When Turkish students chant 'Down with capitalism (or globalization or imperialism)', they do not differ from their like-minded contemporaries in the West. But to rain curses on the infidel has a medieval ring about it. Turkish reformers, of whom Atatürk was the greatest, had dragged the country out of the middle ages, but, as in Bingöl, within standard-issue concrete apartment houses and internet cafés (one of which was operated by a bomber), medieval fanaticism can survive, just as medieval hatred of the Jews survived in civilized Germany until it was harnessed by Hitler. Turkey may not harbour more nasty people than do its European neighbours, but such nastiness as exists within it is fed from distinctly local sources.

Turkey differs from the West in this respect also that it is a young country. Out of a population of some 70 million, it has 22 million children and young people of school age (32 per cent). In the United Kingdom in 1999, the number of people of school age was 11 million out of a total population of 59 million (19 per cent). At the time of the 2000 census in Turkey, the age group between 6 and 30 years accounted for nearly 60 per cent of the population (as against 32 per cent in the United Kingdom). This bulge of young people is Turkey's strength, but also its problem. The novelist Orhan Pamuk has ascribed terrorism to the rage of 'the damned' – of people who feel condemned to poverty and who are denied the fulfilment of their aspirations. But most Turks do not feel condemned to misery, from which they are determined to escape by their own efforts. True, conspiracy theories are rife in Turkey, where personal and national misfortune is often attributed to malevolent outsiders, but in public as in private life rational judgement is the norm.

Parliamentary democracy came to Turkey after the death of Atatürk, but rational government was instituted in his lifetime. This is best seen in foreign policy which has pursued successfully two well-defined objectives: to protect the country's integrity and independence and to safeguard, and where possible to augment, the resources available for its economic development. Development has been at the centre of the political debate in Turkey since the establishment of the republic, as thinkers of all persuasions discussed the means of raising the country's standard of living. Similarly, personal development is the main preoccupation of individual Turks. In seeking to improve their lot, they try to break out of the confines of their immediate environment and to reach out to the outside world. Young religious fanatics and utopian secularist revolutionaries provide a perverse example of this trend as they make common cause with like-minded enthusiasts at home and abroad. But they are on the fringes of Turkish life. The vast majority want to improve their lot by rational means, by making use of the experience of others, by joining the mainstream of human civilization.

This endeavour is seen most clearly among the country's intellectuals. They may simplify choices when they argue, for example, that if Turkey does not enter the European Union it will be condemned to existence in the Third World, to the company of Persians and Arabs. But their enthusiasm for modernity, as represented by the West, is both genuine and rational. Breaking out of isolation, breaking down the walls erected by history, finding past points of contact between Turkey and the West and parallels between Western and Turkish culture is a major preoccupation of Turkish academics and imaginative writers alike. It is the theme, for example, of the prize-winning novel *Romantik: Bir Viyana Yazı* (The Romantic: A Summer in Vienna), by the woman writer Adalet Ağaoğlu, who creates an echo-chamber where Western and Turkish culture meet. The hero is an elderly history teacher in a Turkish provincial *lycée*, who uses his retirement bonus to travel to Vienna where he is seduced by the city's baroque heritage. The Ottoman sieges of Vienna are to the author the symbol of both the confrontation and the cross-fertilization of Western and Turkish cultures. One can discern a similar interest in the work of the young musicologist Emre Aracı who has uncovered the music composed in the Western manner in the nineteenth-century Ottoman palace, or in that of Turkish historians who study the penetration of Western ideas and ideals into Ottoman Turkey. A common aim is to present the Turks not as passive recipients of Western influences, but as parties to a dialogue with the West.

Turkish students who go to Western universities, Turkish professionals who work in the West, traders and contractors who do business with the outside world, and the mass of Turkish migrant workers abroad, are in their own way engaged in the same dialogue. The defeatist tendency of treating the West as a scapegoat for Turkey's ills coexists with the much stronger urge to engage with the West, as far as possible, on equal terms. Although in the nineteenth century the Ottoman empire had become the Sick Man of Europe (and not of Asia), the Turks were never colonized, and are therefore free of the feelings of inferiority of people who were. Their Muslim religion, or in the case of the secularized elite their Muslim background, distinguishes them from the majority of Europeans who, Turks argue, have an opportunity of proving their liberal credentials, and of disproving theories of the inevitable clash of religion-based civilizations, by welcoming them into their midst. It is true, Turkish thinkers admit, that the Renaissance and the Enlightenment started in Europe and originally bypassed the Turks. But the lost centuries can be made good, particularly in the modern age when knowledge is instantly transmissible.

Europe will not be easily convinced by these arguments, particularly since Turkish membership will not be cost-free. Germans, in particular, fear an influx of Turkish workers, even if the right to the free circulation of labour is granted to Turkey only after a long transitional period. With its large agricultural sector, Turkey is bound to benefit from European farm subsidies, however much they may be trimmed. It would be difficult to devise special provisions to stop the flow of European regional aid and cohesion funds to the poor and backward tracts of Turkish territory. Negotiations between the EU and Turkey will therefore be long and difficult, and no one can predict when or even whether Turkey will become a full member.

Turks argue that European delaying tactics risk a backlash in their country and encourage advocates of a truculent isolationism, mistrustful of the West. The risk should not be exaggerated. Convergence with the practices of liberal democracies is a popular cause in Turkey, and it is likely to be pursued irrespective of the contortions of EU policymakers. Although reforms can be facilitated by EU or American advice, Turkey needs them for its own sake and not just in order to satisfy the West. It can even be argued that if Turkey achieved European standards of governance, it would advance to a European level of prosperity more easily if it were unrestrained by EU rules and regulations. In any case, the structure of the EU is changing. It is becoming more diverse as member countries pick and choose the areas in which they want to work in common. A Europe in which the common currency or the common security and foreign policy is optional is already a Europe *à la carte*. If this tendency were to prevail, the EU could accommodate Turkey more easily. But whatever happens in the long-standing relationship between Turkey and Europe, the real question is whether it will be the developed world or the underdeveloped (in plain language, the backward) part of the globe which will serve as a model for Turkey's endeavours. If the question is put in this way, the answer is obvious. The Turks will not turn for inspiration to laggards in the race.

12

Progress and Pitfalls

THE STORY IS told of a German Jewish professor who was so happy with the reception he was given in Turkey, where he had sought refuge from Nazi persecution, that he decided to apply for Turkish nationality. The hosts were flattered and the professor was given a Turkish passport. But his gratitude was strained when he received his next salary slip and discovered that his pay had been halved. He remonstrated with the university authorities, who explained that expatriates were paid twice as much as Turks and that now that he had become a Turkish national he would be subject to the local scale. It may have been easy in his case to acquire a Turkish passport, the university official concluded, but it was not easy to be a Turk.

Zeki Kuneralp, one of Turkey's most successful and best-loved diplomats who served two terms as ambassador in London, ends his memoirs with these words. 'Yes,' he writes, 'it is no easy thing to be a Turk, but is not the privilege of being one all the greater for that?'[1] Kuneralp ended his diplomatic career in 1979 when he retired from the Turkish embassy in Madrid, where his wife and brother-in-law were murdered by Armenian terrorists who thought that by killing Turks they would draw attention to the historic grievances of their people. Commenting on the murders, *The Economist* dwelt on Armenian claims of genocide at the hands of Ottoman Turks in the First World War. In a letter to the editor, Kuneralp pointed out that his wife had not been born at the time. The article was a typical response to terrorism directed against Turkey. Since 1973, when the Turkish consul in Los Angeles became the first victim of Armenian assassins, the Turkish authorities have repeatedly urged Western governments to take action against terrorist groups which use their territory as a base for attacks on Turkey and Turkish interests. The French moved against Armenian terrorists only after four Frenchmen were killed, along with four foreigners, by a bomb attack against the Turkish Airlines at Orly airport in Paris in 1983. The Kurdish PKK and Turkish Marxist-Leninist terrorists had offices throughout western Europe until after the attack on the Twin Towers on 11 September 2001. Long before November 2003 when the British consulate and a London-based bank as well as two synagogues were blasted by terrorists in Istanbul, Turkey had asked that the Islamic terrorist group IBDA-C (Islamic Grand Orient Raiders Front), which was to claim responsibility for the attacks, should be placed on the EU list of banned organizations. There was no response. But immediately after the outrages, British subjects (and others) were advised not to travel to Turkey, international football fixtures were transferred from Turkey to other countries, and it became more difficult for Turks to obtain British visas. It is not easy to be a Turk when terrorists strike your country.

Ambassador Kuneralp did not have much official work in Madrid, since there was little contact between the two countries at the time, and this gave him time to think about the differences and similarities between them. Until the first half of the twentieth century, he wrote,

> Spain was a country whose people were poor and whose rulers were weak, where political leaders fell victim to assassination and one civil war followed another. In recent years the case has altered. The people have grown rich; the per capita income has risen from 300 to 3,000 dollars. New industries have been created, the road network and other infrastructures have developed. Spain, once an underdeveloped country, has become one of the world's ten leading countries in terms of national product.[2]

Kuneralp made these remarks in 1979, when Turkey's gross national product per person was just under 1,900 dollars. By 2001, the Spanish economy was thirteenth in size in the world, with a gross national product of 816 billion dollars, or just under 20,000 dollars per head. Turkey was twentieth in the league table, with a gross national product of 383 billion dollars or 5,800 dollars per head (in terms of the purchasing power of the local currency).[3] As in Spain, so too in Turkey, new industries had been created and the physical infrastructure had been extensively modernized. The growth of income per person in Turkey has been slowed down by a transient factor – the much more rapid rise in population. Is Turkey now likely to follow in the footsteps of Spain and catch up with it in the foreseeable future, in terms of political stability and economic prosperity?

There is much that Turkey and Spain have in common. The Anatolian peninsula and the Iberian peninsula have a similar climate and physical configuration, with a central plateau surrounded by fertile coastlands. Both countries once ruled over extensive empires before retreating to their present boundaries. Both have experienced a struggle between traditionalists and modernizers – clericals and anti-clericals in Spain, secularists and Islamists in Turkey. Both have to accommodate conflicting nationalist ideologies at home: Spanish, Basque and Catalan in Spain, Turkish and Kurdish in Turkey. Both have been plagued by terrorists: ETA in Spain, PKK, left-wing revolutionaries and various Islamist groups in Turkey. Both have armies that have tasted political power. Spain experienced the catastrophe of the civil war, because its army was divided in its allegiance, Turkey avoided it because its army managed to remain united.

There is one crucial difference, however. Spaniards have a Catholic Christian background, Turks a Muslim one. Can Islam and modernity be reconciled? True, the same question had been asked of the Catholic Church, particularly after 1910 when the Holy See published an oath against modernism, and required its clergy to swear it. But the crux of the matter is not religious dogma, but the influence of religion on a country's culture. Zeki Kuneralp gave two reasons for the easy transition in Spain from Franco's dictatorship to democracy: economic and social progress under Franco, and the high level of culture in Spain. Historically, he says, 'Spain has always created culture, and disseminated culture'.[4] Even if one makes allowance for the efforts of nineteenth-century reforming sultans and of the Young Turks, it was only with Atatürk's cultural revolution that the ideals of the Enlightenment became official policy in Turkey, speeding up the dissemination of modern knowledge. Spain was an innovative producer of motor cars before the First World War; Turkey used an American design to build its first motor car in 1960. There was, and there still is, a discrepancy in the stock of modern knowledge and of knowledge of the outside world, held in the two countries. The discrepancy is diminishing, but it is still affecting perceptions. Conspiracy theories, whose prevalence in Turkey is one of the themes of Orhan Pamuk's novel *Kara Kitap* (*The Black Book*), are ghosts that take shape in the fog of ignorance. Can people really believe that the American CIA and the Israeli intelligence service MOSSAD organized the attacks of 11 September 2001 in the United States, and then the bombings of synagogues and British targets in Istanbul in November 2003? Whether they do or not, the Islamist press in Turkey has suggested it repeatedly.

Unlike western Europe where most churchgoers are of the educated middle class, in Turkey religious observance and, with it, support for religious parties decreases as the level of education rises. There are, of course, other factors: people who are born and bred in metropolitan areas are less religious than provincials; within cities rich neighbourhoods are less religious than poor districts (unlike Paris, for example, where the working-class Red Belt had little time for religion); the west is less religious than the east. But geographical distinctions are being blurred by migration. Turkey's Middle East is no longer only in the Kurdish-inhabited south-east, but also in the poor suburbs of Istanbul, Ankara and other cities, where rural migrants have made their home. In his novel *Kar* (*Snow*), Orhan Pamuk juxtaposes a metropolitan atheist with a poor pious provincial. 'Is there then no hope?' asks the poor man. 'Is there no heaven to reward us for our misery?'

The mass of Turks are not prey to such existential despair, primarily because they believe that they can better themselves, and that therefore they can hope for a better life in this world. At the beginning of the new millennium, more than 4 million of the country's 13 million dwellings were new.[5] Life in the multi-storey concrete apartment blocks in poor neighbourhoods, which house an increasing part of the population, brings to mind the scenes shot outside cities like Milan by directors of Italian social-realist films half a century ago. Wages are low; work is scarce; young people get into trouble; children often go out to work rather than to school; mothers, grandmothers and aunts do their best to feed the family, while earning such money as they can as pieceworkers at home or as part-time domestic servants. In Italian films, angry young residents of these neighbourhoods found solace and a sense of purpose in local cells of the Communist Party. In Turkey, Islamist parties sometimes provide a support network, middle-class voluntary organizations give some help, while Marxist and Islamist clandestine groups appeal to a handful of young semi-educated people who, like the hero of Orhan Pamuk's novel *Yeni Hayat* (*The New Life*), have read one book that has changed their lives – usually an Islamic or a Marxist tract. In the Kurdish areas, where most violent fanatics originate, terrorist cells have taken shape in bookshops selling religious tracts. But most residents of poor urban neighbourhoods remember that life was even harder in the village or in their first shanty, and strive to make it better still. Kinsmen and neighbours provide a social context, religion and patriotism fuse to provide a framework of moral reference. If social surveys are to be believed, the Turks are not, on the whole, a trusting people. A hard life makes for hard characters. But the majority do not feel imprisoned: education provides an avenue of escape for many; there are trips to and from the village; work opportunities turn up at home or abroad.

The Turks like to think of themselves as a physically robust people, 'strong like a Turk'. When the republic was established eighty years ago, the authorities began implementing ambitious programmes to combat endemic diseases – TB, malaria, venereal disease, trachoma – which had sapped the vitality of the people. Sanatoriums were built, pools of stagnant water sprayed, health certificates stating that the couple was free of venereal disease had to be produced before marriages could be registered. This last requirement, copied from old French legislation, is still enforced fitfully, perplexing foreigners who want to marry in Turkey. The aim was to increase the numbers and improve the health of a population in a country that had been devastated by war. Gradually, the population began to grow and health improved in the towns. Faced with a soaring birth rate after the Second World War, official and private foundations put in hand birth control programmes against the inclinations of traditionalists, but with the approval of the religious establishment. Now, according to official figures, nearly all women (99 per cent) are aware of contraceptive techniques, and two thirds (64 per cent) practise some form of contraception. The average number of children women wanted was 2.5 at the time of the last survey.

The burden of public debt prevents the state from investing sufficient funds in health care. In 2002, only 9 per cent of the state budget was spent on health services. However, one should add to this the expenditure of insurance organizations, local councils and, of course, private individuals.[6] The government of the Justice and Development Party which took office in 2002 worked out a plan to streamline and decentralize health care by merging the three existing organizations which cater for public employees, all other employees and the self-employed, respectively. Public hospitals recover part of the cost of treatment from patients, unless these have been issued with a means-tested green card entitling them to free care. In 1999, there were some 1,200 hospitals, of which a quarter were private, with a total of just over 150,000 beds to serve a population approaching 70 million.

Some private hospitals can compete internationally on the cost and quality of the care they provide and attract foreign custom. At the same time rich Turks travel abroad for medical care – to Vienna or Switzerland before the Second World War, then to London, and now to the United States. In Istanbul the rich prefer foreign institutions: the International Hospital, the American, French or Italian hospitals. True, these employ mostly Turkish consultants, but care in them is supposed to be better organized. They are not as crowded as public hospitals, whose approaches are filled with patients and visitors, women in headscarves, friends bringing provisions, children. Public emergency services – fire, ambulance, disaster relief – have improved since their deficiencies were exposed by the earthquake which struck the approaches to Istanbul in August 1999. The old-established Red Crescent (the equivalent of the Red Cross) was criticized as sclerotic and riddled with nepotism. It claims to have improved since then. Voluntary relief organizations have become more active.

In the year 2000, the country had 85,000 physicians or approximately one for every 830 inhabitants. While the number is considered adequate, the geographical distribution is uneven, with a high concentration in prosperous urban areas. The average expectation of life – 66 for men and 71 for women in 2002 – is affected by the high rate of infant mortality (40 per thousand, or some eight times the European average). The figure, which has dropped from over 50 per thousand some ten years ago, reflects the backwardness of the east and south-east of the country. Even so, some 80 per cent of births are assisted by trained health staff. Further improvement depends on education, the relief of poverty and public health measures. Here progress has been impressive, given the size and difficult topography of the country: 70 per cent of the population have access to safe drinking water, 85 per cent have adequate drainage; the number of people per room is only 1.3; nearly 80 per cent of all children are immunized against measles, and only 8 per cent are deemed to be clinically underweight. Once again, domestic critics who complain that Turkey lags behind prosperous countries tend to disregard the immense improvements achieved in public health with only limited means.

In the last half century which has witnessed a population explosion, a move from the countryside to towns, industrialization and the advent of mass communications, there has been much discontent, but little revolutionary ferment among the masses. It is in this context, where reason prevails over passion, that progress seems most likely – in the same way that it has been achieved since the Second World War, first by Italy, then by Spain and Portugal, countries that have a much more profound and long-standing tradition both as participants and as creators of European culture. Turks can draw hope also from the success achieved by Greece, which was poor and backward until recently. Now it has become, at least by Turkish standards, a prosperous suburb of Europe.

No country can replicate another's experience. But similarities exist. In the case of Turkey, the most important similarities are with southern Europe and not with the Middle East. Like the countries of southern Europe, Turkey has copied the laws and institutions of republican France. Its social networks are similar to those in Italy. Its economic development through the agency of large family-owned conglomerates was paralleled in Portugal. The *kulturkampf* fought in Turkey between secularists and religious believers has ranged throughout continental Europe. If the Turks speak of 'Europe' as a place outside their borders, so too did Spaniards, Greeks and other peoples now within the European Union. Just as Turks tend to say bitterly that they have no true friends outside their community, so too Greeks saw themselves as a 'people without brothers' (*anadhelfo ethnos*). In any case, what is at issue in Turkey is not so much membership of the European Union as a European standard of life. Many middle-class Turks have already achieved it. Can it be extended to the whole population, 70 million and rising, and, if so, how long will it take?

The answer will depend partly on developments outside Turkey. Turkey needs peace on its borders and orderly neighbours. To its west, both are more or less assured. True, it will take time to recreate the natural unity of the Aegean basin which was torn by the creation of the Greek and Turkish nation states. It will take time also for Cyprus to settle down in whatever shape circumstances dictate. In the meantime, like the unresolved problem of Gibraltar between Britain and Spain, it is likely to be an irritant with which both Turks and Greeks can live. Both peoples appear to have developed a will to live peacefully, but separately, side by side.

The frontier with the former Soviet Union remains uneasy. Turkey has benefited from the fall of Communism. Its security is no longer threatened by Russia, which has become one of Turkey's most important trading partners. True, relations with the small, land-locked republic of Armenia are poor. But it does not pose a threat to Turkey. Developments in the Caucasus and in central Asia will affect the benefits which will accrue to Turkey from economic relations with these areas – the scope for new oil and gas pipelines, for the sale of Turkish consumer goods and for profitable contracts for Turkish construction companies. But Turkey's security is unlikely to be threatened from this direction.

It is Turkey's frontier in the east with Iran, and in the south with Syria and Iraq, which causes most concern. Instability in the Middle East threatens Turkey, because the Middle East extends into Turkey. On the other hand, given a modicum of order, the area could become a major market for Turkish products. In time, Middle Eastern countries will develop their own production of consumer goods, but Turkey has a head start; foreign competitors are further away; and the food Turkey produces will always be in demand in the arid lands south of its borders. However, there is little Turkey can do to bring order to the Middle East, which the Ottoman empire controlled for four centuries.

Turkey's integration in the global market and its membership, however hedged with conditions, of the club of developed countries make it vulnerable to external shocks – wars, threats of war, economic crises, recessions and panics. But from the world depression in 1929 to the Second World War, and then through petrol shocks, regional wars, and defaults in emergent markets, it has weathered storms which may have slowed down but have not arrested the country's development.

While external factors will undoubtedly affect Turkey's prospects, internal developments will be paramount. At the beginning of the millennium, Turkish newspapers habitually carried headlines such as 'Education – the Only Solution to the Crisis' or 'The Other Turkey [meaning the Turkey of the poor] – a Cause for Alarm!' It is right that the country should look to its social problems. But the fact remains that what was a century ago a small educated elite, whose members lived and thought like Europeans, has expanded into a large middle class. It is unfashionable to speak of civilized and uncivilized people, terms that were used uninhibitedly until after the First World War. But provided one does not confuse civilization with morality, the old terminology corresponds to a social reality.

Writing in 1922 about the partition of the Ottoman empire, a French journalist, Maurice Pernot, relates how on a visit to Baghdad in 1912, he heard the Ottoman governor explain to Arab leaders why he was to conduct a census of their tribes – not as a prelude to conscription or taxation, but to deliver services to them. Nevertheless, when the governor sent out his officials, they were assassinated and their bodies were mutilated 'in the customary way'. 'This is the people', Pernot goes on, 'that the Amir Faisal and his British protectors are asking to elect a parliament, pay taxes and obey laws.' Pernot argued that the settlement which Britain tried to impose after the First World War did not take into account either the ancient, advanced civilization of some people in the Near East or the 'ferocious barbarism' of others.[7] The bombings in Istanbul in November 2003 exemplify the 'ferocious barbarism' which survives in Turkey's Middle East and beyond.

Eighty years on, rather than speak of a Europeanized or westernized elite in Turkey, it makes more sense to say that Turkey is, by and large, a civilized country, with a civilized middle class, but with pockets of backwardness. It is precisely because Turkey is a civilized country that Europeans and other Westerners feel at home in it, that it is a popular posting for expatriate executives and a popular destination for Western tourists. Turkey has an increasingly active civil society. It is governed rationally, if not always competently. Its foreign policy is well informed and based on a rational calculation of the national interest, which does not mean that it is immune to miscalculation.

The Turkish republic has entered the third phase of its development, after the first phase in which the foundations were laid, and the second in which the motto was 'get rich quick and cash in on your strategic importance if you run out of resources'. Like the oil revenue of backward countries, which comes as the free gift of their geology, strategic rent – the unearned gift of geography – delays the adaptation of society to modern needs. The reforms which are being or about to be implemented in Turkey have been compared with the Tanzimat, the reordering of the Ottoman empire by the combined pressure of domestic modernizers and foreign advisers in the nineteenth century. The primary aim of the Tanzimat was equality before the law and the equal protection of the lives, property and honour of the sultan's subjects. It fell short of its ideal, but improved the lives of the population and increased prosperity, particularly among non-Muslims. Now the ideals are democratic accountability, transparency, zero tolerance of corruption, popular participation in decision-making, an end to gender discrimination, the recognition of multiculturalism, an improved delivery of justice and of public services – in short, more democratic and more effective governance. Inevitably, not all these fine ideals will be realized in full in our time. But the demand for them is real and it will yield results. Habits will change. The current drive for liberalization and democratization will limit people's freedom to do as they please. Tax laws, planning and building regulations, international standards of accountancy and a host of other rules imposed by the state will cease to be purely formal. Opinion-formers are urging the country to abandon the easy, and often dishonest, ways which advanced its prosperity for half a century, but at the cost of coups and crises.

One fashion which Turkey has recently imported from the West is the interest in roots – in the ethnic, geographical and social origins of its citizens. The spread of this fashion suggests that the task which Atatürk had set of creating a nation out of ethnically and socially disparate communities has largely been completed, and that, with the exception of the Kurds, fragmentation is no longer a serious danger. Turkish citizens now speak freely of their diverse origins – Turkoman, Albanian, Bosnian, Circassian, Crimean or Volga Tartar, Hungarian convert or whatever – or of the countries from which their ancestors came – the Balkans, the Aegean islands, the former Russian empire, the Arab Middle East. But the vast majority consider themselves Turks, united by language, culture and common destiny. Fault lines remain in Turkish society – between Turks and Kurdish nationalists, Sunnis and Alevis, secularists or Islamic traditionalists. But these are overridden by a strong feeling of Turkish national solidarity, which has withstood political conflict and economic hardship. There is a common pride in the achievements of Turkish businessmen, professionals or sportsmen.

Turks ceaselessly criticize themselves, their habits and their society, as well, of course, as each other. It is a well-known joke that no devils are needed to torment the Turks in Hell – they torment each other. But the currency of criticism and self-criticism can mislead outsiders, who are best advised not to corroborate it. Turkish society is more knowledgeable and open than ever, more willing than ever to learn from the experience of rich countries, as eager as ever to obtain the seal of foreign approval for its achievements, but it still presents a common front to the world whose motives it subjects to close, and not always charitable, scrutiny. The transformation through which the country is passing will inevitably increase internal tensions. The traditional solidarity of Turkish society should be strong enough to contain them.

Turkey is important not only because it is the only secular, democratic state inhabited by Muslims. It deserves attention also because it is the prototype of a non-Western country which is trying to organize its society on Western lines. Turkey lies close to the European countries in which our modern Western civilization was born. It has interacted with them ever since the Turks conquered the remnants of the Eastern Roman Empire just as the Renaissance was opening the way to the modern age. For close on two centuries, Turkey's expanding ruling class has adopted European ways. In the words of the

Turkish former foreign minister, İsmail Cem, Turkey's condition has been one of 'privileged backwardness' – privileged because of its long imperial administrative tradition, its social cohesion, and its closeness to the West. If in spite of these privileges, Turkey cannot extend to the whole of its burgeoning population the ways of thinking, working and living which have made the West prosperous, what hope is there for other countries which the West wishes to draw into its orbit? The history of Turkey is also an object lesson for those who want to implant Western institutions in non-Western soil. It suggests that this object can be achieved, but that it takes a long time.

Western prosperity does not depend on the possession of natural resources, but rather on the acquisition of new knowledge and the ability to organize society to make the most productive use of it. Paul Stirling, a British social anthropologist who spent a lifetime studying a Turkish village, remarked in a seminar, 'We're better off, because we organize better. Our whole success depends on this.' The most striking and most saddening characteristic of developing countries (which used to be called the Third World) is the waste of human lives. Human lives are still being wasted in Turkey, where the energy of the unemployed and the underemployed and the knowledge acquired through modern education are denied an adequate outlet. In the nineteenth century Europeans who were similarly denied an outlet for their energy could seek new lives in the empty spaces of the New World. Today there are no empty spaces left and emigration to rich countries can only offer a palliative. The cure must be sought at home, as it is being sought in Turkey. Turkey has travelled a long way to modernity, with its rewards and also its problems. There are still pitfalls on the way, but the goal is in sight.

Chronology

1071   Seljuk Sultan Alp Arslan defeats Byzantines at Malazgirt and opens the way to Turkish settlement in Asia Minor and to the establishment of the Seljuk sultanate of Rum with its capital at Konya.

1299   Osman I, ruler of a Turkish principality in north-western Anatolia, proclaims his independence and lays the foundations of the Ottoman state.

1453   Mehmet II conquers Constantinople (Istanbul), which becomes Ottoman capital.

1699   Treaty of Karlowitz marks end of Ottoman expansion in Europe.

1839   Beginning of Ottoman reforms (*Tanzimat*).

1856   Peace of Paris at the end of the Crimean War marks the entry of the Ottoman empire into the concert of Europe.

1876   Promulgation of the first Ottoman constitution, followed by the opening of the first parliament in 1877 and its dismissal in 1878.

1908   The Young Turks (Committee of Union and Progress/CUP) force Sultan Abdülhamit II to summon parliament. The Sultan is deposed the following year.

1912–13   Ottoman defeat in Balkan Wars leads to loss of all European possessions except for eastern Thrace.

1914   Ottomans enter First World War on the side of Germany.

1915   Allies land in Gallipoli; Mustafa Kemal (Atatürk) distinguishes himself in battles leading to allied withdrawal. Mass deportation of Armenians from Anatolia and flight of Muslims from Russian advance in the east: hundreds of thousands die.

1918   Armistice signed with Allies following Ottoman defeat in World War.

1919   Mustafa Kemal places himself at the head of Turkish resistance in Anatolia as War of Independence starts.

1922   Turkish nationalist troops defeat Greeks on 30 August and drive them out of Anatolia.

1923   Turkish victory confirmed in Treaty of Lausanne. Internationally recognized independent Turkish state becomes a republic on 29 October, with Mustafa Kemal as its first president, İsmet (İnönü) prime minister, and Ankara its capital. Mustafa Kemal retains leadership of ruling Republican People's Party (CHP), which remains in power until 1950.

1924   Caliphate abolished; republican constitution replaces provisional constitution of the resistance movement; first opposition party formed. İsmet resigns, but returns to power the following year, when the opposition party is suppressed following a Kurdish rebellion. Mustafa Kemal pushes on with his reform programme.

1930   Second experiment with a parliamentary opposition lasts for a few months.

1937   Atatürk replaces İnönü by Celal Bayar as prime minister.

1938   Atatürk dies on 10 November, and is succeeded by İnönü.

1939   Bayar is replaced by Refik Saydam as prime minister. Second World War begins; Turkey stays neutral.

1942   Saydam dies and is succeeded by Şükrü Saracoğlu.

1945   Turkey issues a formal declaration of war against Germany and Japan and becomes founder member of United Nations. Soviet Union ends treaty of friendship with Turkey.

1946   Democrat Party (DP) formed as first serious challenger to CHP, which wins elections, but is accused of fraud. Saracoğlu is replaced by Recep Peker as prime minister.

1947   Truman Doctrine protects Turkey against Soviet threat. Peker is replaced by Hasan Saka.

1949   Şemsettin Günaltay becomes prime minister in run-up to elections.

1950   DP wins republic's first free elections. Bayar becomes president and Adnan Menderes prime minister.

1952   Turkey joins NATO.

1954   DP re-elected.

1955   Turkey becomes party to Cyprus conflict following Greek campaign against British rule. Anti-Greek pogrom on 6–7 September in Istanbul marks end of friendly relationship established with Greece in 1930.

1960   Cyprus becomes independent with Greek president and Turkish vice-president. DP government overthrown and leaders arrested in military coup of 27 May. Junta (National Unity Committee/ NUC) under General Cemal Gürsel takes power.

1961   DP leadership sentenced; Menderes and two ministers hanged; DP dissolved. Elections held under new constitution. Gürsel becomes president, CHP leader İnönü prime minister at head of coalition with newly established Justice Party (AP).

1962   İnönü forms new coalition with New Turkey Party (YTP).

1963–4   Cypriot Turks come under attack on 21 December. US President Lyndon Johnson warns President Gürsel against military intervention. United Nations peace force (UNFICYP) sent to Cyprus.

İnönü forms minority government. On 1 December 1964, Turkey becomes associate member of European Economic Community (EEC, later EC, then EU).

1965   AP wins elections under new leader Süleyman Demirel, who becomes prime minister.

1966   Cemal Gürsel is succeeded by General Cevdet Sunay as president.

1969   Demirel re-elected, as student agitation mounts.

1971   'Coup by memorandum': military impose national government under Nihat Erim, which amends constitution. Martial law declared and order restored.

1972–3   Erim succeeded as prime minister first by Ferit Melen then by Naim Talu. İnönü ousted from CHP leadership by Bülent Ecevit; CHP emerges from elections as single strongest party. Admiral Fahri Korutürk elected president. İsmet İnönü dies in December 1973.

1974–5   Ecevit forms coalition with Islamist leader Necmettin Erbakan's National Salvation Party (MSP). Cyprus president Makarios ousted on 15 July in coup organized by Greek junta in Athens. Turkish troops land on 20 July and occupy over a third of the island by mid-August. Ecevit breaks with Erbakan. A transitional government formed by Sadi Irmak is replaced in March 1975 by Nationalist Front coalition under Demirel (main partners: AP, MSP and Nationalist Action Party/MHP led by Alpaslan Türkeş).

1977   Ecevit wins plurality in general elections and forms minority administration which lasts for one month and is succeeded by second Nationalist Front coalition (AP, MSP, MHP) under Demirel, as internal security deteriorates.

1978–9   Ecevit replaces Demirel at the head of a weak coalition, which resigns in November 1979 in the midst of an economic and security crisis. Demirel returns with a minority government.

1980   On 14 January government introduces wide-ranging stabilization programme drawn up by state planning organization head Turgut

Özal. Military high command assumes direct rule in coup on 12 September and restores law and order. All political parties dissolved.

1982   New constitution approved in referendum. Former chief of general staff General Kenan Evren becomes president. Military allow establishment of three new political parties (Nationalist Democracy Party/MDP, Populist Party/HP and Motherland Party/ANAP, led by Turgut Özal).

1983   ANAP wins elections and Turgut Özal forms new government which launches successful export drive. İsmet İnönü's son Erdal forms Social Democracy Party (SODEP), which absorbs HP the following year and is renamed SHP.

1984   Kurdish separatist PKK begins insurgency in south-eastern Turkey.

1986   Celal Bayar dies at the age of 103.

1987   On 14 April, prime minister Turgut Özal applies for membership of EC. (European Commission advises that neither party is ready for it.) Referendum allows leaders of political parties dissolved by the military in 1980 to resume political activity. Demirel becomes head of True Path Party (DYP); Bülent Ecevit refuses to cooperate with Erdal İnönü and heads his own Democratic Left Party (DSP); Necmettin Erbakan assumes leadership of Islamists in Welfare Party (RP); Alpaslan Türkeş resumes control of his party which after an interval reverts to the name of MHP. Özal is returned to power in general elections.

1989   President Evren dies and is succeeded by Turgut Özal. Yıldırım Akbulut becomes leader of ANAP and prime minister.

1991   Mesut Yılmaz replaces Akbulut. ANAP comes in second place in general elections in November. DYP emerges as the strongest party, and Demirel forms a coalition with Erdal İnönü's SHP.

1993   Turgut Özal dies; Demirel becomes president. He is succeeded as ANAP leader and prime minister by Tansu Çiller who continues coalition with SHP.

1995–6   Erbakan's RP emerges as single strongest party in general elections in November 1995. Çiller clings to power by forming coalition with SHP, which reverts to its old name CHP under a new leader, Deniz Baykal, as Erdal İnönü steps aside. In March 1996, Çiller changes partners and teams up with ANAP led by Mesut Yılmaz, who becomes prime minister. Four months later the coalition collapses, and Erbakan becomes the republic's first Islamist prime minister, with Çiller as his junior partner. In January 1996 a customs union between Turkey and EU comes into force.

1997   'Post-modern coup': at a meeting of the National Security Council on 28 February the military demand that 'the forces of reaction' should be confronted. As Erbakan procrastinates, Çiller's DYP is split and the coalition collapses. On 30 June ANAP leader, Yılmaz, forms a secularist coalition with DSP and DYP dissidents (Democratic Turkey Party/DTP). Erbakan's RP banned and is reconstituted as Virtue Party (FP) under Recai Kutan. Istanbul Islamist mayor Recep Tayyip Erdoğan deprived of office and briefly imprisoned.

1999   In January PKK leader Abdullah Öcalan is snatched from Kenya by Turkish commandos and is taken to Turkey where he is sentenced to death (sentence later commuted to life imprisonment). Yılmaz gives way to Bülent Ecevit, whose DSP forms minority government in run-up to elections, from which Ecevit's DSP and Türkeş's MHP emerge as the strongest two parties. Ecevit forms coalition with MHP and ANAP. A stand-by agreement is reached with IMF and a new stabilization programme is introduced. In December EU grants Turkey candidate status and promises to decide in December 2004 whether to set a date for accession negotiations.

2000   In May, Demirel is succeeded in the presidency by Ahmet Necdet Sezer. In November, crisis of confidence hits stabilization programme which has to be amended.

2001   A public quarrel between Sezer and Ecevit leads to economic crisis in February. Lira is floated and halves in value; GNP falls by nearly 10 per cent. Fresh credits secured from IMF under new stabilization programme; World Bank vice-president Kemal Derviş

(AKP) under Erdoğan and Felicity (SP) under Kutan. Process to amend the constitution in line with EU requirements goes ahead.

2002   Ecevit falls ill. As he refuses to resign, a number of his ministers quit (some of them forming the New Turkey Party/YTP); coalition collapses. In early elections in November, AKP wins absolute majority. CHP is only other party to win seats in parliament. As Erdoğan is still banned from politics, AKP deputy leader Abdullah Gül becomes prime minister. Economy begins to revive. In December EU grants Turkey candidate status and promises to decide in December 2004 whether to set a date for accession negotiations.

2003   On 1 March a government proposal to allow US troops passage through Turkey to open northern front against Iraqi regime of Saddam Hussein fails in parliament. As ban on Erdoğan is lifted, he is elected to parliament and becomes prime minister in March. In October, agreement by parliament to the dispatch of Turkish peace-keeping troops to Iraq has no effect, as Iraqi provisional governing council opposes their deployment. Economic revival continues.

2004   AKP makes gains in local government elections on 28 March. Turkey endorses UN plan to reunite Cyprus. On 24 April the plan is approved by Turkish Cypriots, but rejected by Greek Cypriots.

Abbreviations

Turkish Political Parties

AKP	*Adalet ve Kalkınma Partisi*	Justice and Development Party
ANAP	*Anavatan Partisi*	Motherland Party
AP	*Adalet Partisi*	Justice Party
CHP	*Cumhuriyet Halk Partisi*	Republican People's Party
DEHAP	*Demokratik Halk Partisi*	Democratic People's Party
DEP	*Demokrasi Partisi*	Democracy Party
DP	*Demokrat Parti*	Democrat Party
	Demokratik Parti	Democratic Party
DSP	*Demokratik Sol Parti*	Democratic Left Party
DTP	*Demokrat Türkiye Partisi*	Democratic Turkey Party
DYP	*Doğru Yol Partisi*	True Path Party
FP	*Fazilet Partisi*	Virtue Party
GP	*Genç Parti*	Young Party
HADEP	*Halkın Demokrasi Partisi*	People's Democracy Party
HEP	*Halkın Emek Partisi*	People's Party of Toil
HP	*Halkçı Parti*	Populist Party
HP	*Hürriyet Partisi*	Freedom Party
MDP	*Milliyetçi Demokrasi Partisi*	Nationalist Democracy Party
MHP	*Milliyetçi Hareket Partisi*	Nationalist Action Party
MKP	*Milli Kalkınma Partisi*	National Development Party
MNP	*Milli Nizam Partisi*	National Order Party
MP	*Millet Partisi*	Nation Party
MSP	*Millî Selâmet Partisi*	National Salvation Party
PKK	*Partiya Karkeren Kurdistan*	Kurdistan Workers Party
RP	*Refah Partisi*	Welfare Party
SHP	*Sosyal Demokrat Halkçı Parti*	Social Democratic Populist Party
SODEP	*Sosyal Demokrasi Partisi*	Social Democracy Party

SP	*Saadet Partisi*	Felicity Party
TİP	*Türkiye İşçi Partisi*	Turkish Workers Party
TKP	*Türkiye Komünist Partisi*	Turkish Communist Party
YTP	*Yeni Türkiye Partisi*	New Turkey Party

International Organizations

CENTO	Central Treaty Organization
EC	European Community
EEC	European Economic Community
EU	European Union
IMF	International Monetary Fund
OECD	Organization for Economic Cooperation and Development
OEEC	Organization for European Economic Cooperation
NATO	North Atlantic Treaty Organization
UN	United Nations

Notes

PROLOGUE

1. www.undp.org.
2. Şahin Alpay in *Zaman*, 10 April 2003.
3. Ildikó Bellér-Hann and Chris Hann, *Turkish Region* (Oxford: James Currey, 2001), 215.
4. *Radikal*, 29 August 2002.
5. 258,000 women and 501,000 men in 1991–2; 621,000 women and 887,000 men in 2000–1.
6. Paul Henze, *Turkey and Atatürk's Legacy* (Haarlem: Sota, 1998), 159.
7. Erik Cornell, *Turkey in the Twenty-first Century* (Richmond, Surrey: Curzon, 2001), 117.
8. David Shankland in Brian Beeley (ed.), *Turkish Transformation* (Hemingford Grey, Cambs.: Eothen, 2002), 79.

I   STATE BEFORE NATION 1938–1945

1. İsmet İnönü, *Hatıralar* [Memoirs] (Ankara: Bilgi, 1987), II, 326.
2. Mahmut Gologlu, *Millî Şef Dönemi* [The Era of the National Leader] (Ankara: Turhan, 1974), 54–5.
3. Selim Deringil, *Turkish Foreign Policy During the Second World War* (Cambridge: Cambridge University Press, 1989), 38.
4. Gologlu, 63.
5. Ibid., 80.
6. İsmail Soysal, *Türkiye'nin Siyasal Anlaşmaları* [Turkey's Political Treaties] (Ankara: Türk Tarih Kurumu, 1983), I, 270.
7. Baskın Oran (ed.), *Türk Dış Politikası* [Turkish Foreign Policy] (Istanbul: İletişim, 2001), I, 392.
8. Rıfat Bali, *Cumhuriyet Yıllarında Türkiye Yahudileri* [Turkey's Jews in the Years of the Republic] (Istanbul: İletişim, 1999), 467, 472.

9. Rıfat Bali, *Aliya: Bir Toplu Göçün Öyküsü* [Alia: The Story of a Mass Emigration] (Istanbul: İletişim, 2003), 258.

10. For a detailed account see Rıfat Bali, *Musa'nın Evlatları Cumhuriyet'in Yurttaşları* [Children of Moses, Citizens of the Republic] (Istanbul: İletişim, 2001), 181–205.

11. Goloğlu, 240.

12. Ibid., 245–55.

2 THE HIGH COST OF FREE ELECTIONS
1945–1960

1. Çağlar Keyder, *State and Class in Turkey* (London: Verso, 1987), 126, 129.

2. Şevket Süreyya Aydemir, *İkinci Adam* [The Second Man] (Istanbul: Remzi, 1991), 343 and Mahmut Goloğlu, quoting Menderes.

3. Goloğlu, 327–37.

4. Ibid., 408.

5. Ekavi Athanassopoulou, *Turkey: Anglo-American Security Interests 1945–1952* (London: Frank Cass, 1999), 69–72.

6. Paul Stirling, *Turkish Village* (London: Weidenfeld & Nicolson, 1965), 269.

7. Adil Temel, 'Büyüme, Ekonomik Yapı Değişmeleri (1946–1997)' [Growth and Structural Change in the Economy (1946–1997)] in Zeynel Rona (ed.), *Bilanço 1923–1998* [Balance-Sheet 1923–1998] (Istanbul: Tarih Vakfı, 1999), II, 73–6.

8. Captain Muzaffer Özdağ to the author in June 1960.

3 YEARS OF STRIFE 1960–1980

1. Baskın Oran (ed.), I, 520.

2. In a private conversation with the author.

3. Metin Toker in private conversation with the author.

4. In private conversation with the author.

5. Hasan Cemal, *Kimse Kızmasın, Kendimi Yazdım* [Don't Get Angry Anyone, I've Written About Myself] (Istanbul: Doğan, 1999), 347.

6. Quoted in ibid., 332.

7. Baskın Oran (ed.), I, 850–1.

8. Zeki Kuneralp (trans. Geoffrey Lewis), *Just a Diplomat* (Istanbul: Isis, 1992), 109.

9. Private conversation with the author.

10. William Hale, *Turkish Politics and the Military* (London: Routledge, 1994), 238.
11. Ibid., 232.

4   CONFLICT CONTAINED 1980–2003

1. M. Ali Birand, *12 Eylül Saat 04.00* [12 September 0400 hours] (Istanbul: Karacan, 1984), 320.
2. Ibid.
3. Baskın Oran, *Kenan Evren'in Yazılmamış Anıları* [The Unwritten Memoirs of Kenan Evren] (Istanbul: Bilgi, 1989), 8–11.
4. Emin Çölaşan, *Turgut Nereden Koşuyor* [Where's Turgut (Özal) running away from?] (Istanbul: Tekin, 1989), 25–7.
5. In private conversations with the author.
6. Morton Abramowitz (ed.), *Turkey's Transformation and American Policy* (New York: Century Foundation Press, 2000), 27–8.
7. Revised English edition published in 1991 by K. Rustem, (Turkish) Nicosia; first French edition published in 1988.
8. Ibid., 346.
9. Meltem Müftüler-Bac, *Turkey's Relations with a Changing Europe* (Manchester: Manchester University Press, 1997), 64.
10. In private conversation with the author.
11. Do.
12. Official text, 11, 12, 18.
13. In private conversation with the author.

5   CATCHING UP

1. Ruşen Çakır and Fehmi Çalmuk, *Recep Tayyip Erdoğan: Bir Dönüşüm Öyküsü* [Recep Tayyip Erdoğan: The Story of a Transformation] (Istanbul: Metis, 2001), 17.
2. Ibid., 50.
3. Survey by STRATEJI-MORI, published on 27 October 2002.
4. Statement by public service union KAMU-SEN on 10 September 2003.
5. In 2002, prices in Turkey amounted to 47 per cent of the OECD average, while the gross national product per person, calculated in purchasing power parities, was only 25 per cent of the average (www.oecd.org).
6. ANKA Risk Review, 25 November 2003.

7. Gallup poll reported on www.ntvmsnbc on 14 August 2003.
8. Daily *Türkiye*, 20 June 2003.
9. Statement by Prime Minister Erdoğan to mark the beginning of the school year, www.ntvmsnbc, 12 September 2003.
10. Figures from website of State Institute of Statistics, www.die.gov.tr.
11. *2001 Statistical Yearbook of Turkey*, 234.
12. Quoted by Erdal Bilallar in the daily *Sabah*, 20 March 2002.
13. Turkish Ministry of Women's Affairs, *The Status of Women in Turkey*, a Report on the Fourth World Conference on Women, May 1994, 61.
14. For a full analysis see Women for Women's Human Rights, *The New Legal Status of Women in Turkey* (Istanbul: New Ways, 2002).
15. Article by Mehmet Ali Yılmaz in *Milliyet*, 4 December 2003.
16. Sevim Timur, *Türkiye'de Aile Yapısı* [Family Structure in Turkey] (Ankara: Hacettepe Üniversitesi, 1972).
17. See Deniz Kandiyoti, 'Pink Card Blues: Trouble and Strife at the Crosssroads of Gender' in Deniz Kandiyoti and Ayşe Saktanber (eds.), *Fragments of Culture: The Everyday of Modern Turkey* (London: I.B.Tauris, 2002), 277–93.
18. Reported by ntvmsnbc on 15 July 2003.
19. Ibid.
20. Anadolu Ajansı reported by www.haber.turk.net.
21. www.ntvmsnbc.com/news/49978.asp?om=N11Q
22. Orhan Pamuk, *Kar (Snow)* (Istanbul: İletişim, 2000), 409–10.
23. www.tesev.org/projeler/proje_yolsuzluk.
24. www.ntvmsnbc.com/news/231878.asp?Om-N1AJ on 3 September 2003.
25. www.hrweb.org/legal/catsigs.html.
26. *Hürriyet*, 24 July 2001.
27. ntvmsnbc, 2 September 2002.
28. In an interview with the newspaper *Zaman*, which is close to the Fethullahçı brotherhood, published on 27 November 2003.
29. Ali Çarkoğlu and Binnaz Toprak for TESEV [Turkish Economic and Social Studies Foundation], *Türkiye'de Din, Toplum ve Siyaset* [Religion, Society and Politics in Turkey] (Istanbul: 2000).
30. Ibid., table 6.1.2.
31. Ibid., pp. 16–17.
32. Ibid., table 6.4.9.
33. Ibid., table 6.2.1.
34. ntvmsnbc, 2 September 2003.
35. ntvmsnbc, 14 August 2003.
36. www.tsk.mil.tr/genelkurmay.

6 ECONOMIC SURPRISES

1. Sencer Ayata, 'The New Middle Class and the Joys of Suburbia' in Deniz Kandiyoti and Ayşe Saktanber (eds.), *Fragments of Culture: The Everyday of Modern Turkey*, 30, 41.
2. Rıfat Bali, *Tarz-ı Hayat'tan Life Style'a: Yeni Seçkinler, Yeni Mekânlar, Yeni Yaşamlar* [From Way of Life to Lifestyle: New Elites, New Places, New Lives] (Istanbul: İletişim, 2002), 115.
3. Quoted in *Radikal*, 23 August 2003.
4. Discussed in Alexander Stille, 'Italy: The Family Business', *New York Review of Books*, 9 October 2003, 23–5.
5. Report of parliamentary commission into corruption, p. 34 (www.tbmm.gov.tr), quoting State Institute of Statistics.
6. EU Annual Report on Turkey, November 2003, pp. 73–4.
7. Annex 6 to EU Annual Report on Turkey, November 2003.
8. www.tursab.org.tr.
9. Bülent Kahraman in *Radikal*, 1 August 2003.
10. Annex to EU Annual Report on Turkey, November 2003.

7 EDUCATION AND CULTURE

1. All the figures in this chapter are taken from DİE (State Institute of Statistics), *Statistical Indicators 1923–1995* (Ankara: 1996), and *Statistical Yearbook of Turkey* for 2000 and 2001, published in Ankara in 2001 and 2002.
2. UN Human Development Report (http://hdr.undp.org/reports/global).
3. DİE, *Statistical Yearbook of Turkey 2001*, 64.
4. Feride Acar and Ayşe Ayata, 'Discipline, Success and Stability: The Reproduction of Gender and Class in Turkish Secondary Education' in Deniz Kandiyoti and Ayşe Saktanber (eds.), *Fragments of Culture: The Everyday of Modern Turkey*, 102–7.
5. Güngör Uras in *Milliyet*, 23 August 2003.
6. I thank Prof. Ziya Öniş of Koç University for the Turkish text of this 'Student's Oath'.

8 ANKARA GOVERNS

1. Ertuğrul Özkök in *Hürriyet*, 23 April 2003.
2. *Radikal*, 5 November 2003, quoting report by the office of the prime minister.
3. Ibid.

9 ISTANBUL LIVES

1. Ruşen Çakır and Fehmi Çalmuk, 118.
2. ntvmsnbc, 31 January 2003, corrected by DİE and Istanbul Büyükşehir Belediyesi [Metropolitan Municipality], *Sayılarla İstanbul* [Istanbul in Numbers], n.d.
3. Cem Behar, *Osmanlı İmparatorluğu'nun ve Türkiye'nin Nüfusu 1500–1927* [The Population of the Ottoman Empire and Turkey], DİE, Ankara, 1996, II, 71.
4. Ali Neyzi, *Hüseyin Paşa Çıkmazı No. 4* [No. 4 Hüseyin Paşa cul-de-sac] (Istanbul: Karacan, 1983), 8–10.
5. Can Yücel, *Ölüm ve Oğlum* [Death and My Son] (Istanbul: Cem, 1976), 24–6.
6. Latife Tekin, *Berci Kristin Çöp Masalları* [The Rubbish Tales of Berci Kristin] (Istanbul: Adam, 1984), 9.
7. Gül Özyeğin, 'The Doorkeeper, the Maid and the Tenant: Troubling Encounters in the Turkish Urban Landscape' in Deniz Kandiyoti and Ayşe Saktanber (eds.), *Fragments of Culture: The Everyday of Modern Turkey*, 43–72.
8. *Sayılarla İstanbul*, 603.
9. *İstanbul Belediyesi 2000 Yılı Faaliyet Raporu* [Activity Report by the Istanbul Municipality for the Year 2000], 14.
10. *Sayılarla İstanbul*, 242.
11. *Milliyet*, 29 August 2002.
12. *Sabah*, 20 March 2002.
13. ntvmsnbc, 10 August 2002.
14. Istanbul police presentation, reported in NTVMSNBC, 31 January 2003.
15. ntvmsnbc, 28 June 2002.
16. Rıfat Bali, *Tarz-ı Hayat'tan Life Style'a*, 229.
17. Ayşe Öncü, 'Global Consumerism, Sexuality as Public Spectacle, and the

Cultural Remapping of Istanbul in the 1990s' in Deniz Kandiyoti and Ayşe Saktanber (eds.), *Fragments of Culture: The Everyday of Modern Turkey*, 171–90.

10 EASTERN APPROACHES

1. Survey by Prof. Naci Bostancı, quoted by Taha Akyol in *Milliyet*, 4 April 2002.
2. There is a considerable literature on Öcalan and his PKK. The factual information in this chapter is drawn from Michael M. Gunter, *The Kurds in Turkey: A Political Dilemma* (Boulder, CO: Westview, 1990); İsmet G. İmset, *PKK: Ayrılıkçı Şiddetin 20 Yılı (1973–1992)* [PKK: Twenty Years of Separatist Violence (1973–1992)] (Ankara: Turkish Daily News, 1993); Nihat Ali Özcan, *PKK (Kürdistan İşçi Partisi: Tarihi, İdeolojisi ve Yöntemi)* [PKK (Kurdistan Workers Party): Its History, Ideology and Methods)] (Ankara: ASAM, 1999); Ümit Özdağ, *Türkiye Kuzey Irak ve PKK: Bir Gayri Nizamî Savaşın Anatomisi* [Turkey, Northern Iraq and PKK: The Anatomy of an Irregular Conflict] (Ankara: ASAM, 1999); Oktay Pirim and Süha Örtülü, *Ömerli Köyünden İmralı'ya PKK'nın 20 Yıllık Öyküsü* [From Ömerli Village to İmralı: The PKK Story over Twenty Years] (Istanbul: Boyut, 2000); Attila Şehirli, *Türkiye'de Bölücü Terör Hareketleri* [Separatist Terror Movements in Turkey] (Istanbul: Burak, 2000) and Paul White, *Primitive Rebels or Revolutionary Modernizers: The Kurdish National Movement in Turkey* (London: Zed, 2000).
3. Oktay Pirim and Süha Örtülü, 33.
4. Figures issued by the governor of the provinces under a state of emergency, www.ohal.gov.tr/ist3.asp.
5. The figures are taken from the indictment served on Öcalan at his trial (quoted in Pirim and Örtülü, 283) and from a briefing letter sent to members of the US Congress by the Turkish General Staff at the end of 2001.
6. The information on Hizbullah has been taken from Ercan Çitlioğlu, *Tahran-Ankara Hattında Hizbullah* [Hizbullah on the Line from Teheran to Ankara] (Ankara: Ümit, 2001); Mehmet Faraç, *Batman'dan Beykoz'a Hizbullah'ın Kanlı Yolculuğu* [The Bloody Journey of Hizbullah from Batman to Beykoz] (Istanbul: Günizi, 2001), and Hikmet Çiçek, *Hangi Hizbullah* [Which Hizbullah?] (Istanbul: Kaynak, 2000).

7. Mehmet Faraç, 246.
8. The indictment drawn up in July 2000 against seventeen alleged members of Hizbullah lists the links between Iranian intelligence and Hizbullah terrorists in Turkey (Mehmet Faraç, 254–5).
9. Ibid., 235–8.
10. Servet Mutlu, 'Economic Bases of Ethnic Separatism in Turkey' in *Middle Eastern Studies*, 37/4, October 2001, pp. 101–27.
11. Report by Anti-Terror Department of the Turkish Directorate of Security, quoted in *Hürriyet*, 1 May 2002.
12. Özden Bilen, *Turkey and Water Issues in the Middle East* (Ankara: GAP, 1997), 114.

11   RED APPLE OR SOUR GRAPES

1. Quoted by NTV on 7 March 2003.
2. Ferenc Váli, *Bridge Across the Bosphorus: The Foreign Policy of Turkey* (Baltimore, MD: Johns Hopkins, 1971), 335.
3. *Milliyet*, 4 January 2003, quoting a report of the Turkish Studies Centre in Germany.
4. *Atatürk'ün Söylev ve Demeçleri* [Atatürk's Speeches and Statements] (Ankara: Atatürk Araştırma Merkezi [Atatürk Research Centre], 1989), III, 87.
5. Turkistan Newsletter, 14 October 2003.
6. *Hürriyet*, 2 July 2003.
7. Witnessed by the author.

12   PROGRESS AND PITFALLS

1. Zeki Kuneralp (trans. Geoffrey Lewis), *Just a Diplomat*, 138.
2. Ibid., 148–9.
3. World Bank revised figures quoted in haber.tnn.net on 11 September 2003.
4. Kuneralp, 135.
5. For total housing stock, see www.ntvmsnbc.com/news/241545.asp; for occupancy permits of newly constructed dwellings, DİE and DPT. The fact that many more construction permits are issued than occupancy permits suggests that, in addition to buildings which are never completed, some at least of the new dwellings are used illegally without an occupancy permit.

6. In 2003, the health ministry worked out the cost of health care at 150 dollars per person or 5 per cent of GNP in total. This remarkably low figure probably represents only direct state expenditure. (Anatolian Agency, reported by haber.turk.net on 18 January 2003.)

7. Maurice Pernot, *La Question turque* (Paris: Bernard Grasset, 1923), 249–50.

Further Reading

Turkey has attracted a great deal of attention of late, and the list of books examining the country's present state and future prospects is lengthening by the day. Readers who wish to acquaint themselves with the past could begin with Erik Zurcher, *Turkey: A Modern History* (I.B. Tauris, revised edition, 1998). The latest biography of the founder of the republic is Andrew Mango, *Atatürk* (John Murray, paperback 2004). For Atatürk's antecedents, the standard work is Bernard Lewis, *The Emergence of Modern Turkey* (Oxford University Press, paperback 2001). Roderic Davison, *Turkey: A Short History* (Eothen, 1981), gives a convenient summary of events to the mid-1960s. The standard detailed history to 1975 is Stanford Shaw's *History of the Ottoman Empire and Modern Turkey* (Cambridge University Press, Volume 1, 1976; Volume 2 (with Ezel Kural Shaw), 1977).

William Hale, *Turkish Foreign Policy, 1774–2000* (Frank Cass, second edition 2002), provides the best general account of the subject. More detailed studies will be found in his bibliography. Cyprus and Greek-Turkish relations need separate bibliographies of their own, but readers who do not have a special interest in the matter would be well advised to content themselves with Hale's succinct account, as the situation on the ground is changing constantly. Turkish foreign policy since the Cold War is analysed in Philip Robins, *Suits and Uniforms* (Hurst, 2003).

For domestic politics up to the date of publication, consult Hale's *The Political and Economic Development of Modern Turkey* (Croom Helm, 1981) and *Turkish Politics and the Military* (Routledge, 1994). Both have useful bibliographies. Metin Heper and Sabri Sayarı (eds.), *Political Leaders and Democracy in Turkey* (Lexington, 2002), describes the personalities of the politicians who have shaped modern Turkey. Hugh

Poulton, *Top Hat, Grey Wolf and Crescent: Turkish Nationalism and the Turkish Republic* (Hurst, 1997), discusses the political ideologies at work. There are useful essays on political and social aspects of Turkish life in Andrew Finkel and Nükhet Sirman, *Turkish State, Turkish Society* (Routledge, 1990).

The new millennium has prompted a number of books which take stock of developments in Turkey. They include: Morton Abramowitz (ed.), *Turkey's Transformation and American Policy* (Century Foundation, 2000); Brian Beeley (ed.), *Turkish Transformation: New Century, New Challenges* (Eothen, 2002); İsmail Cem, *Turkey in the New Century* (Rustem, 2001); Erik Cornell, *Turkey in the Twenty-first Century* (Curzon, 2001); Heinz Kramer, *A Changing Turkey: The Challenge to Europe and the United States* (Brookings, 1999); Amikam Nachmani, *Turkey: Facing a New Millennium* (Manchester University Press, 2003); Onur Öymen, *Turkish Challenge* (Rustem, 2000).

Change in the Turkish economy is so rapid that most books on the subject are of historical interest only. For recent economic history, consult Anne Krueger and Okan Aktan, *Swimming Against the Tide: Turkish Trade Reform in the 1980s* (International Centre for Economic Growth, 1992) and Ayşe Buğra, *State and Business in Modern Turkey* (SUNY, 1994).

Turkish and international statistical services and business organizations provide up-to-date information on-line. They include: the [Turkish] State Institute of Statistics (DİE/SIS) (www.die.gov.tr), the State Planning Organization (DPT/SPO) (www.dpt.gov.tr), the Turkish Central Bank (www.tcmb.gov.tr), the (Turkish) Foreign Economic Relations Board (DEİK) (www.deik.org.tr), the Turkish Industrialists' and Businessmen's Association (TÜSİAD) (www.tusiad.org.tr), the Turkish Union of Chambers of Commerce (TOBB) (www.tobb.org.tr), the Turkish Economic Development Foundation (İKV) which reports on relations between Turkey and the EU (www.ikv.org.tr), and among international organizations, OECD (www.oecd.org), IMF (www.imf.org), the World Bank (www.worldbank.org), the EU (for Turkey's accession, (www.europa.eu.int/com/enlargement). The Directorate General of Press and Information in Ankara (www.byegm.gov.tr) publishes a useful press review in English on weekdays, in addition to official documents. The NTV television channel has a free on-line news service in English (www.ntvmsnbc. com). Many Turkish national newspapers also provide free internet editions in English (for the mass-circulation Istanbul daily *Hürriyet*, www.hurriyetim.com).

Some of the best insights into life in Turkey today can be found in the work of social anthropologists. The two most recent studies on Islam in Turkey are: David Shankland, *Islam and Society in Turkey* (Eothen, 1999), and Richard Tapper (ed.), *Islam in Modern Turkey* (I.B. Tauris, 1991). David Shankland has also published a study of the heterodox Alevi community: *The Alevis in Turkey: The Emergence of a Secular Islamic Tradition* (Routledge, 2003). Other notable recent studies are: Ildikó Bellér-Hann and Chris Hann, *Turkish Region* (James Currey, 2001); Deniz Kandiyoti and Ayşe Saktanber (eds.), *Fragments of Culture: The Everyday of Modern Turkey* (I.B. Tauris, 2002); Michael Meeker, *A Nation of Empire: The Ottoman Legacy of Turkish Modernity* (University of California, 2002), and Jenny White, *Islamist Mobilization in Turkey: A Study in Vernacular Politics* (University of Washington, 2002).

Many books have been written by journalists stationed in Turkey. A classic of this genre, describing the scene in the 1960s, is David Hotham, *The Turks* (John Murray, 1971). The two most recent works by foreign correspondents are Nicole and Hugh Pope, *Turkey Unveiled: Atatürk and After* (John Murray, 1997), and Stephen Kinzer, *Crescent and Star* (Farrar, Straus & Giroux, 2001).

There is a large literature on the Kurds. The standard history is David McDowall, *A Modern History of the Kurds* (I.B. Tauris, second edition 2000). Martin van Bruinessen, *Agha, Shaikh and State: The Social and Political Structures of Kurdistan* (Zed, 1992), is a classic study by a social anthropologist. Books dealing specifically with the Kurdish problem in Turkey include: Michael Gunter, *The Kurds and the Future of Turkey* (Macmillan, 1997) and *The Kurds in Turkey* (Westview, 1990); Kemal Kirişçi and Gareth Winrow, *The Kurdish Question in Turkey* (the only book on the subject in English co-authored by a Turkish scholar; Frank Cass, 1997); Robert Olson, *The Emergence of Kurdish Nationalism and the Sheikh Said Rebellion, 1880–1925* (University of Texas, 1989): Olson has also edited *The Kurdish Nationalist Movement in the 1990s: Its Impact on Turkey and the Middle East* (University of Kentucky, 1996);

Jonathan Rugman and Roger Hutchings, *Atatürk's Children: Turkey and the Kurds* (a lavishly illustrated book by a foreign correspondent; Cassell, 1996); and Paul White, *Primitive Rebels or Revolutionary Modernizers? The Kurdish National Movement in Turkey* (Zed, 2000).

The controversy on the deportation of Armenians from Turkey in 1915 has produced a large and growing literature. For the Armenian case, consult Christopher Walker, *Armenia: The Survival of a Nation* (Croom Helm, 1980); for the Turkish response, Kamuran Görün, *The Armenian File: The Myth of Innocence Exposed* (Rustem/Weidenfeld & Nicolson, 1985).

As far as contemporary Turkish literature is concerned, the novels of Yaşar Kemal and Orhan Pamuk, and the poems of Nazım Hikmet are widely available in English translation. Some of the work of a few other authors (the novelists Adalet Ağaoğlu and Latife Tekin, the short-story writer Sait Faik, the poet Can Yücel and others) has also been published in translation.

Finally, there is no lack of up-to-date guidebooks for travellers, in the Blue Guide, Rough Guide and other series. On Istanbul, John Freely, *Istanbul, the Imperial City* (Penguin, 1996), and Philip Mansel, *Constantinople: City of the World's Desire* (Penguin, 1995), deserve special mention.

Index

Index

Turkish personal names classified by forename. Letters with diacritical marks treated as separate letters.

Kurdish safe haven, 90–1; support for Allies criticized, 91; belief in a free Turkey, 92; dies, 93; recruits from private sector, 186; local government reforms, 195

Turkey: society compared to other Islamic countries, 5; urban life, 7–8; unevenness of modernization, 9; first appearance of in history, 17; and international relations during WWII, 28; signs alliance with Britain and France, 29; receives foreign aid after earthquake, 30–1; WWII threat draws closer, 31–2; relations with Soviet Union, 32; agrees in principle to enter WWII, 36; declares war on Germany and Japan, 37; becomes member of Organization for European Economic Cooperation, 44; transformation under Democrat rule, 47; problems of under Democrats, 54–5; becomes associate member of European Economic Community, 77; rejected by EEC, 89; Kurdish policy, 96; attempts to gain EU membership, 235; attempts to decentralize, 238; between the West and the Third World, 240; comparisons with Spain, 245; integration into global market, 250–1; drive for liberalization, 252

Turkish Business Bank (*Türkiye İş Bankası*), 29

Turkish Cypriots: engaged in anti-terrorist operations, 49

Turkish nationalists: founders of Republican People's Party, 32; violence against Greek property, 49

Turkish republic: established, 25; in third phase of development, 252

Turkish state: secularized, 21; citizenship, 26; and religion, 43; police allow anti-Greek violence, 49; paternalism, 107; human rights violations, 123–4; anti-terrorist policy, 124; total secularization of, 132; concerns for integrity of, 137; relationship with private enterprise, 203; well-informed foreign policy, 252

Turkish War of Independence, 21, 34

Turkish Workers Party (TİP): formed, 62; loses votes, 66

Turkomans, 221, 253

Turks: strong national identity, 4; determination of, 9; origins of, 15; early Turkish tribes, 16; ethnic variety of, 17, 253; xenophobia among Turks, 18; Turkish diaspora, 65; surge of nationalism, 98; want EU membership, 113; living standards of, 115; morality, 126; migrant communities in Europe, 236; enthusiasm for modernity, 11, 240; national solidarity, 253

unions: strikers close factories, 77; militant action, 79; banned from politics, 81; reduction in power of, 113; labour organizations, 114

United Nations: Turkey in human development index, 2, 4; Turkey a founding member of, 28; intervenes in Cyprus crisis, 60; peace force dispatched to Cyprus, 61; sanctions on Iraq, 91; convention on eliminating discrimination against women,